JOHN DOBSON

Architect of the North East

John Dobson, c.1850

Fig. 1 'Photographic portrait' of John Dobson published at the time of his death in 1865 by Messrs. W. & D. Downey of Eldon Square, Newcastle upon Tyne.

Northern Architectural Association; by courtesy of the Literary and Philosophical Society of Newcastle upon Tyne.

JOHN DOBSON

Architect of the North East

"Mr. Dobson may fairly be styled the father of the architectural profession in Newcastle"

(The Newcastle Weekly Chronicle, 1 January 1887)

Thomas Faulkner

and

Andrew Greg

Tyne Bridge Publishing

Newcastle Libraries and Information Service

with Tyne and Wear Museums

Acknowledgements
Tyne Bridge Publishing at Newcastle Libraries & Information Service, and Tyne and Wear Museums, gratefully acknowledge the invaluable support of, the University of Northumbria at Newcastle, the Grainger Town Project, and FaulknerBrown Architects in the production of this book.

Photographic Acknowledgements:
Authors' photographs: figs 6, 8, 18, 23, 52, 62, 64, 72, 82, 88, 89, 91, 92, 94, 96, 99, 100, 101, 102, 104, 108, 110, 111, 112, 113, colour plates ix, x; Bildarchiv Foto Marburg: fig. 53; Cheshire Libraries and Museums, Warrington Library: fig. 87; Durham County Record Office: colour plate ii; His Grace the Duke of Northumberland: fig. 5; James A. Johnson and Associates, Vermont, Victoria, Australia: fig. 106; Lord Hastings: fig. 13; Newcastle Document Services: fig. 114; Newcastle Libraries & Information Service: figs 14, 20, 21, 22, 34, 35, 37, 38, 44, 50, 55, 59, 65, 69, 70, 73, 83, 86, 90, 93, 97, 98, 103, 109; Northumberland County Record Office: fig. 95; Philipson Studios, Newcastle upon Tyne: figs 10, 11, 12, 16, 57; South Shields Library: fig. 68; The British Architectural Library: figs 49, 60; The Laing Art Gallery, Newcastle upon Tyne: back cover illustration; front cover illustration; figs 2, 3, 4, 26, 33, 43, 46, 54, 66, 67, 75, 80, 84, colour plates i, iii-viii, xi-xvi; The Literary and Philosophical Society of Newcastle upon Tyne: figs 76, 79; The National Monuments Record: figs 32, 39, 45, 107; The Northern Architectural Association: figs 1, 105; Tyne and Wear Archives: figs 15, 25, 85; Tyne and Wear Museums Service: figs 27, 29, 30, 71, 74, 115; University of Northumbria at Newcastle: figs. 7, 9, 17, 19, 24, 28, 31, 36, 40, 41, 42, 47, 48, 51, 56, 58, 61, 63; Whitby Literary and Philosophical Society: fig. 81
(Note: illustrations are of buildings or designs by Dobson unless otherwise stated.)

Front cover illustration: John Dobson as a young man. From an oil painting by J. Dixon, c.1820. *Laing Art Gallery, Newcastle upon Tyne*

Back cover illustration: The Central Station, Newcastle upon Tyne, begun 1847. The interior, from a watercolour by Dobson and J.W. Carmichael. *Laing Art Gallery, Newcastle upon Tyne*

Published by
City of Newcastle upon Tyne, with Tyne and Wear Museums
Education & Libraries Directorate
Newcastle Libraries & Information Service
Tyne Bridge Publishing
2001
www.newcastle.gov.uk/tynebridgepublishing

ISBN: 185795131X

Printed by Elanders Hindson, North Tyneside

Contents

ABBREVIATIONS

AA *Archaeologia Aeliana*

CL *Country Life*

Collard and Ross W. Collard and M. Ross, *Architectural and Picturesque Views in Newcastle upon Tyne*, 1841

DCRO Durham County Record Office

Dobson M.J. Dobson, *Memoir of John Dobson, etc.*, 1885

Faulkner and Lowery T.E. Faulkner and P.A.S. Lowery, *Lost Houses of Newcastle and Northumberland*, 1996

Fordyce W. Fordyce, *The History and Antiquities of the County Palatine of Durham*, 2 vols, 1857

Hodgson J. Hodgson, *A History of Northumberland*, 3 vols, 1820-58

Hodgson 1832 J. Hodgson, *A History of Morpeth*, 1832

ICBS Incorporated Church Building Society

Latimer J. Latimer, *Local Records*, 1857

Mackenzie 1811 E. Mackenzie, *A Historical and Descriptive View of the County of Northumberland*, 2 vols, 1811

Mackenzie 1825 E. Mackenzie, *A Historical and Descriptive View of the County of Northumberland*, 2nd edn., 2 vols, 1825

Mackenzie 1827 E. Mackenzie, *A Descriptive and Historical Account of ... Newcastle upon Tyne*, 2 vols, 1827

Mackenzie and Ross E. Mackenzie and M. Ross, *A Historical, Topographical and Descriptive View of ... Durham*, 4 vols, 1834

Manders F.W.D. Manders, *A History of Gateshead*, 1973

Meadows and Waterson P. Meadows and E. Waterson, *Lost Houses of County Durham*, 1993

NA *The Newcastle Advertiser*

NC *The Newcastle Courant*

NCh *The Newcastle Chronicle*

NCL Newcastle City Library

NCRO Northumberland County Record Office

NDJ *The Newcastle Daily Journal*

NJ *The Newcastle Journal*

NMR National Monuments Record

NWC *The Newcastle Weekly Chronicle*

Oliver T. Oliver, *A New Picture of Newcastle upon Tyne*, 1831

Pevsner 1992 N. Pevsner et al., *The Buildings of England: Northumberland*, 1992

Proc. Soc. Ant. Proceedings of the Society of Antiquaries of Newcastle upon Tyne

RIBA Royal Institute of British Architects

Sykes J. Sykes, *Local Records*, 2 vols, 1866

TWA Tyne and Wear Archives

Wilkes L. Wilkes, *John Dobson, Architect and Landscape Gardener*, 1980

Wilkes and Dodds L. Wilkes and G. Dodds, *Tyneside Classical*, 1964

Fig. 2 John Dobson's bookplate, c.1820
Laing Art Gallery, Newcastle upon Tyne.

Foreword

In 1987 we organised a major exhibition at the Laing Art Gallery, Newcastle upon Tyne, to commemorate the bicentenary of the birth of John Dobson, the North East's most eminent architect. Our accompanying book, *John Dobson: Newcastle Architect, 1787-1865* (Tyne and Wear Museums), which also served as an exhibition catalogue, was kindly acknowledged as having superseded previous biographies. However, it rapidly sold out after a limited print run and has become extremely hard to find. This present book comes in response to the longstanding demand for some kind of second edition of this earlier work, but has been substantially rewritten and enlarged, incorporating more recent research as well as material not included hitherto. It is in a completely different format and includes a much fuller appraisal of Dobson's overall achievement. It also places him even more firmly in his local and national context by relating him more extensively to his contemporaries, especially those in the North East.

Similarly, it has now been possible to incorporate a considerable amount of additional information in the revised and extended Catalogue of Works (Chapter 8). It should also be noted that at the request of the publishers a short glossary of architectural terms has been appended, in line with their policy of encouraging the widest possible readership for books of this kind.

Dobson, from North Shields, educated and trained in Newcastle and London, brought to the region London's most fashionable ideas effectively combined with a North Easterner's down-to-earth practicality. He was also the first architect from the North East to achieve a measure of national as well as local status. Immensely versatile in the range and styles of his buildings, he designed fine houses for the local gentry, noble crescents and squares for the middle classes, hotels and railway stations for travellers, and churches, schools, hospitals and other public buildings for everyone. Thus in 1987 we wrote: "Dobson is a figure of great importance, of whom all of us who live and work in the North East can justifiably feel proud." Arguably the significance of Dobson is even greater today, given the increased awareness since that date of conservation and 'heritage' issues. Evidence of this is provided, for example, by the existence of Newcastle's new Historic Environment Team, charged with the task of encouraging the long overdue appreciation of Newcastle as a place of considerable historical and architectural importance. This is something to which the work of Dobson contributed enormously.

Those who helped us in our research for *John Dobson: Newcastle Architect, 1787-1865* were gratefully acknowledged at the time, but it would not be inappropriate to reiterate our thanks to Angus Fowler, Peter Meadows, Denis Perriam, Graham Potts, David Rogers and Dr. Peter Willis.

For this present book we are indebted to those who kindly drew our attention to various errors and omissions in the earlier work, especially Sir Howard Colvin and Dr. R.W. Rennison, as well as to those, including Jimmy Donald and A. Desmond Walton, who suggested revisions to it. Also important have been those whose subsequent research, published and unpublished on Dobson and related matters has proved invaluable. Noteworthy in this context is the work of Peter Addyman, H.F. Dobson, Andrew Everett, Bill Fawcett, Phoebe Lowery, Grace McCombie and Alan Morgan. For private information we are most grateful to Mr. J.W.H. Boon, Mr. P.R.B. Brooks (on Holeyn Hall), Dr. Bob Giddings (on the Oliver dynasty of architects), Mr G.R. Hawkins, Mrs Grace McCombie (on numerous matters), Mr. D.J. Price (on Lymm Parish Church), Ms Jane Rees (on Bonnyrigg Hall), Mr. H.C.N Scott (on Dobson's family), Mr. A.H. Tweddle and Dr. Lynne Walker.

We are also especially grateful to Ian Chilvers, who kindly wrote the glossary and read the proofs of the book as a whole. Moreover, at an earlier stage Mr. Chilvers checked the manuscript and effected many improvements both of style and content. Similar thanks in this regard should also be accorded to Dr. Martin Harrop of the University of Newcastle upon Tyne. Lavinia Down not only prepared the index but also undertook the equally monumental task of typing the original manuscript. She again made many helpful comments, as did our publisher, Anna Flowers of Tyne Bridge Publishing at Newcastle Libraries & Information Service, whose encouragement has been much appreciated throughout.

Among the many staff of institutions, too numerous to mention all by name, who have provided us with invaluable help, were those of Durham County Library, Durham County Record Office, the Laing Art Gallery Newcastle upon Tyne, the Literary and Philosophical Society of Newcastle upon Tyne, Newcastle City Library (Local Studies Section) Northumberland County Record Office (Melton Park), North Yorkshire County Record Office (Northallerton), the Royal Institute of British Architects (Newcastle upon Tyne), Tyne and Wear Archives, and Tyne and Wear Museums. We are also indebted to the Literary and Philosophical Society and the Society of Antiquaries, both of Newcastle upon Tyne, for permission to reproduce historic material in their collections, as well as to all the persons and organisations specifically mentioned in the photographic captions and in the Photographic Acknowledgements section above. Finally, it should be emphasised that the publication of this book has been facilitated by the generous financial support of the University of Northumbria at Newcastle.

Thomas Faulkner
Andrew Greg
Newcastle upon Tyne, 200

1 The Making of an Architect, 1787-1823

By the end of the 18th century, North Shields had grown from a decaying and impoverished fishing village into a prosperous and fashionable port (see fig. 3). Its quays sent coal from the newly developed coalfields of Northumberland down to London, and its roperies and anchor foundries supplied the local shipyards. High on the banks of the Tyne, smart Georgian terraces and squares had been built for the shipowners, mariners and manufacturers of the area. A few miles inland the villages of Chirton and Preston lay as yet relatively untouched by industry and commerce; Chirton, with a population of fewer than 1,000, was dominated by the mansion houses of the Collingwoods and the Lawsons. However, a wagon way just west of Chirton crossed the muddy Newcastle turnpike and carried coal from Shiremoor and Murton down to the staithes at Whitehill Point; smoke from the steam engine at nearby Percy Main colliery would often have drifted over the village.

John Dobson was born at his parents' home in Chirton on 9 December 1787[1]. His father, John Dobson snr., in addition to owning a public house, was in business on a large scale as a market gardener. "The beautiful and extensive fruit gardens of Mr. Dobson", wrote the local historian Eneas Mackenzie, "render Chirton a place of fashionable resort during the summer

Fig. 3 *The Mouth of the Tyne*. From an aquatint by W.H. Timms after R. Parker, c.1800.
Laing Art Gallery, Newcastle upon Tyne.

months. They are tastefully laid out with pleasant walks and convenient seats and arbours for the accommodation of parties of pleasure. Mr. D. has other gardens for the growth of vegetables, of which great quantities are consumed by the town and shipping of Shields."[2] He was also occasionally employed to lay out ornamental pleasure grounds, a talent he was to pass on to his son. Dobson later remembered the Tyne of his youth as being "little short of Paradise"[3] covered in trees and flowering shrubs down to the water's edge, from Newcastle to Shields. Within his lifetime it was to be transformed from rural bliss to a hive of industrial activity. His father evidently intended him to follow in the gardening profession and gave him instruction to that end. He also gained some experience on the Earl of Strathmore's estate at Gibside in County Durham. The young boy's artistic talent soon showed itself, however, and with the encouragement of the local schoolmaster and eventually his father, he became well known locally for his botanical drawings. This led to occasional employment, while still in his early teens, as draughtsman to a damask and linen weaver at nearby Preston, Mr. J. McGlashan, and to a grazier and butcher at North Shields, Mr. Ratcliffe.

At some time in the early 1800s Dobson went to Newcastle to study under Boniface Muss, who taught perspective and landscape painting, fencing and Italian, some of the necessary elements in the education of young gentlemen and women. There he was a fellow pupil of his almost exact contemporary, the eccentric John Martin (1789-1854), later to achieve great fame as a painter of dramatic literary, historic and biblical subjects, often incorporating immense architectural perspectives.

The Newcastle of 1800 was a town still largely confined within its medieval walls. However, in the previous two decades it had struggled to accommodate its narrow, steep thoroughfares to the demands of its burgeoning commercial and industrial economy. Mosley Street and Dean Street were built from 1784 to 1788 to improve the road route from the Tyne Bridge northwards. The walls and gates along the Quayside were being demolished; the Tyne Bridge itself was widened in 1801. New public buildings, such as the Assembly Rooms, All Saints' Church and the remodelled Guildhall and Exchange, introduced a previously unknown classical purity to the provincial architecture of the town and were evidence of the growing prosperity and sophistication of its inhabitants. The town itself was expanding northwards, above and beyond the overcrowded chares, tenements and warehouses of the Close, the Quayside and Sandgate. Elegant new residential streets and squares were rising beyond the town walls. Westgate Hill and Saville Row lay newly built among open fields.

On the river an ever-widening range of industry was spreading along both banks. Staithes unloaded coal wagons from the Tyneside pits onto ships for transport to London and abroad. Steam engines were allowing deeper and more productive pits to be sunk. Iron, glass, paper and soap works, roperies, shipyards and potteries were rapidly expanding. The Tyne served as a port for the whole North East of England, exporting lead, grain and grindstones as well as local manufactures. Much of the investment for all these new enterprises came from local landowners, who were involved not only in the traditional rural industry of agriculture, but also the new industries of coal extraction, lime-burning and lead-mining. The interrelation of many of these industries made the Tyne a centre of the country's fledgling chemical industry, and the financial requirements of such large-scale and complex investments had given rise to some of Britain's earliest provincial banks.

Carried along by this flourishing industrial environment were the necessary trades and professions that formed the increasing middle class in Newcastle and created a continuing demand for sophisticated urban housing. The industrialists and landowners themselves had houses and estates in the country. Some were medieval castles, most of them decayed and severely uncomfortable; others were the result of new wealth from coal and the shipping trade. All were to become ripe for further improvement and restoration in the 19th century.

Soon after beginning to study with Muss, Dobson took more practical instruction in mechanical and architectural drawing from Mr. Hall of Stamfordham, bridge surveyor for the county of Northumberland. He confirmed his commitment to the architectural profession around 1804 by entering into an apprenticeship with David Stephenson (1757-1819), then Newcastle's and the North East's leading architect. Stephenson had made his name with All Saints' Church in Newcastle (1786-96, fig. 4). All Saints' typifies Stephenson's brand of delicate neoclassicism, combining an inventive

Fig. 4 David Stephenson: All Saints' Church, Newcastle upon Tyne, 1786-96. From an aquatint by Robert Pollard after Robert Hardy, 1799.
Laing Art Gallery, Newcastle upon Tyne.

11

oval plan with a finely detailed spire, the exterior decorated with the characteristic urns, swags and fluted columns of the late 18th century. He had been architect to Newcastle Corporation from 1788 and in 1794 designed the new north front of the Guildhall and Exchange with William Newton, architect of St. Anne's Church and the Assembly Rooms (pp121-22), all also in Newcastle. At the time of Dobson's apprenticeship Stephenson was about to be appointed architect to the Duke of Northumberland, for whom his most important design was to be the uncompleted project for a new Market Place and Quay at North Shields.

By 1800 apprenticeships had become the usual mode of formal architectural training. The years of Dobson's late teens were thus spent in Stephenson's office assisting him in his work and thereby learning all the skills necessary to the work of the professional architect: dealing with clients and contractors, estimating and surveying, drawing up designs and working drawings and supervising contractors' work. Stephenson's practice does not seem to have been very large, however; his works after 1800 are almost all connected with the Duke of Northumberland. But the most important of these, the North Shields Market Place, was planned and begun during the time of Dobson's apprenticeship. This was one of the most ambitious pieces of neoclassical public architecture in the North of England, comparable to the urban designs by Robert Adam for the Adelphi (1768-72) and Fitzroy Square (1790) in London, and for Edinburgh in the 1780s. As a northern architect, Stephenson would certainly have had ample opportunity to witness the dramatic transformation of Edinburgh as the building work progressed. Of particular relevance in this context are the designs for Edinburgh University, Charlotte Square and the South Bridge development.

However, by 1810, when Dobson drew the attractive oval perspective view of the intended Market Place appended to a large plan of North Shields (fig. 5), Stephenson's architectural style was outdated and Dobson had

Fig. 5 David Stephenson: Intended New Market Place and Quay, North Shields. From a watercolour by Dobson, 1810.
The Duke of Northumberland.

already won his first important commission, for the Royal Jubilee School in Newcastle, in a characteristically robust expression of the newly fashionable Greek Revival style (see below and colour plate i).

Richer or better-connected architectural apprentices would travel abroad at the end of their apprenticeships, to study the monuments of classical antiquity and Renaissance architecture in Italy and Greece. Dobson, of lesser means, travelled to London after completing his time with Stephenson in 1809, remaining in the capital for about a year. He spent some time studying watercolour painting with the successful watercolourist John Varley, who was an influential and fashionable teacher, both in person and through his publications. He had toured the North East of England in 1808, sketching the picturesque sites of the region and giving lessons to the families of the Northumberland gentry. It is possible that Dobson first met him on this occasion. A watercolour by Varley of c.1810-11 in the Victoria and Albert Museum is inscribed on the back "Mr. Dobson", identifying it as a drawing Dobson was required to copy. The relationship later matured into friendship.

Dobson probably sought out Varley in order to acquire the facility in watercolour that was necessary for him to produce the newly fashionable architectural perspectives. Later however, as we shall see, Dobson was to employ the well known Newcastle artist John Wilson Carmichael (1799-1868) to work up his perspective drawings into dramatic and effective watercolours with which to impress clients. A large and conventional landscape watercolour supposedly made by Dobson during his time with Varley is in the Laing Art Gallery, Newcastle; it certainly bears some of the characteristics of the master's style. More obvious in the surviving early architectural drawings by Dobson is a distinctly 18th-century flavour, in the elongated figures in the large perspective of the Royal Jubilee School, or the Bewick-like vignettes in the album of William Clark's Estates, for example. The perspective of St. Thomas's Church of c.1827 is the first surviving drawing of the partnership of Dobson and Carmichael, and in this the talent of an accomplished landscape watercolourist is more evident.

Apart from Varley, another important figure that we can be sure that Dobson knew was the architect Robert Smirke, then a rising star on the architectural scene. His recently completed Covent Garden Theatre was a pioneering example of the Greek Revival style. Smirke may also have been an influence in matters constructional, being an early exponent of the use of iron and, importantly, concrete in architecture. His younger brother, Sydney (1798-1877), also a noted architect, was to marry Dobson's eldest daughter Isabella in 1840. Meanwhile, Sir John Soane, then commencing his Royal Academy lectures on architecture – possibly even attended by Dobson – may have been a further indirect influence, especially with his advanced concept of architectural professionalism. Also while in London Dobson may have seen illustrations of the designs of the contemporary German neoclassicist Schinkel, whose work bears a resemblance to some of his own.

The Greek Revival

In London Dobson was able to study the current architectural scene at a time – an important one in the history of architectural design – when the Greek Revival was coming to the fore. The new enthusiasm for Greek art was epitomised by the reception given to the Elgin Marbles from the Parthenon in Athens, which were available to selected observers from 1807 and went on public exhibition at the British Museum in 1817. (The present British Museum building was soon to be designed in a Grecian style by Robert Smirke.) The Marbles excited controversy between enthusiastic artists and sceptical connoisseurs, but finally helped convince architects of the supremacy of Greek forms.

The leaders of the Greek Revival in architecture, William Wilkins and Robert Smirke, were both travelling in Greece in the early 1800s. The discoveries, excavations, surveys and publications of architects and collectors fuelled the Greek mania that soon pervaded not only architecture but also novels, poetry, fashion and all aspects of design. The first large-scale examples of the Greek Revival in English architecture were built in this decade: Wilkins's Grange Park, Hampshire (1804-09) and Downing College, Cambridge (from 1807) and Smirke's Covent Garden Theatre (1808-09). Before 1800 the Greek Revival was regarded as the plaything of a few private patrons; after 1810 it became the established style of public buildings throughout the country.

The powerful austerity of the style seems particularly well suited to Scotland, where it continued with undimmed vigour into the 1850s, and to

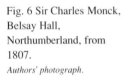

Fig. 6 Sir Charles Monck, Belsay Hall, Northumberland, from 1807.

Authors' photograph.

Fig. 7 John and William
Stokoe, The Moot Hall,
Newcastle upon Tyne,
1810-12.
*Photograph: R. Walton,
©University of Northumbria at
Newcastle.*

the North of England. Thomas Harrison's Chester Castle of 1785-1820 pioneered the style for public buildings; in Northumberland, Sir Charles Monck was his own architect at Belsay Hall, arguably the finest Greek Revival mansion in the country, begun in 1807 (fig. 6); and in Newcastle John and William Stokoe's Moot Hall of 1810-12 (fig. 7) was one of the best of the provincial responses to Smirke's Covent Garden Theatre. Dobson's involvement in the design of Belsay Hall has never been proved, but there is no doubt that on his return to Newcastle in 1810 he would have found the existence of Belsay and the Moot Hall powerful encouragement to promote Greek Revival architecture of the purest and highest quality in the North East of England.

When Dobson set up practice on Tyneside, initially basing himself in Chirton, he and his friend Ignatius Bonomi were, in his own words, "the only professional architects in the counties of Northumberland and Durham".[4] Dobson was careful to maintain the distinction of status between the profession of architect and the trade of the builder. He had entered the architectural profession at the very time that it was struggling to create and define its identity. By 1834, with the creation of the Institute of British Architects, the process was nearly complete, but in 1810 builder-architects, like John Stokoe, who, with his son William, was the designer and the builder of the Moot Hall, were more typical. On leaving Stephenson's office Dobson made

15

the deliberate decision, with the former's advice, to set up in Newcastle as a professional architect, in the modern sense.

However, although in London the architectural profession was already overcrowded, the provinces were as yet unused to this new breed of practitioner. Dobson acknowledged that in the first few years of his career there was little demand for his services, but it seems that his first success, and a major coup for a young architect, may have been obtained before he had even returned to settle in the North East.

Dobson arrives

The Royal Jubilee School in City Road, Newcastle, was built to designs by Dobson that were approved by the subscribers on 23 March 1810, although Dobson's absence in London may have forced him to entrust the supervision of the building of the school to the builder-architect John Stokoe.[5] It was built to honour George III's Jubilee wish that "every poor child in the Kingdom be able to read the Bible" and consisted of a stark rectangle in pure Greek temple form. The Doric portico is taken straight from Robert Smirke's recently completed Covent Garden Theatre, but returned to its 'correct' position at the gable-end of a roof. It is also more correct than the Stokoes' contemporary north entrance to the Moot Hall, where the columns are unevenly spaced. However, in a strange foreshadowing of the incomplete execution of Newcastle's Central Station at the climax of Dobson's career, this school, his first building, was built without its portico.

On his return to the North East and for the first two years of his professional practice, Dobson was based at Chirton, presumably in his parents' house. His work in these early years was split between North Shields and Newcastle; local contacts in and around North Shields enabled him to build up a solid base of domestic, institutional and industrial work there.

Fig. 8 Scottish Presbyterian Church, Howard Street, North Shields, 1811.
Authors' photograph.

In view of the relative sophistication of this early design, it is somewhat surprising to find a year later, in 1811, the rather crude Greek Revival Meeting House for the Scotch Presbyterians in Howard Street, North Shields (fig. 8). This is another severe neoclassical building, its three-bay facade with Doric pilasters bearing some resemblance to that of the Royal Jubilee School as built. However, the Greek temple effect, with steps leading up to the front in both designs, is less pronounced in the case of the Meeting House since it has no pediment, its entablature being surmounted by a tall attic storey. The

Fig. 9 St. Nicholas's, Gosforth, Newcastle upon Tyne, enlarged by Dobson 1818-20.

Photograph: R. Walton, ©University of Northumbria at Newcastle.

mouldings above the windows on the ground floor are supported by brackets embellished with a curious motif of animal skulls. The Meeting House was followed in 1812 by a Methodist Chapel in Newcastle, sited opposite the Royal Jubilee School on New Road, an extremely plain classical building of two storeys.

Dobson's first major work for the local Anglicans was carried out between 1818 and 1820, when he made extensive alterations to Gosforth Parish Church, a handsome but under-sized structure of 1799. He added a north and south aisle with galleries, connecting with a gallery already present at the west.[6] Dobson followed the simple classical style of the existing church by providing Tuscan columns supporting elegant shallow arches to divide the aisles from the nave (see fig. 9). He also built at the edge of the churchyard a little rustic cottage for the sexton in a rudimentary Tudor style, now demolished.

Dobson had made further inroads into Newcastle in 1811 by selling building sites in Jesmond for Thomas Burdon, who was an important figure in Newcastle at the time. He had been elected Mayor in 1810 and was to be knighted in 1816 as a reward for putting down the 1815 sailors' strike. To work for Burdon, even in such a humble capacity, was a valuable introduction into the influential Northumberland and Newcastle oligarchy of squires, merchants and landowners. Dobson was later to win an important architectural commission from him in 1817 for the design of West Jesmond House (see below).

With this and the contacts he had made through the Royal Jubilee School, Dobson felt able to move to Newcastle in the early summer of 1812, to an office in Pilgrim Street. In the years 1810-12 only four buildings by Dobson are recorded, but immediately after his move to Newcastle work came considerably faster and soon expanded to include his first houses and his first work in County Durham.

Home improvements

Field House in Gateshead, built in 1813 for George Barras, was Dobson's first identifiably recorded house, a plain classical design with a hipped roof undisguised by a parapet.[7] The major remodelling undertaken in the same year for Henry Riddell at Cheeseburn Grange, near Stamfordham in Northumberland, is more interesting: the survival of both the house and of Dobson's original album of designs[8] gives us the opportunity to look in

17

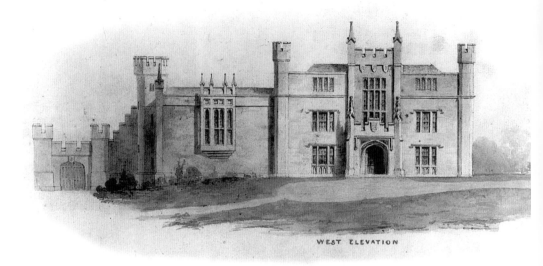

WEST ELEVATION

Fig. 10 Cheeseburn Grange, Northumberland, Dobson's proposed entrance front, 1813. *Major Philip Riddell; photograph: Philipson Studios.*

detail at several aspects of Dobson's work at this time.

Cheeseburn was a 17th-century farmhouse, embellished in the 18th century with a baroque doorcase in the centre of the south front and, according to Dobson's drawing of the house before he began work on it, Tudor-style drip mouldings around the windows. Dobson took the opportunity to extend the Tudor treatment to the whole house. He moved the entrance to the side and raised a short tower over it. He embellished the skyline with turrets and small hexagonal towers, crowned with castellations at the corners, and raised a high parapet, pierced with Gothic openings, to hide the old roof. Castellated offices completed the ensemble (see fig. 10).

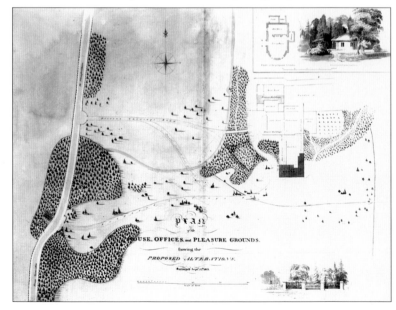

Fig. 11 Cheeseburn Grange, Northumberland, Dobson's proposed improvements to the park, 1813. *Major Philip Riddell; photograph: Philipson Studios.*

18

PLAN of the proposed LODGE.　　　　ELEVATION of the LODGE.

Fig. 12 The lodge, detail
from Dobson's proposed
improvements to
Cheeseburn park.
*Major Philip Riddell; photo-
graph: Philipson Studios.*

Dobson's proposals are important for also including major alterations to
the surrounding parkland. He built a ha-ha to visually link the house and its
park, suggested a whole new scheme of tree planting to shelter the house,
designed a new gateway and lodge and replanned the driveway to enable the
visitor on his approach to the house to fully appreciate the siting of the house
in its landscape (see fig. 11). The lodge (fig. 12) is a deliberately 'primitive'
cottage, set deep in trees, with a thatched roof and diamond-paned windows.
These landscaping elements follow the fashionable and influential example
of Humphry Repton, who, inspired by then-current theories of the
'Picturesque', reshaped the rather formulaic approach to landscape gardening of his famous predecessor 'Capability' Brown. Repton revived formal
elements, such as terraces, borders, paths and lawns, in the immediate vicin-
ity of a house; he emphasised the siting of a house within a landscape, and
had a thorough botanical knowledge of trees and shrubs. Dobson's own
background put him in a good position to benefit from the popular and practical books through which Repton publicised his theories.

Dobson's interest in landscape gardening is also illustrated by his work
at Bolam in Northumberland for the Hon. W.H. Beresford in 1816. There he
laid out an artificial lake, "necessary islands" and adjoining plantations, so
that the estate might be both attractive and productive. Thirty years later he
commented knowledgeably on the lack of attention that the estate had subsequently received.[9]

At Cheeseburn, Dobson was engaged in modernising a plain old house;
in two other well-documented commissions of the following years we can
study other aspects of his increasingly popular role as an improver of older
houses.

Two beautiful drawings made by Dobson in 1814 for the Earl of
Strathmore[10] concerned alterations to Gibside in County Durham, an early
17th-century house which had already been much enlarged in 1805. Here the

Perspective View of the South Front of the HOUSE showing the proposed Addition & Alteration

Earl had inherited one of the finest 18th-century landscape gardens in the
North of England and he continued his predecessors' interest in horticulture
and gardening by perhaps commissioning Dobson to design a large conservatory which was to be added to the west end of the house. This charming
building, of cast iron and glass, fed by rainwater and heated by hot air from
an adjacent furnace, combined these practical considerations with an expression of the Regency period's delight in being able to walk directly from the
house into a conservatory full of luxuriant and exotic plants (see colour plate
ii).

At Seaton Delaval in Northumberland, the most important 18th-century
country house in the North East of England, Dobson proposed to Sir Jacob
Henry Astley alterations and additions intended to improve the appearance
of the house. Sir John Vanbrugh's superb, but impractical, house of 1718-28
had been seriously marred around 1770 by the addition of a large wing,
extending the south elevation seven bays to the east. Dobson proposed, in an
elaborate album of drawings[11] dating from 1814-17, to rebuild the east end
of the wing so as to conform more closely to Vanbrugh's architectural style,
with octagonal corner towers repeating exactly the form of those on the central block. More grandiosely, Dobson also proposed the building of a matching west wing that would have created an enormous south front of 23 bays
(see fig. 13). However, these proposals did not survive the death of Sir Jacob
Henry Astley in 1817. Sir Jacob Henry may have intended to carry them out
(they appear in contemporary engravings and paintings of the house) but his
successor, Sir Jacob Astley (d.1859), seemed little interested in building.
When the main block of the house was gutted by fire in 1822, Dobson may
also have been consulted concerning its restoration. In 1838 he exhibited in
Newcastle a watercolour of its restored state (having 20 years earlier exhibited at the Royal Academy another fine watercolour of Seaton Delaval, now
in the Laing Art Gallery, Newcastle), but in the event it was not until 1860
that Dobson eventually re-roofed the block and enabled what remained of
the house's architectural glories to survive to the present day.

At Gibside and Seaton Delaval, Dobson was dealing with old aristocratic families. The elaborateness of both sets of designs and the fact that neither was carried out suggest that they were perhaps unsolicited; that Dobson made them purely in order to bring his talents and ambition to the notice of potentially important and influential patrons. Much of his work of the next few years suggests that this presumption was justified. In his 1859 Presidential Address to the Northern Architectural Association,[12] Dobson stressed how the formal planning of 18th-century houses encouraged the continual cold draughts that plagued inhabitants and visitors. A north or south entrance, always overlooking an open view, led directly into the staircase hall and thence into the principal corridors and rooms. As we have seen, Dobson's solution at Cheeseburn, as in his own later houses, was to place the entrance in a sheltered position at the side. In his alterations to James Paine's 18th-century houses in the region (Axwell Park in County Durham, Belford Hall, Bywell Hall and Gosforth Park in Northumberland), he moved the principal entrance to the north, more sheltered, side. At Belford Hall in 1817 an Ionic colonnade and a new entrance hall were built across part of Paine's rear courtyard. Other work in the village of Belford, including small terraced houses, also suggests Dobson's hand. At Belford he was working for a patron, William Clark, for whom he had previously made a charming series of estate plans including land at Cullercoats, Little Benton, Monkseaton and New Whitley around 1812-13.[13]

The classical houses of the previous century may have been relatively uncomfortable, but the older country seats were mostly in a far worse state. Not only were the castles and Jacobean mansions of the region inconvenient and decayed to such a degree that few were habitable at all, but architecturally they were often mongrel affairs consisting of work of several different periods. As patrons and architects became more sensitive to the architecture of the Gothic and Elizabethan periods, they regretted the 'improvements' of the 18th century, such as the introduction of large sash windows. At Chipchase Castle, for example, both the 14th-century tower and the attached Jacobean house of 1621 had received a complete set of regular sash windows in 1784. Dobson's work on the house in 1819 included the restoration of Jacobean-style fenestration to the bay windows. It is also typical of this period that the patron of this work was not a family of ancient Northumbrian lineage, but Colonel John Reed, a partner in the Newcastle bank Blake, Reed and Co. The new industrial and commercial middle classes were replacing the old country families as patrons and landowners.

Greek and Gothic

The 18th century is rightly seen as a period of classical architecture, an age which admired and promoted the rational aspects of architecture and its association with the intellectual traditions of the well ordered and 'democratic' societies of Greece and Rome. But a thread of Gothic design survived and ran through the century, principally as a superficial decorative style, seen as

Fig. 14 John Nash and
T.H. Liddell,
Ravensworth Castle,
County Durham, 1807
onwards, largely
demolished.

*Newcastle Libraries &
Information Service.*

more appropriate for ornamental buildings in parks. Towards the end of the century, the irregularity and visual potential of the Gothic style was encouraged by theories of the Picturesque, which stressed qualities of variety, texture and informality. So Gothic, 'Tudor-Gothic' and castellated styles flourished side by side with classically derived architecture. Again among the most important proponents of these styles in the early 19th century was Robert Smirke who, as well as being at the forefront of the Greek Revival, was highly influential for his dramatic compositions in the castle style. Smirke's first architectural success, Lowther Castle in Cumberland (1806-11), is in the castellated Gothic style and as a highly important northern example must have been familiar to Dobson. Another stimulating local example of domestic Gothic Revival architecture must have been the 'monster castle' of Ravensworth (fig. 14), a few miles south west of Gateshead. Based on designs made by John Nash in 1807-08, Ravensworth evolved over the next 40 years, long after Nash's death, under the direction of Lord Ravensworth's son, Thomas Henry Liddell. Nash's original plans show a house that would have been the largest Gothic house in the North of England. In contrast to Smirke's symmetrical castellated houses, Ravensworth was to be consciously asymmetrical in the manner pioneered by the theorist of the Picturesque Richard Payne Knight at Downton, Herefordshire, in the 1770s and later adopted by Nash.

Thus, at the time Dobson was building up his professional practice, the two traditions of design, classical and Gothic, were well established and Dobson was well supplied with new and important examples. In addition he had access to numerous, if superficial, books of Gothic designs from which

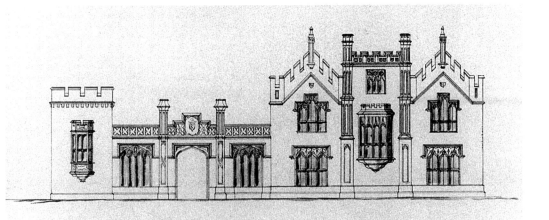

Fig. 15 Thomas Oliver jnr., the former West Jesmond House (now La Sagesse School), Newcastle upon Tyne, in 1865. The south front showing Dobson's work of 1823-27.

Tyne & Wear Archives.

to gain inspiration. Early designs by Dobson for new Gothic houses were made for Sir Thomas Burdon at West Jesmond House (later Jesmond Towers) and for Thomas Emerson Headlam at Black Dene House (later Jesmond Dene House). Burdon, we have already met; Headlam was a leading local Whig politician, twice Mayor of Newcastle, a strong supporter of Earl Grey's moves towards Reform, and also an important local surgeon. Both these houses, in the fashionable and picturesque suburb of Jesmond, have complicated building histories that reveal the varied phases of the 19th-century Gothic Revival.

Black Dene House, worked on by Dobson in 1822 and 1851, was completely rebuilt by F.W. Rich in 1896 and nothing is now visible of the earlier work. Dobson's work at Jesmond Towers is embedded in substantial additions by Thomas Oliver jnr. of 1869 and T.R. Spence of 1885. The appearance of the house before 1869 is fortunately recorded in Oliver's drawing of the house as it then existed (fig. 15).[14] Two phases of building, corresponding presumably to Dobson's two periods of work there of 1817 and 1823-27, are clearly visible. The north side, with its wide, relatively plain windows and solid octagonal corner turrets, represents the earlier house, reflecting the solidity of the Smirke castle style and Dobson's own work at Cheeseburn. This front, overlooking Jesmond Dene, originally had a high terrace hiding the basement and was of only three floors; the fourth was added by Oliver. The south side is Dobson's work of 1823-27, also symmetrical, but with corner towers and battlements elaborately decorated, the windows more richly traceried. Like his contemporary Lying-in Hospital in Newcastle, the details, though well observed, are a mixture of Decorated and Perpendicular elements.

Early houses in the Greek Revival style

Dobson's assured handling of the Greek Revival style came early, as is obvious in the designs for the Royal Jubilee School. Within a few years of beginning work he had adopted and was promoting the style in his domestic work.

None of these early houses, Gothic or classical, was large; they were what their contemporaries would have called villas, houses for men of moderate means, or country retreats for the gentry of the towns.

The notion of the villa had been given architectural form in the mid 18th century by architects such as Sir Robert Taylor and James Paine, and became the ideal vehicle of expression for the variety of picturesque styles prevalent at the end of the century. Despite its serious intellectual overtones, the Greek Revival was just one more decorative style available for the rural architect. The Grecian villa in its landscaped parkland was as picturesque an object as the ruined church or rustic bridge. Nonetheless the Greek style did have serious meaning to a young gentlemen returning from the Grand Tour or to a patron with artistic and intellectual leanings. It tended to appeal to the mind, while Gothic appealed to the heart. The Greek style also had the useful advantage of economy. The flat expanses of wall, regular windows with uncomplicated mouldings, and comparative lack of external ornament saved the work of expensive craftsmen.

Fig. 16 Prestwick Lodge, Northumberland, 1815. Interior of hall.
Philipson Studios, by courtesy of Mr. and Mrs. Wilson.

Many of Dobson's earliest houses, the majority of which were probably Greek, have been demolished, especially those around North Shields, but three excellent examples survive: Prestwick Lodge in Northumberland; the Villa Reale in Newcastle; and Doxford Hall in Northumberland. Prestwick Lodge, of 1815, is very plain; Greek detail is confined externally to the pilasters of the porch, the entrance hall being divided with two sturdy Greek Doric columns (see fig. 16). At the slightly later Villa Reale (1817) the exterior is enlivened with a perhaps over-large Doric portico on the entrance front and a large bay on the garden front (see fig. 17), foreshadowing his mature houses of the 1820s and 1830s. But the sources for this attractive and ultimately 'picturesque' variation of design on the three facades of a house

Fig. 17 Villa Reale,
Newcastle upon Tyne,
1817.

*Photograph: R. Walton,
©University of Northumbria at
Newcastle.*

lie in the villas of John Soane and James Wyatt in the 1790s.

The interiors of these two houses are plain and conventional, decorated with the characteristic motifs of the Greek Revival, though with the addition of some more provincial naturalistic floral plasterwork that suggests the use of craftsmen not yet familiar with the 'correct' ornamental vocabulary. (In contrast, at Newbrough Hall in Northumberland, with which Dobson was evidently associated around 1821, the plasterwork copies motifs from Thomas Hope's *Household Furniture and Interior Decoration* of 1807, an influential compendium of the most fashionable Greek decorative designs.)

The most impressive house of Dobson's early years is Doxford Hall (fig. 18), a beautifully crafted Greek design of 1817-18 with a projecting Doric portico *in antis* (i.e., set into the facade, rather than projecting in front of it) and, a rather old-fashioned feature, two string-courses between ground and first floors. It is set in one of Dobson's most spectacular situations, high on a terrace above a wood-shrouded lake, surely also laid out by Dobson. The

25

Fig. 18 Doxford Hall,
Northumberland, 1817-18.
Authors' photograph.

entrance front is a close relative of the even more sophisticated facade of
Linden Hall, also in Northumberland, designed in all probability by Sir
Charles Monck of Belsay in 1812. Doxford would appear to be the first of
Dobson's houses that benefited from the exceptional masonry skills that
Monck bequeathed to Northumberland following the completion of Belsay
Hall. Dobson had good reason to acknowledge the influence of the masons
employed at Belsay:

> "Sir Charles Monck ... made the masonry of his new house equal to any
> of the polished marble temples of that classic land; this at once intro-
> duced a style of masonry previously unknown ... The masons employed
> at Belsay ... branched off into different parts of England, and since that
> time a Northumbrian mason has been considered amongst the best that
> could be found in any part of the country."[15]

The importance that Dobson gives in his later houses to the hall and
staircase is not apparent in these early designs; even at Doxford, one of the
largest houses of this period, the hall led into a transverse corridor, off which
leads a narrow staircase. No rooms intercommunicated; all led off the long
corridor (this arrangement was altered in the early 20th century). This situation is further evidence of the influence of Cresswell Hall, a now-demolished
mansion in Northumberland of 1820-24, itself inspired by Belsay Hall, on

Dobson's later country house planning in the 1820s (see below, p.xx).

The overwhelming majority of Dobson's early designs were concerned with domestic architecture and arguably it is as a domestic architect that he was to produce his greatest achievements in the forthcoming decades.

Notes

1 The principal sources for Dobson's early life are Fordyce, II, p.765, and Dobson.

2 Mackenzie 1811, II, p.560.

3 J. Dobson, *Presidential Address to the Northern Architectural Association* (April 1859), reprinted in Wilkes, p.104.

4 *Ibid.*

5 See *NC*, 28 April 1810. In this there is the following advertisement, referring to the Royal Jubilee School: "To Builders: Committee appointed for building the New School having determined upon the Plan. Proposals to Mr. John Stokoe at the Manors." The building was completed within a year (see *NC*, 23 February 1811). For confirmation of Dobson's authorship, however, see *Royal Jubilee School Reports*, 1-12 (1811-20), in NCL (L372 N536R), p.2.

6 Drawings by Dobson are in NCRO (NRO 1875/A(50)).

7 Reproduced in a newspaper cutting in Gateshead Central Library illustrations collection.

8 Collection of Major Philip Riddell.

9 NCRO (ZMI B/13/12).

10 DCRO (D/St/X/46A & 81A).

11 Album at Seaton Delaval Hall.

12 Wilkes, p.105.

13 NCL (Cr 428975).

14 TWA (T186/3615).

15 Wilkes, p.108.

Fig. 19 The Fishmarket, Newcastle upon Tyne, 1823-26.
Photograph: R. Walton, ©University of Northumbria at Newcastle.

2

The Spirit of Improvement:
Public Architecture, 1820-1840

Town planning became an increasingly important part of an architect's work during the 19th century. In the previous century landowners in the most fashionable and prosperous cities, such as London, Bath and Edinburgh, had been developing land on the borders of the older parts of the cities to build not only high-quality terraced houses, but also shops, offices and public buildings. In many cases, they employed the best architects of their day (the brothers Adam were particular favourites) to design and carry out these speculative undertakings. In Newcastle too, in the late 18th and early 19th centuries, population pressure on the crowded town encouraged many landowners to sell off fields as building plots. Westgate Hill was created in this period, and Saville Row and Ridley Place extended the town eastwards. The degree to which these developments had architectural character depended on the landowner and on the Town Council, which required an Act of Parliament to create new streets and could specify the quality of the buildings to be erected. Small civic improvements had been made in Newcastle in the 18th century, the creation of Mosley Street and Dean Street from 1784 for example, but until the 1820s most new developments were privately financed and took place on the fringes of the town.

Building the suburbs

We have already noted Dobson's involvement in the selling of building land in Jesmond for Thomas Burdon in 1811 and 1814 – perhaps represented today by the part of Burdon Terrace to the east of Clayton Road. In the following years more sales of this kind were advertised through Dobson's office: in Chirton and North Shields as we would expect, at Forth Banks, at Westgate and off the Shields turnpike at Wallsend, for example.[1] These were probably fairly modest unplanned developments; some may have come to nothing. Of more architectural interest were: a proposal in 1817 for a crescent off Percy Street, not carried out, but perhaps reflected in one of the speculative 'projected streets' on Thomas Oliver's 1830 map of Newcastle, which closely resembles it, as well as the much later St. Thomas's Crescent development; the proposed formation in 1820 of a new road extending Jesmond Road in a straight line to the Great North Road, shortcutting the straggling Sandyford Lane and providing adjoining sites for villas; and the extensive new developments around Pandon Dene, across which John Stokoe's new bridge had been built in 1812.

Like the bridge over the Wear in Sunderland, the Pandon Dene Bridge

Fig 20 The Bridge over
Pandon Dene, Newcastle
upon Tyne.
*Newcastle Libraries &
Information Service.*

(see fig. 20) opened up new land conveniently placed for the town centre
Dobson advertised the fact that building sites were available in thi
favourable location on many occasions between 1813 and 1833. On the wes
side of the Dene, later to be known as Picton Place, and on either side of New
Bridge Street beyond the Dene to the east were built villas, some semi
detached, and terraced houses of some architectural quality, some to design
by Dobson. He had built his own house in this newly fashionable street (see
p.54); similar neat Greek Revival villas overlooked the Dene in Picton Place
around the corner. Ridley Villas, on the north side of New Bridge Street eas
of the bridge, and the terrace on the south side opposite, are, with Dobson'
house, the sole survivors of this rash of development. The semi-detached
Ridley Villas, built on sites leased from Sir Matthew White Ridley, probabl
date from 1823, when Dobson was advertising sites for villas on the north
side of New Bridge Street, so they too may be to his design. By 1827 nine
pairs had been built.

These building schemes around the bridge linked it to the newly extend
ed Ellison Place, "the genteelest and best built part of the town",[2] where
Dobson was also active. Around 1825, he designed David Cram's large
house at the end of the terrace, overlooking the Dene. This house merited a
detailed description in Mackenzie's *History of Newcastle*. He considered i
"noble and capacious" and "the most chaste and elegant specimen of mason
ry exhibited in any private house in the town" and admired the quality o
workmanship and the gardens, "the whole ... designed by, and proceeding

30

under the direction of, Mr. John Dobson, architect".[3] It must have been Dobson's most important town house and its loss has created an irreparable gap in our knowledge of his architecture. Rather later, around 1850, he closed the tree-lined street with Gresham Place, also now demolished, for the coal-owner James Morrison. All these activities resulted in what must have been, before the arrival of the Blyth and Tyne Railway in 1861-63, one of the most attractive residential parts of the town.

Fig. 21 Detail of Thomas Oliver's map of Newcastle of 1844 showing New Bridge Street and the surrounding developments.

Newcastle Libraries & Information Service.

Disease and drains

However, the same cannot be said of the new streets being laid out by Dobson at the opposite end of the town for Isaac Cookson jnr.[4] Cookson was a leading Tyneside industrialist, being particularly involved in the glass industry. Dobson may have worked for the Cooksons before, at their South Shields glassworks in 1817, but no solid evidence has come to light. More importantly, he was later to design one of his most important country houses, Meldon Park, for Cookson (see pp.58-59).

At Westgate, on part of an estate he had acquired in the early 1820s, Cookson decided to sell off freehold building sites, possibly in order to recoup his expenses in the contested Northumberland election of 1826. He employed Dobson to lay out the proposed streets and to design the elevations to which builders and other purchasers of the sites had to conform. From 1827 sites were put up for sale, at 19 guineas each, but were slow to sell. The terraces were named after Cookson's sons, John, Edward and William (see fig. 22), and the whole 'village' was named Arthur's Hill. It is probable that some of the shorter streets above William Street, which included a public house, 'The Cooksons' Arms', were also part of Cookson's estate. The ter-

31

Fig. 22 Edward Street,
Westgate Road, Newcastle
upon Tyne, from 1827,
demolished.

*Newcastle Libraries &
Information Service.*

races had some architectural character, being built with stone from
Cookson's adjacent quarries, with projecting doorcases and an attempt at
overall symmetry along the length of the terraces and in the ends of the terraces facing Westgate Hill. Unfortunately, we have little idea of what these
terraces looked like in detail since they were cleared before the Second
World War. Now only 'The Balmoral' public house remains to remind us of
the architectural pretensions of these early to mid 19th-century streets.

Another nearby estate was to share the eventual sad fate of Arthur's Hill
Thomas Anderson inherited on his uncle's death in 1831 not only the historic
mansion of Anderson Place in the heart of Newcastle, but also other lands
close to the town centre, in particular 30 acres of fields south of Westgate
Road, around what is now Blenheim Street. Anderson began to develop this
land in 1834, the same year he sold Anderson Place to Richard Grainger (see
below, p.47), in the same manner as Cookson, that is by selling freehold
plots to builders or other buyers, on a street plan laid out by Dobson. The
houses were to be built to elevations supplied by Dobson and were to conform to a particular architectural standard. They had to be of brick with stone
bases, sills, window heads, cornices and doorcases. Despite the clearance of
most of these houses during the last century a few remain on Blenheim Street
to give us an idea of their relatively humble yet classically derived facades

The streets themselves were broad and the houses provided with gardens
at the front and lanes at the back. The conditions of sale required that sewers were laid and that the back lanes were paved and provided with drains
However, in the great 1853 cholera epidemic the Westgate township was to
have one of the worst death rates in Newcastle. One person in 57 died of

cholera there, one in 30 in Blandford Street, one in 19 in Blenheim Street and one in 18 in George Street, streets that contributed most to the eventual toll of 291 deaths in the area. What had happened to these apparently elegant new streets in the suburbs of the town to have made them as desperately unhealthy as the ancient tenements on Sandgate and the Quayside? First, the builders had failed to carry out the conditions of sale; few drains and sewers were laid and little paving was carried out. Secondly, the Corporation had utterly failed to use the powers it had under the 1837 and 1846 Local Improvement Acts to force owners to bring their property up to the legal minimum standard. Thirdly, the houses themselves had rapidly become tenemented and overcrowded, because of a shortage of working-class housing. The Report of the Cholera Inquiry Commissioners in 1854 did not hesitate to lay blame on the "deliberate intentions" and "criminal cupidity"[5] of the builders and on the gross inefficiency of the Council in making no attempt to improve matters, despite having full and specific powers to do so. Cookson's streets, for the same reasons, were also centres of the cholera outbreak.

It is sad that Dobson, when called as a witness to the Inquiry, was careful to distance himself from the problem, stating that "small villas I have had very little to do with. It has generally been with buildings on a large scale", and, more evasively, when asked, "I think you said that you had not had much to do with building small houses here?", replied "No".

"Nor do you probably know much about them?"

"I do not at all."[6]

Yet in the 1820s, as we have seen, Dobson was deeply involved in the planning of just such developments at the west and east ends of the town. Dobson's apparent lack of familiarity with the requirements of a healthy water supply is evident also in his work on Gateshead's main sewer in 1849, built while a cholera epidemic raged in the town.[7] The sewer, however, was largely ineffective as it was of too wide a diameter to allow the water it carried to empty it thoroughly. Dobson also considered it a great advantage to have the drainage of Newcastle and Gateshead directed straight into the Tyne. However, the connection between drinking water and cholera did not influence legislation until the 1870s and Dobson was by no means alone in his ignorance.

Richard Grainger had been proud of the quality of water supply and sewerage in his developments, and health and cleanliness became increasingly public concerns in the early 19th century. There had been public baths in Newcastle since at least 1781, and a subscription was opened in 1836 for shares in New Public Baths to designs by Dobson on the site of the present City Baths in Northumberland Road. (However, part of them was shortly afterwards converted into an inn, so presumably they were not a great commercial success.) The Whittle Dene Water Company, of which Richard Grainger was a director, provided Newcastle's first clean water supply from

reservoirs near Welton in Northumberland, with Dobson designing the pretty little "keeper's cottage and Directors' Rooms" (fig. 23) overlooking the reservoirs in 1848.[8]

Cholera, meanwhile, was also a factor in the decision to encourage the creation of new cemeteries in the 1820s and 1830s. Westgate Hill Cemetery had been opened in 1831 to designs by John

Fig. 23 Whittle Dene Reservoir, Northumberland, Keeper's Cottage and Directors' Rooms, 1848.
Authors' photograph.

Fig. 24 Newcastle General Cemetery (Jesmond Old Cemetery), 1834-36, chapels and north entrance.
Photograph: R. Walton, ©University of Northumbria at Newcastle.

Green of Newcastle (see Chapter 6) while Dobson was probably responsible for laying out the new Gateshead Cemetery in 1834. But it was the Newcastle General Cemetery Company that employed Dobson in 1834 to create what is now recognised as one of his finest surviving works.[9] The Newcastle General Cemetery, in Jesmond, is triangular, bounded by a high stone wall. The south entrance is made through two massive gate piers of uncompromising severity. The larger north entrance (fig. 24) incorporates two chapels, one for Anglicans and one for Dissenters. These entrances are among Dobson's purest Greek Revival designs, of great originality and comparable with the work of the great German neoclassical architect Schinkel. Here Dobson exploited the intrinsic character of Greek architecture, its noble monumentality and timelessness, and employed to the best his

own talents for scholarly detail, fine construction and, most importantly, superb architectural design. However, it is interesting to note that Dobson's initial proposal for the cemetery (fig. 25) was even grander. This scheme, which also illustrates Dobson's interest in picturesque landscaping, would have been on an adjacent site slightly to the west of the present cemetery, with a projected street

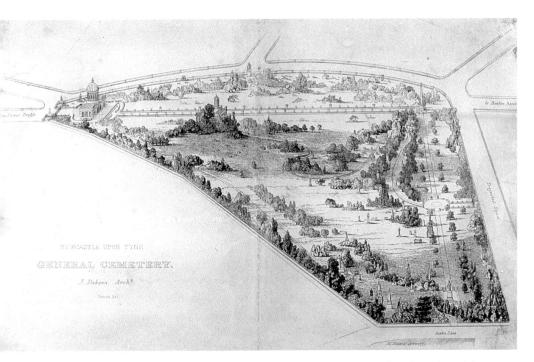

Fig. 25 Dobson's initial
proposal for the Newcastle
General Cemetery, 1834.
Tyne & Wear Archives.

running north-south on the eastern side and the main orientation of the cemetery running east to west. A central dome would have surmounted the main
pair of chapels (to the west), with an obelisk at or near the east entrance, and
a colonnaded mausoleum in the centre of the layout.[10]

In any event, J. C. Loudon, who illustrated several of Dobson's designs
in his prolific architectural publications[11] and became an authority on cemetery design, particularly admired Dobson's principal entrance to the cemetery as built. Loudon would have approved too of the layout and planting
within it, though perhaps not of the weeping willows. However, with its
numerous excellent classical funerary monuments and mature trees, the
Newcastle General (Jesmond Old Cemetery) is the North East's finest
Victorian cemetery. Dobson's daughter Margaret wrote in 1885:

> "Mr. Dobson's design for the Jesmond Cemetery exhibits very striking-
> ly one of the great characteristics of his works – namely, their appropri-
> ate sentiment. The cemetery is ornamentally laid out, and yet there is no
> mistaking it for a mere garden, or in fact for anything but a place devot-
> ed to the sacred purpose for which it is intended. The church and the
> Dissenters' chapel grouped together form a most imposing entrance to
> our Campo Santo. The designer, with a true artistic hand, has made all
> the existing features to form part of his plan, and nowhere has his taste
> and skill as landscape gardener been more effective. Even the long blank
> wall facing the road, marked by a dwarf railing enclosing a shrubbery
> and plantation covered with trailing ivy, is pleasing to the eye."[12]

The cemetery is also an architectural memorial in more ways than one, for it contains the graves not only of John Dobson himself but also of his Newcastle architectural contemporaries William Stokoe, Thomas Oliver and John Green.

Working for Richard Grainger

In contrast to his denial of association with the building of small houses, Dobson, in his evidence to the Cholera Inquiry Commissioners, was happy to claim responsibility for Eldon Square, the sort of urban architecture he was proud to have been associated with. Eldon Square was indeed remarkable, the first formal town planning scheme in Newcastle and the first of the Corporation's 19th-century ventures into large-scale town improvement. The scheme originated with the creation of Blackett Street in 1824, just beyond and parallel to the town wall. Previously the road had consisted of "a few straggling houses and workshops ... the street, being unpaved, was dirty and almost impassable ... a useless waste, where manure was deposited".[13] Dobson had surveyed and valued the old street for the Blacketts, on whose land it lay, as early as 1815,[14] and Mackenzie, who was writing at the time of building and with information supplied by Dobson, attributes the design of the brick houses in Blackett Street to Dobson. However, Thomas Oliver, the cartographer and Dobson's architectural contemporary, claimed[15] that the Council had originally commissioned plans for Blackett Street and Eldon Square from him and that drawings and a model had been submitted Dobson had been asked for his opinion and on receiving his proposed alterations the Council decided to build Eldon Square according to Dobson's elevations. Oliver states that Blackett Street was built to his own designs and plans. It is at any rate clear that Dobson was responsible for the facades of

Fig. 26 Eldon Square, Newcastle upon Tyne, 1825, largely demolished. From an etching after T.M. Richardson.
Laing Art Gallery, Newcastle upon Tyne.

Eldon Square, facades that contributed greatly to the its distinction not just in Newcastle, but nationally.

Unlike most large urban developments of the Regency period, such as John Nash's contemporary Regent's Park terraces in London, Eldon Square (fig. 26) was characterised by high-quality ashlar masonry rather than stucco, and was one of the earliest uses of stone for domestic architecture in Newcastle. In addition, Eldon Square was comparatively plain and undecorated, with the notable exception of the Greek honeysuckle motifs in the cast iron balconies. In the true neoclassical manner, the angles of the three terraces that composed the Square were accented with shallow Doric pilasters, and the centre of the north side was stressed with a higher roofline and, in the original design, though unbuilt, an Ionic portico. The design seems an unconscious echo of David Stephenson's North Shields Market Place, but dressed in the severer clothes of the Greek Revival. The centre of the Square was filled with an ornamental garden for the use of residents.

The builder of Eldon Square and Blackett Street, and the man on whom the commercial risk of the venture rested, was Richard Grainger (1797-1861). For the next fifteen years it was to be impossible to separate the architectural developments of Newcastle from the ambitions, financial skills and enthusiasms of this man.[16] Unlike Dobson, ten years his senior, Grainger was of the most humble origins, having been the son of a Quayside porter who died when the boy was 13, and of an "industrious, clever and neat handed"[17] mother, who supported her family by washing, starching and glove making. Grainger had a respectable schooling and an apprenticeship with a builder and house-carpenter. Success as a builder on his own account and a profitable marriage gave him the resources to undertake the Eldon Square project with confidence. What cannot be doubted was his desire to see the town benefit commercially, culturally and architecturally from his speculations. In 1827 he made available a site in Blackett Street for T.M. Richardson and H.P. Parker's Northern Academy of Arts, built to Dobson's designs for £2,000. The Northern Academy of Arts (fig. 27) had on the first floor a recessed central bay with columns *in antis*, in a style echoing that of John Shaw's Cresswell Hall, Northumberland, of 1820-24 (see p.126). About the same time Grainger leased on favourable terms a further site for the Library of the Literary, Scientific and Mechanical Institution, opened in 1828. The Institution, a less familiar building, had a rather more elegant facade, though it was of stucco rather than stone. There is no evidence that Dobson was its architect, but he was a full member of the Institution's Governing Committee and lectured to its members.

Fig. 27 The Northern Academy of Arts, Blackett Street, Newcastle upon Tyne, 1827, demolished. From an engraving. *Tyne & Wear Museums.*

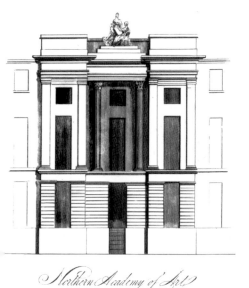

Northern Academy of Art

NEWCASTLE UPON TYNE.

Working for the Corporation

In the same period Dobson was also engaged in some other public buildings. For Newcastle's Common Council he made a semicircular addition to the east end of the Guildhall to replace the ancient decayed Maison de Dieu, originally a charity almshouse, but by then used as a Quayside warehouse. Dobson's addition consisted of a new covered fish market, a new Merchants' Court, offices for the town clerk, his deputy and the protonotary, and a fireproof room for the Corporation records. It was built from 1823 to 1826 and comprised a bold semicircular colonnade (see fig. 19 and colour plate iii), with two storeys of offices above, joined to William Newton and David Stephenson's earlier neoclassical refacing work at the Guildhall of 1796. With reference to this new structure, Margaret Dobson relates an amusing anecdote:

> "Mr. Dobson designed the Fish Market, Sandhill, Newcastle, the business of which was previously carried on in the open air. The good ladies who presided the stalls seriously objected to be removed from their old quarters, and for some time Mr. Dobson received such an impolite reception from them that he was obliged to avoid their presence. But when bad weather came, and they realised the comfort of their new abode, they relented, and a deputation of fair dames arrived at his residence in New Bridge Street with a peace offering of fish for a Christmas dinner. Ever after that he was their 'Cannie Mr. Dobson'."[18]

In any event, despite the fishwives' initial lack of enthusiasm for their new market, the building was considered "one of the handsomest architectural ornaments of the town which has cleared the Sandhill of the number of fish stalls and widened the entrance to the Quay".[19] Inside the Merchant Adventurers' Court on the first floor Dobson refitted their 17th-century carved oak panelling and elaborate fireplace and concocted a new cornice and ceiling in early 17th-century style, with a fictitious date of 1620. His double-glazed windows were considered an innovation.

While the fish market was building, in 1824 Dobson made additions to William Newton's Newcastle Lunatic Asylum, off Gallowgate, of 1767. He enlarged and improved it for the Corporation, who were introducing a more humanitarian regime into what had been little more than a private prison. The next year Dobson designed his first important public building in the Gothic style, the former Lying-in Hospital in New Bridge Street (fig. 28). He gave his plans for

Fig. 28 The former Lying-in Hospital, New Bridge Street, Newcastle upon Tyne, 1825.

Photograph: R. Walton, ©University of Northumbria at Newcastle.

this charitable 'asylum for poor married pregnant women' free and they do not as yet speak of great confidence in the Gothic style. The building is a rectangular block with hipped roof, the facade of ashlar with windows and niches in a mixture of Decorated and Perpendicular styles. The side elevations of the building are of coursed rubble with plain rectangular windows with Tudor drip mouldings. The individual elements are well detailed and based on observation of medieval originals, but the whole is unconvincingly composed.

The great prisons

By far the most important civic enterprise with which Dobson was concerned at this time was the new Gaol and House of Correction at Carliol Square, Newcastle, built between 1823 and 1828 at the cost of a little over £35,000.[20] His plans were selected by the Gaol Committee of the Common Council from a number of competing designs in October 1822. But the choice must have been a foregone conclusion since Dobson had accompanied the prime mover of the scheme, the municipal reformer and Mayor of Newcastle Archibald Reed, on a fact-finding visit to London in December 1818, and in July 1820 attended a meeting of the Gaol Committee to advise its members on possible designs. The decision to build a new prison had been formally taken earlier that year after the old gaol in the New Gate (demolished in 1823) had been criticised at the Spring Assizes as insufficient, insecure, inconvenient, too small and out of repair.

At first, the Castle Garth was favoured as a site for the new complex, and Dobson seized on the opportunity to propose a substantial scheme of improvement. This would have cleared surrounding property and converted the old castle into a debtors' prison, with a new gateway to the south east, linking to a governor's house, magistrates' hall, gaol and house of correction, all in a castellated style and enclosed by corner towers and an encircling wall. A new street was to have connected the complex with St. Nicholas's Church, and, as Mackenzie observed, "the county courts, the old Castle, the new prisons, and St. Nicholas's steeple, would have presented an incomparably grand and imposing group".[21] The Council was too timid to accept this plan, probably on grounds of expense, though for a time it was prepared to consider the dubious idea of having the house of correction within the Castle Garth and the gaol elsewhere. Ultimately they decided on an entirely new but controversial site at the south end of the Carliol Croft, now Carliol Square.

During the late 18th and early 19th centuries many prisons were being built as a result of the general impetus towards public improvement. Prison reform was specifically influenced by philanthropists such as John Howard, who had thoroughly investigated gaols in Britain and Europe and argued ceaselessly for more humane conditions capable of improving rather than degrading a criminal's moral worth. Most new designs represented a major advance on the old system of manacled prisoners huddled together in a single space or confined indiscriminately in insanitary cells. They embodied

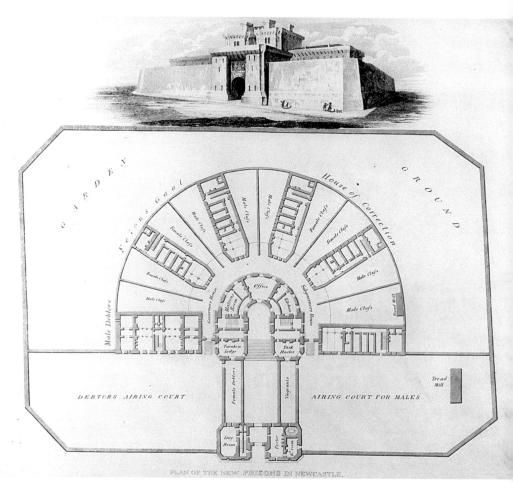

PLAN OF THE NEW PRISONS IN NEWCASTLE.

Fig. 29 Gaol and House of Correction, Newcastle upon Tyne, 1822-28, demolished. From a plan published in Mackenzie 1827.

Photograph: Tyne and Wear Museums.

more modern and sophisticated notions of correction and reform, reflecting the rationalist virtues of the Enlightenment, and in particular the idea of classification, whereby different classes of prisoner were separated according to sex, age and the nature of the crime. As a result such plans tended to be especially typical of public architecture during the neoclassical age, being extremely ordered, and geometrically arranged. Some were variations of the Greek cross system favoured by Howard himself, others were radiating or concentric designs influenced by the 'Panopticon', an all-purpose if ultimately impractical proposal formulated by the philosopher Jeremy Bentham in 1791. This extended the idea of surveillance to an extreme degree, featuring a masonry cylinder with cells arranged around the outside walls and partitions radiating from a central inspection tower.[22]

Dobson addressed the problem with characteristic thoroughness, studying other examples of prison designs such as that at Liverpool, which he admired, and at Edinburgh, where the circular arrangement of cells gave too much opportunity for the inmates to converse. He also canvassed the opinions of prison governors and other experts on his plan, and would certainly have been aware of the 'Panopticon' idea. Another influence might have been the Millbank Penitentiary, then under construction on concentric lines, which he must surely have seen during his London visit with Archibald Reed to examine the famous Newgate Prison, built by George Dance the younger between 1769 and 1778.

The most up-to-date concepts of punishment, security and reform were reflected in Dobson's design for the Newcastle Gaol. It consisted of a horse-shoe-shaped central block containing offices and supervisors' rooms, linked to a gatehouse and overlooking six radiating wings (of which only five were initially built). The whole formed a semicircular complex closed off from the outside world by a walled area, which created a garden, exercise courts, and yards. There are minor discrepancies between the plan published by Mackenzie (illustrated here, fig. 29) and Dobson's original design,[23] but it is clear that the central block was flanked by two slightly larger wings, one for debtors and one for the most hardened criminals. The remaining four radiat-ing wings as proposed were identical cell blocks giving separate accommo-dation for males and females, and with cells arranged on one side only (alter-nating floor by floor), thus preventing communication between the blocks. These were further separated by dividing walls. Construction was of stone with intermediate floors supported by iron columns, as advocated for the 'Panopticon', to reduce the risk of fire. The result was an outstandingly orig-inal design, combining the merits of a radiating scheme with the main fea-tures of London's Newgate Prison, a central block with flanking wings. The overwhelming visual severity of the Carliol Square Prison, though more like a feudal fortress than Dance's awe-inspiring classical design, also continued the tradition of symbolic or associational expression in architecture, where-by its function was expressed through the choice of 'appropriate' styles and forms.

Dobson's other major prison schemes were also pro-duced at about this time. In 1821 he won a competition for the design of the Northumberland Gaol, House of Correction and Sessions House at Morpeth. Built (1822-28) like its Newcastle counterpart of local stone and equivalent in scale, size and cost, it was more authentically castellated in style – the architect himself stated that Conway, Beaumaris and Caernarvon Castles had inspired the design[24] – with a plan (fig.

Fig. 30 Northumberland Gaol, House of Correction and Sessions House, Morpeth, 1821-28, partly demolished. Plan as pub-lished in Mackenzie 1825.
Photograph: Tyne and Wear Museums.

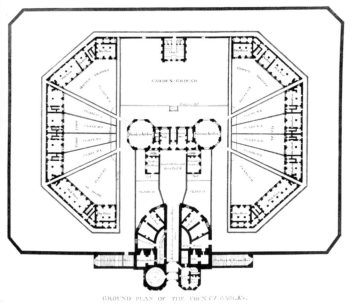

GROUND PLAN OF THE COUNTY GAOL.

41

30) largely based upon the concept of the medieval castle keep and curtain wall. There may also have been a more contemporary influence from the castellated designs of Robert Adam and his followers, such as John Paterson's Brancepeth Castle, County Durham (1818-21). Dobson would also have known Robert Smirke's massive Citadel and Law Courts complex in Carlisle (1810-11). Thus the horseshoe-shaped structure, the central feature of the Newcastle design (which had not needed to incorporate a court house), is here combined into a gigantic gatehouse 72 feet high (fig. 31) containing a porter's lodge with a monumental staircase leading to the Sessions House above. Although now converted to a different use, this survives largely intact as a splendid semicircular space with gallery and rib-vaulted ceiling (see fig. 32). The rather simplified quasi-medieval detailing of this and other surviving rooms resembles that of Dobson's contemporary Tudor-Gothic country houses. Under the Sessions House an arched entrance led via a court to a central building, part of which survives, containing offices and the governor's house, and which overlooked sets of vaulted cells facing inwards over walled courts, all within an overall octagonal plan. Again the whole complex was surrounded by two sets of walls.

A comparison of Morpeth and Newcastle gaols, two of the most important designs of Dobson's whole career, suggests that he was influenced also by the most famous new prison of the day, the 'Maison de Force' near Ghent. Begun in 1773, it incorporated eight trapezoid courts joined to each side of a central octagon, with cells (arranged in this case back to back) placed around the circumference and along the divisions between the courts; it was described by John Howard in several of his works. The Morpeth and Newcastle designs, minus the gatehouse element, would if com-

Fig. 31 Northumberland Gaol, House of Correction and Sessions House, Morpeth, 1821-28. Gatehouse as surviving.
Photograph: R. Walton, ©University of Northumbria at Newcastle.

Fig 32. Northumberland Gaol, House of Correction and Sessions House, Morpeth, 1821-28. Interior of former Sessions House.
©Crown copyright NMR.

bined closely resemble the plan of the 'Maison de Force'.

At this time Dobson was also commissioned to make additions to the Hexham House of Correction (1822), which he executed in the severest block-like style. In the following year he built small prisons at Belford (an informal neo-Tudor design, unexpectedly domestic in type) and Wooler, both in Northumberland. More importantly, Dobson had won a competition in March 1822 for the design of the Carlisle County Gaol. Soon afterwards, however, his plans were rejected on the advice of John Orridge, the Governor (and designer) of Bury St. Edmunds Gaol, which was a fully developed radial type. A completely new design formulated by William Nixon in consultation with Orridge, an internationally respected expert, was substituted; this was further modified after Nixon's death by Christopher Hodgson and the building completed in Gothic style in 1827.[25] No trace can be found of Dobson's design, but it was almost certainly castellated and probably resembled his Morpeth plan. Its rejection may well have been a further reason for Dobson to adopt the radiating principle, at least in part, in his Newcastle scheme.

Creating the "City of Palaces"

B y the mid 1820s, the spirit of improvement was flourishing as never before. Eneas Mackenzie, who clearly had Dobson's advice on all aspects of architectural activity, devoted a whole chapter of his *History of Newcastle* to "Improvements Effected and Projected" and described in detail several extravagant proposals.[26] One, "according to the plans ... by Mr. Dobson", was to continue Blackett Street in a straight line across Gallowgate, eventually joining the Carlisle turnpike; another, soon abandoned, was to continue the line of villas at Picton Place in a bold sweep to Vine Lane along the banks of Pandon Dene; a third was to continue Trafalgar Street down to the Pandon Burn and thence to the Quayside, thus providing a further and gentler means of ascent from the river to the higher parts of the town. It is interesting that the first and third of these schemes appear as proposals on Thomas Oliver's 1830 map. In the same map Oliver also partially adopted Dobson's plans, described in detail by Mackenzie, to exploit the open spaces of Anderson Place and The Nuns.

The 13 acres of ground attached to the Elizabethan mansion of Anderson Place had once been the seat of the Blacketts and was a unique feature to find within the walls of a town. In 1783 the Blacketts had offered the house to the Corporation, who felt unable to purchase it, perhaps because of their simultaneous involvement in one of their rare 18th-century enterprises, the creation of Mosley and Dean Streets. The rejection was lamented by Mackenzie who no doubt hoped, with Dobson, that the detailed publication of the latter's grand and ambitious scheme would help to bring about its fulfilment.

Dobson proposed that on the site of Anderson Place itself should be built a Mansion House with "four handsome stone fronts, the north, south and west sides to rise from a bold terrace; and the latter to be ornamented with eight beautiful pillars. The east front to face Pilgrim Street, and to have a lofty grand portico, capable of admitting carriages."[27] With the sensitive eye of the landscape gardener, he proposed retaining the avenue of trees leading from Pilgrim Street to Anderson Place as part of the ceremonial approach to this new 'civic palace'.

To the west of the Mansion House was to be a large open market place bounded by four wide new streets lined with new buildings. These streets were carefully planned to make the most of existing features in the town: the west street was to run from Blackett Street, opening opposite and perpendicular to the centre of Eldon Square, to the junction of Newgate and the Bigg Market, then a severe bottleneck; the east street would have begun at the junction of Blackett Street and High Friar Street, running in front of the proposed Mansion House and into High Bridge opposite the then New Butcher Market, which was to be given a more imposing entrance. The north and south bounds of the new square would have run off Pilgrim Street on either side of the Mansion House, towards Newgate Street. However, these proposed streets would have had no impact on the town beyond the area bounded by Blackett Street, Pilgrim Street, High Bridge Street and Newgate Street.

Dobson's plan for the exploitation of Anderson Place and its grounds would undoubtedly have resulted in a most splendid centrepiece of the town, even if limited in its scope. That it was not built and was eventually superseded by Grainger's successful and substantially different proposal reflects Dobson's lack of financial and Council backing and probably the scheme's lack of commercial viability. Compared to Grainger's, it seems to have lacked sufficient street frontage and building area. Moreover, Grainger included several additional public buildings in his plan and, although this echoes some of Dobson's ideas, it takes into account to a greater extent the geography of the town. For a more detailed discussion of Grainger's scheme and of Dobson's involvement in it see below and Chapter 6. In the meantime, three of Dobson's proposed new streets appeared in John Wood's 1827 map of Newcastle, and one of them, that leading off Eldon Square, is shown as a 'projected street' on Oliver's 1830 map, thus keeping at least part of the scheme alive.[28]

Meanwhile, in 1829 Oliver achieved his first major architectural success by designing Leazes Terrace for Grainger. Leazes Terrace (see p.125) is over twice the length of any of the Eldon Square ranges and is more heavily ornamented, with fluted Corinthian pilasters at the corners and a richly decorated frieze. It was built on Grainger's own land and was a building speculation of magnificent proportions, the most splendid early 19th-century terraced development in the country outside John Nash's contemporary 'Metropolitan Improvements' in London.

While Leazes Terrace and Eldon Square were still under construction, Grainger was undertaking yet another major speculation. In 1830 he sent to Newcastle's Common Council plans and a model of a proposed Corn

Exchange to be built on land he had acquired in Pilgrim Street, opposite the end of Mosley Street. The building, designed by Dobson, was to cost just over £5,000, excluding an ornamental stone front. However, we know that Dobson had previously, around 1825, made plans for a Corn Market or Exchange on a site occupied by the "ancient and crazy dwellings" of Middle Street, between the Groat Market and the Cloth Market, opposite St Nicholas's Church.[29] The designs were probably made for a private consortium, which had been negotiating with the Council for approval to build such a new Corn Market. A covered Corn Market was evidently a very much-needed public improvement, but there were to be years of argument between the various interested parties within and outside the Council before one was eventually built in 1838 on the Middle Street site, to John and Benjamin Green's designs, though left uncompleted. What Dobson's earlier design looked like we do not know, except that, in Mackenzie's ambiguous words, its entrance was to consist of "a noble colonnade, executed in a simple and grand style, to harmonize with the architecture of the adjoining Christian temple",[30] i.e. St. Nicholas's. This suggests a design in the Gothic style. Grainger was set against the Middle Street site; as late as 1838 he was offering his Central Exchange site free to the Council, for use as a Corn Exchange, despite a committee of the Council having in February 1831 decided on the Middle Street location in preference to Grainger's earlier Pilgrim Street offer.

Even so, Grainger felt himself committed to erecting a major public building on the rejected Pilgrim Street site. In June 1831 work began on the Royal Arcade (colour plate v and fig. 33), which was finished, almost miraculously, in May 1832. As a Corn Exchange the site would seem to have had distinct advantages, being near to the quayside, but also close to the other principal markets, the New Butcher Market to the north of Mosley Street, and the older markets opposite St. Nicholas's. Instead, Grainger decided

Fig. 33 The Royal Arcade, Newcastle upon Tyne, 1831-32, demolished. The interior, from an engraving of 1833 after T. Allom.
Laing Art Gallery, Newcastle upon Tyne.

45

to create a shopping arcade, a fashionable building type not yet seen in Newcastle, but common in London and Paris.[31] The Royal Arcade was a major contribution to Newcastle's public architecture and one that well deserved the presentation to Grainger of a silver tureen and salver at a public dinner held in his honour in July 1833. The arcade itself was based closely on the highly successful Lowther Arcade in London, designed by Witherden Young in 1830, which was held to surpass the famous Burlington Arcade. In its turn, Newcastle's Royal Arcade was considered to be superior, particularly in its lighting, to the Lowther Arcade, and thus to be the finest in the country. It was 250 feet long and 20 feet wide, floored with chequered stone and black marble and contained 16 shops. Lighting was by eight conical skylights set in domes.

The Royal Arcade was the first building of its kind to be built as part of a self-contained commercial development. Thus it was a single vast structure containing, in addition to the shopping arcade, banks, auction rooms, professional offices, Government offices, a post office and a steam and vapour bath. The front to Pilgrim Street dominated the 18th-century houses of the nearby streets, rising to a height of 75 feet, with giant Corinthian columns above a severe Doric ground floor. A heavily ornamented cornice, an attic storey with figures and a large figure group by David Dunbar the younger lay above. A similar block at a lower level at the east end of the Arcade faced Manor Chare.

The Arcade did, however, have commercial problems. Shops were still unlet in 1841 when the topographers Collard and Ross recognised that the exit to the unattractive Manor Chare discouraged the use of the Arcade as a thoroughfare,[32] which would have been a desirable attribute; the most successful arcades were U-shaped, or led from one fashionable shopping street to another. The post office moved out in the 1860s and demolition of the Arcade was first proposed as early as the 1880s, by which time Manor Chare was regarded as an unsavoury neighbourhood. The Arcade was eventually lost in the 1960s, blackened and dilapidated (see Chapter 7). The Royal Fine Art Commission's recommendation that the facade be rebuilt close to its original site was not carried out; the elegant but sadly ignored interior was recreated in the Swan House office complex, itself now due for redevelopment. The Arcade's commercial failure must lie at Grainger's feet; architecturally it amounted to one of Dobson's most dignified compositions, showing his mastery of bold large-scale forms, perhaps not to be surpassed until his early designs for Newcastle's Central Station 15 years later.

Dobson in the centre of Newcastle

The climax of Dobson's association with Richard Grainger was the work he did for Grainger's major redevelopment in the centre of Newcastle, centred on the Anderson Place site. Grainger presented his plan, notably different from Dobson's earlier scheme of c.1825, to the Common Council in May 1834, while he was in negotiation with Thomas Anderson over the purchase of Anderson Place. The plan was soon published, was briefly controversial on account of its effect on property prices in the lower part of the town, but was by mid July 1834 overwhelmingly approved by popular acclaim and by the Common Council itself. Essential to the latter's approval was the support and advice Grainger had from the solicitor John Clayton, Newcastle's Town Clerk since 1822. The story of Grainger's great enterprise, which resulted in "the best designed large city in England",[33] has been well told elsewhere.[34] It is clear that Grainger had architects working in his office full time who probably laid out the streets and designed most of them. John Wardle and George Walker seem to have been most active in this respect (when setting up on their own account in 1841, they said they had worked for Grainger since 1834). John and Benjamin Green were the architects of the new Theatre Royal and the rest of the block between Market Street and Shakespeare Street. Dobson's designs seem to have been confined to the new Markets,[35] perhaps including their street elevations, the varied institutions – Cordwainers Hall, Dispensary, Music Hall, etc. – on the north side of Nelson Street, and the east side of Grey Street between Shakespeare Street and Mosley Street (see fig. 34 and colour plate xi).[36] There is no evidence of Thomas Oliver's involvement; the rest of the street elevations must have been the responsibility of Wardle and Walker.

For the most part the streets are plain and untheatrical, certainly when compared with John Nash's contemporary 'Metropolitan Improvements', and again have the advantage over them in being solidly built in finely

Fig. 34 Grey Street, Newcastle upon Tyne, 1834-37, the lower east side.
Newcastle Libraries & Information Service.

carved stone rather than cheaper painted stucco. The excellence of the design lies in the careful way each range is composed with balancing central and terminal emphases. The highlights are the Theatre Royal, and the Central Exchange triangle with its three domed corners. Dobson's portion of Grey Street is notably distinct in design from the typical Wardle and Walker pattern. In some respects Dobson's style is heavier and coarser, but it is also more varied, more three dimensional; less elegant perhaps, but more characterful.

Grey Street was not completed until 1837 and its termination, the Grey Monument, for which Dobson had unsuccessfully submitted a design, was erected in 1838; the Markets, however, were the first part of the scheme to be finished, having been opened on 24 October 1835, within one year of the contract being signed. The building cost the Corporation £36,290, less the £15,000 which Grainger had paid for the Corporation's existing Butcher Market, south of High Bridge. Dobson's enormous covered market (see colour plates xv, xvi), the largest in the country, was divided into two parts, an open-plan Vegetable Market, 318 feet by 57 feet, with a complex roof structure designed originally without the cast iron pillars later inserted, apparently at the request of the Corporation's architects,[37] and a Butcher Market housed in a network of avenues and arcades with classical detailing. The whole was contained within four streets of shops and houses "surpassing anything in street architecture hitherto witnessed in this neighbourhood",[38] a foretaste of the quality of Grainger's street architecture elsewhere.

Fig. 35 St. Thomas's Place, Newcastle upon Tyne, c.1840, demolished.

Newcastle Libraries & Information Service.

The 1820s and 1830s saw other streets being laid out and built up in Newcastle and beyond. Neville Street was planned by Dobson in 1828, to link the commercial centre of the town to the rapidly developing west end,

and opened in 1835; St. Mary's Place, designed by Dobson as his only non-classical street, to complement his church of St. Thomas's opposite, was being built, perhaps for Grainger, from 1829.

Stately terraces of the 1830s and 1840s along the Great North Road – Jesmond Terrace, St. Mary's Terrace (the only one remaining), St. Thomas's Place (fig. 35) and Jesmond High Terrace – can be attributed to Dobson, as can Carlton Terrace on the north side of Jesmond Road, itself first proposed by Dobson in 1820, but probably not laid out until the 1830s. Carlton Terrace dates from c.1840 and is a late example of a terraced residential development treated as an architectural whole with projecting and slightly raised centre and wings. Shallow Doric pilasters and paired brackets are the only remaining classical details, but the composition is in a tradition that originated over 100 years earlier in John Wood the elder's Queen Square at Bath of 1729 onwards.

Terraces and towns elsewhere

Tynemouth and North Shields were entering a period of rapid growth encouraged by the creation of the railway link from Newcastle. At North Shields Dobson had surveyed land between Tynemouth and the present Linskill Terrace for William Linskill as early as 1816 for proposed housing development.[39] This having been achieved in the following decades, in 1860 Dobson designed crescents in the same area, east of Washington Terrace, for the same family.[40] Overlooking the sea at Tynemouth, Percy Gardens was laid out by Dobson in 1839 close to his Crown Hotel and public baths of 1838. Dobson was probably also responsible for the group of streets around Prior's Terrace, close to his later Collingwood Monument.

At Monkwearmouth in the 1830s, the Wear Bridge was still encouraging growth north of the river, where Sir Hedworth Williamson was developing his land. In 1835 Dobson laid out Bonner's Field, a new street linking the bridge to Sir Hedworth's North Quay, and built a small dock office at his North Dock in about 1837; for the same patron he later laid out several residential streets north of Dame Dorothy Street. At nearby Roker, where industry gave way to recreation, Dobson designed another group of hotel, terrace and baths for the Abbs family. Shares in the Monkwearmouth Bath Company were obtainable through Dobson's office.

Dobson's other important County Durham patron was Lord Londonderry, who, with Lord Lambton, was one of the richest landowners in the country. Their wealth originated with coal and between them the two families owned over half the coal shipped from Sunderland around 1820. Lord Londonderry was determined to avoid the harbour dues at Sunderland by building his own harbour on land he had just acquired at Seaham. To complement this he invited Dobson to design a new town.[41] Initial consultations took place in 1823, but by the time the foundation stones of the harbour (planned by the civil engineer William Chapman) and town were laid in November 1828, Dobson's proposals had already been largely abandoned. In the previous month Londonderry had written at length to Dobson, giving detailed analysis and criticism of the plan, including the following:

"I entertain no doubt if we adopt in the first instance what is most convenient to ourselves & to all the ramifications which are to establish the work, that embellishments will follow in due time. Large & expensive foundations of overgrown buildings, will not inspire confidence in the completion of the work but the reverse. Small neat compact buildings suitable for the concerns of trade are all we should endeavour to [have]. If your plan has any fault it appears to me to be on too expensive a scale ... The portico in the Inn and in the shops need not be contemplated at first. The former building will be built by ourselves and I fear is a dead lay out of ready cash".[42]

Londonderry was determined not to invest money in the town when it was more urgently needed for the harbour. So Dobson's design, delicately Italianate, with the railway running down to the harbour beneath the colliery offices, and flanked by an hotel, shopping area, and two large stone built crescents, with workers' houses behind, was not carried out. The street plan was revised and leaseholds were sold haphazardly with little enforcement of architectural standards. Londonderry's resources were being spent on the harbour, which cost over £118,000, and on the massive rebuilding of Wynyard Park, his country house.

Notes

1 Numerous newspaper references collected in A.G. Chamberlain, *North East Architects and the Building Trade to 1865: References in Local Newspapers*, 1986 (typescript deposited in NCL), have been invaluable in identifying Dobson's lesser activities, many examples of which follow.

2 Mackenzie 1827, I, p.190.

3 *Ibid.*

4 W.R. Foster, *Some Notes on House Building in Newcastle upon Tyne, 1820-1860*, 1981 (typescript deposited in NCL), provided several details for the following account.

5 *Report of the Cholera Inquiry Commissioners*, 1854, p.x.

6 *Ibid.*, pp.312-13.

7 F.W. Rogers, 'Gateshead and the Public Health Act of 1848', *AA*, 4th series, vol. xlix, 1971, pp.153ff.

8 R.W. Rennison, *Water to Tyneside*, 1979, p.57.

9 *CL*, 2 July 1981, pp.68-69.

10 See A. Morgan, *A Fine and Private Place, Jesmond Old Cemetery*, 2000, p.6. Dobson's initial proposal is illustrated in a Prospectus of 29 January 1834 for a proposed "Cemetery in Jesmond Fields", in TWA (DT/NGC/5).

11 As for example 'A Cottage in the Gothic Style for an Upper Servant' (for R. Ellison, Esq., of Sudbrooke, Lincolnshire), a 'Double Cottage for Two Upper Servants' and 'A Cottage in the Old English Style', in J.C. Loudon, *An Encylopaedia of Cottage, Farm and*

Villa Architecture and Furniture (first additional supplement to 1st edn. of 1833), 1842, pp.1185-89.

12 Dobson, pp.46-47.

13 Mackenzie 1827, I, p.188.

14 NCRO (ZBL 62/4).

15 Oliver, p.97.

16 For detailed accounts of Grainger's activities see I. Ayris, *A City of Palaces: Richard Grainger and the Making of Newcastle upon Tyne*, 1997, and Wilkes and Dodds.

17 Quoted in Wilkes and Dodds, p.23.

18 Dobson, p.69.

19 Mackenzie 1827, I, p.217.

20 See the Minutes of the Gaol Committee, TWA (279/1).

21 Mackenzie 1827, I, p.203.

22 For a discussion of late 18th- and early 19th-century prisons, see T. A. Markus, 'Pattern of the Law', *Architectural Review*, vol. 116 no. 694, October 1954, pp.251-56.

23 The drawings are in TWA (279/1).

24 J. Dobson, *Presidential Address to the Northern Architectural Association* (April 1859), reprinted in Wilkes, p.107.

25 Reported in the *Carlisle Patriot*, 3 March and 17 August 1822.

26 Mackenzie 1827, I, pp.197ff.

27 *Ibid.*, pp.200-201.

28 Curiously, Dobson announced in the *NC* on 7 January 1826 that "Major Anderson has been induced to divide the said field [Nun's Field] into sites for let." But no developments seem to have followed.

29 Mackenzie 1827, I, pp.199-200.

30 Ibid., p.199.

31 M. Mackeith, *The History and Conservation of Shopping Arcades*, 1986, pp.104-105.

32 Collard and Ross, pp.63-64

33 N. Pevsner, *The Buildings of England: Northumberland*, 1957, p.56.

34 Wilkes and Dodds, pp.56-102; Ayris, op. cit., pp.40-58; and T.E. Faulkner, 'The Early Nineteenth Century Planning of Newcastle upon Tyne', *Planning Perspectives*, 5, 1990, pp.149-67.

35 Perspectives in the Laing Art Gallery, Newcastle upon Tyne.

36 Perspectives in the Laing Art Gallery, Newcastle upon Tyne, and plans and elevations in the Getty Museum, California.

37 Dobson's roof structure was destroyed by fire in 1901, to be replaced by the present railway station-like arched system with lattice girders. See J. Addyman and B. Fawcett, *The High Level Bridge and Newcastle Central Station: 150 Years Across the Tyne*, 1999, p.80.

38 *NJ*, 31 October 1835.

39 NCRO (ZMD 68/7).

40 NCRO (ZMD 68/5).

41 Mackenzie and Ross, 1834, II, p.374 and Seaham Community Association, *History of Seaham*, 1985, p.81. Drawings in DCRO (D/Lo/E 596 (386)).

42 Correspondence in DCRO (D/Lo/E610).

Fig. 36 Lilburn Tower, Northumberland, 1828-29. The dining room.
Photograph: R. Walton, ©University of Northumbria at Newcastle.

3 Country Houses, Greek and Gothic, 1820-1862

Dobson's maturity as a country house architect lies in the 1820s as far as his classical houses are concerned and in the 1830s with regard to his Tudor and Gothic houses. This distinction reflects a national change in attitude towards styles in domestic architecture. The prolific architectural writer J.C. Loudon felt by 1833 that the classical style was unsuitable for the English countryside and should be confined to the town. The Catholic architect and writer A.W.N. Pugin, increasingly influential from the 1830s, added the moral argument that classical styles were pagan and only for the proud and worldly; the Gothic was both Christian and more patriotic. Architects themselves could combine the symmetry of the classical and the detailing of the native Gothic by adopting Tudor and Elizabethan styles.

Greek Revival houses

The successful formula of the small square Greek country villa had been adopted effortlessly by Dobson in the 1810s and continued into the 1820s. They were simple, even severe, in style and their craftsmanship in stone and plaster was in the spirit of the greatest Greek Revival house of all, Belsay Hall in Northumberland. There are several of these houses on agricultural estates surviving throughout Northumberland and Durham. With their attached service wings and stables they represent a development of the plain but noble farmhouse tradition laid down by David Stephenson in his work for the Duke of Northumberland. Architects and landowners benefited from both the agricultural improvements of the period and contemporary industrial developments. Rural landowners often found coal on their land; successful urban merchants, industrialists and professionals bought country estates. The first house of the 1820s in this tradition is South Hill House, in County Durham, built for the banker Thomas Fenwick in 1821. Here, as at Mitford Hall, the house is, however, somewhat spoilt by the perhaps overheavy arrangement of projecting cornice and parapet.

In all other respects Mitford Hall,[1] near Morpeth in Northumberland (fig. 37), achieves the crisp subtlety of Doxford Hall. It was designed in 1823 for Bertram Osbaldeston Mitford, but building was delayed, perhaps because of the impending marriage of the owner, until 1828-29. Like the Moncks at Belsay, the Mitfords decided to leave their decaying medieval house and build anew nearby. The siting is typically Dobsonian, designed to give the optimum view, looking south over water, in this case the River Wansbeck. Here for the first time we find the full expression of Dobson's great subtlety

Fig. 37 Mitford Hall,
Northumberland, 1823-29.
*Newcastle Libraries &
Information Service.*

Fig. 38 Dobson's house,
New Bridge Street,
Newcastle upon Tyne, 1823.
*Newcastle Libraries &
Information Service.*

of surface articulation, as in the way the wall surface projects and recedes across the facade, and in the varied fenestration on the three principal facades. The entrance front has a projecting Greek Doric portico *in antis* placed in front of a slightly recessed central bay. The south front is plain and regular, the east of a different rhythm again with a wider recessed central section containing three closely spaced windows. From this facade a low wing leads to a conservatory. The horizontal emphases are delicate and restrained: a slightly projecting base, a thread-like string-course carrying the line of the porch's cornice round beneath the first floor windows, and a thin, deeply projecting cornice.

Mitford Hall was designed in the same year that Dobson designed his own house in New Bridge Street (fig. 38) as part of the development around the west end of the New Bridge over Pandon Dene in Newcastle (see p.30). It is the sole survivor of this development. Originally of plain ashlar, it is now brightly painted, but still illustrates the crisp simplicity of Dobson's 1820s classical style. The facade is uncomplicated by an entrance, which was placed to the side. A long garden behind once contained his collection of architectural fragments.

Picton Place nearby, which contained the best of Dobson's urban villas, was destroyed by the gradual expansion of the nearby railway sid-

54

Fig. 39 Picton House
('Dobson's Villa'), Picton
Place, Newcastle upon
Tyne, c.1825, demolished.
©*Crown copyright NMR.*

ings; but one of the larger houses, Picton House, later known as 'Dobson's Villa' (fig. 39), survived until recent times as the terminus of the Newcastle and Blyth Railway and later as an employment exchange.[2] It was a substantial house, three by four bays, with an Ionic portico *in antis* in a slightly recessed centre bay, as at Mitford, and shallow Doric pilasters topped by isolated brackets.

Mitford Hall and Dobson's own house were rapidly followed by one of the architect's very finest classical designs, Longhirst Hall near Morpeth (1824).[3] Longhirst is not a large house, but its refinement of detail in masonry construction and carving, in plasterwork and in architectural design is almost faultless. Its general plan follows Mitford and conforms to a common pattern that Dobson may have derived from the important but now lost mansion of Cresswell Hall in Northumberland (see p.126). Cresswell was built to the designs of the London architect John Shaw under the supervision of John Green from 1820 to 1824. It was a large square house with masonry work of Northumbrian quality and many design features shared by Dobson's best houses.

The archetypal Dobson house plan of the period places the reception rooms, various combinations of drawing room, library and dining room, along the south and east sides of the main square block of the house. Within this L-shape a smaller L-shape contains an entrance hall, entered from the west, and a staircase. The remaining corner contains a study or business

55

Fig. 40 Longhirst Hall, Northumberland, 1824-25.

Photograph: R. Walton, ©University of Northumbria at Newcastle.

room, not entered directly from the hall. To the north is the service wing and off that, to the east, a conservatory at the end of a linking wing.

At Longhirst the plan is so compact that the dining room is squeezed out into the service wing, a departure from the architect's normal practice that has the advantage of placing the dining room nearer the kitchen. Externally, the entrance front is dominated by the great portico of two giant Corinthian, or perhaps more accurately, Composite, columns set *in antis* under the pediment (see fig. 40). The use of a pediment is rare in Dobson's architecture, but here it allows him to omit his often-unattractive parapet by making a virtue of the slope of the roof as echoed in the shape of the pediment.

In addition the powerful vertical emphasis of the portico balances the usual horizontal character of the Greek Revival style to create a perfectly satisfying composition. This is refined with immaculate masonry work, the most delicate and subtle cornice mouldings and pilaster strips at the corners, and superb stone carving in the capitals over columns and pilasters. The south front features a large central bow window, while the east front consists of a rank of five tall evenly spaced windows.

The quality of Longhirst's architecture is continued inside. The long oval entrance hall (fig. 41), entered through a lobby, is an uncompromisingly severe space. Constructed of bare, unplastered masonry as solid as the exterior, it rises through two storeys and is lit by three domes. On the ground floor, decorative features are kept to a minimum: a narrow honeysuckle

Fig. 41 Longhirst Hall,
Northumberland, 1824-
25. The entrance hall.

Photograph: R. Walton,
©University of Northumbria at
Newcastle.

frieze and brackets, and two
Ionic columns that frame the
fine staircase. The ceiling of the
first floor is made up of a series
of coffered domes and a vault of
austere character, but enlivened
with excellent winged figures
deeply carved in the pendentives.

The reception rooms con-
tain some of the finest plasterwork to be found in Dobson's
houses. It employs a wide variety of the usual neoclassical and
Greek Revival motifs, of a
refinement and sophistication
that suggests the use of the best
pattern books. The three drawing rooms at Longhirst were
originally one long room with moveable partitions and have very fine ceilings. The dining room is exceptional for Dobson in having a pictorial frieze
depicting a procession of classical figures and animals. Giant brackets,
which indicate a shallow recess at the end of the room that would have held
the sideboard, repeat exactly the carved oak brackets either side of the doorcase.

The flexibility of planning indicated in the drawing room is a sign of the
growing informality of lifestyle enjoyed by early 19th-century country house
owners. So too are the large windows reaching almost from ceiling to floor,
which encourage the enjoyment of the view over garden and parkland and
the blending of house and garden so typical of the period.

The owner of Longhirst Hall was William Lawson, from a farming family with long though relatively humble connections with Longhirst, and a relative of the Lawsons of Chirton, Dobson's home village. He had acquired his
wealth through the exploitation of coal beneath his land. William Orde of
Nunnykirk, the patron of Dobson's next major classical work, was by contrast a traditional member of the landed gentry. He lived the life of a country
squire and became famous for his racehorses.

Dobson's work for Orde of 1825 involved the remodelling and enlargement of an earlier house, which is represented by the tall central portion of
the existing Nunnykirk Hall (see fig. 42). Dobson refaced this part and added
lower wings to west and east that project forward and are linked by an Ionic
colonnade. The western addition is terminated by a grand bow window,
while the east wing is carried back all along the east side of the house and
forms the new entrance front. Here the details of the south colonnade reap-

Fig. 42 Nunnykirk Hall,
Northumberland, 1825.

Photograph: R. Walton,
©University of Northumbria at
Newcastle.

pear in the form of an Ionic screen and projecting *porte-cochère*. Indeed, the horizontal line of the colonnades is carried all round the house and is one of the elements that tie together the varied parts of the house. Another is the extensive use of banded rustication that covers the entrance front and the facades of the old house. This is a unique feature in Dobson's work and one that is more characteristic of his Durham friend and contemporary Ignatius Bonomi (see Chapter 6), whose Burn Hall of 1821-34 and Windlestone Hall of 1830-34, both in County Durham, have banded rustication throughout. Bonomi's interest in French neoclassicism pervades his work and it must have been through Bonomi that this French characteristic made such a successful appearance in Dobson's work. A final touch of sophistication on the exterior is the unusual richness of the honeysuckle friezes that embellish the parapets.

Inside, the principal feature is a great hall, larger and lighter than that at Longhirst, and boasting a splendid ceiling featuring an ornate coffered central dome and two segmental vaults. A semicircular staircase (see colour plate x) is rather hidden away at one end. As we have come to expect, the quality of plasterwork is superb throughout, though with a slight French emphasis in contrast to the Greek elegance of Longhirst.

The last classical house of importance in this period of Dobson's career is Meldon Park, also near Morpeth, begun in 1832 on a newly created estate purchased by Isaac Cookson III from the Greenwich Hospital Trust in the same year.[4] Cookson was the third in a line of important Tyneside manufacturers and had taken charge of his father's glass interests to become one of the leading glass manufacturers in England and an important figure in Tyneside's chemical industry. Cookson had already employed Dobson in the late 1820s to lay out streets for development in Newcastle (see pp.31-32), and with the examples of Mitford, Longhirst and Nunnykirk all within ten miles of his new estate, he would have needed no further evidence of Dobson's capabilities.

In plan, siting and design, Meldon is the most characteristic Dobson classical house. The entrance front is a refined and elaborated version of that at Mitford. The portico is Ionic and deeper; the windows have moulded surrounds and the parapet is more delicate. The south front, with a splendid view across a terrace over the Wansbeck valley, has a canted bay in the centre. The east front is also a variation on that at Mitford, with three closely spaced windows in the centre and a 'Wyatt' window at either end. Dobson and Carmichael's watercolour (colour plate vi) illustrates how important Dobson felt the relationship between the house and landscape to be. It shows the characteristic shrubbery protecting the entrance front and the dramatic placing of the south front, discreetly separated from the park by ha-ha and terrace, yet surrounded by woodland and pasture. The interiors follow the standard Dobson plan, but are comparatively plain, the details less purely Greek and characterised by a restraint more typical of the 1830s. The hall is very large with a grand staircase. The two drawing rooms lead into one another through double doors and into the library through a false bookcase.

Meldon has justifiably been described as the last flowering of the Georgian country house tradition.[5] Like Dobson's earlier classical houses it combines neat but flexible planning with a deep appreciation of the relationship between the house and its setting, all contained within the discipline of the classical tradition.

Gothic and Tudor houses

If the 1830s saw a decline in commitment to the purity of the Greek Revival, it saw a burgeoning of interest in Gothic styles. This change is evident in Dobson's own work. Indeed, even earlier, his first major Gothic house, Lilburn Tower in Northumberland (colour plates vii, ix), can be considered a classical house in Gothic clothing, while Dobson then rapidly developed a mature, if ultimately unimaginative, Gothic style of his own in the years 1830-37.

Lilburn Tower is in all respects, except its architectural style, a perfect example of the Dobson country house of the 1820s.[6] Designed in 1828 for Henry Collingwood to replace an earlier house, it is, as is to be expected, beautifully sited over the Lilburn Burn, with the land dropping away sharply on two sides. The plan is once again the standard Dobson one as seen at Longhirst and Meldon. The entrance front was originally perfectly symmetrical, as is the south, though the east front does not quite achieve symmetry. The service wing and conservatory are also placed in the usual position.

In style Lilburn is a Tudor-Gothic amalgam typical of the period, but considerably more sophisticated than Dobson's Gothic efforts of only a few years earlier, for example, at West Jesmond House. The spiky angularity of those earlier designs has been replaced by a smoother compactness, with a sophistication and accuracy of detail that is evidence not only of his increased knowledge of medieval prototypes, but also of the work of the two most fashionable proponents of Tudor-Gothic, William Wilkins and William Burn. Burn was two years younger than Dobson, but by the 1820s was already one of the most respected and successful country house architects in Britain. Lilburn can be compared stylistically to a Burn house such as Ratho Park in Midlothian of 1824, though Burn's planning, for which he was so admired, has little in common with Dobson's at this stage.

It is a sad fact, in view of Dobson's self-proclaimed success in combating draughts in large houses, that he had to make major alterations to Lilburn Tower following its purchase by E.J. Collingwood of Chirton in 1843, largely in the interests of improved comfort; the *porte-cochère* was moved to the left to enter the hall via a lobby and the great staircase was separated off from the hall. Inside there is an ensemble, unique in Dobson's work, of surviving fireplaces, fitted furniture, such as the library bookcases and the great oak dining room sideboard, and a largely unaltered decorative finish, especially the large areas of oak-grained plasterwork in the ceilings, of which that in the library is the most notable (colour plate ix). The ceilings are heavily ribbed and encrusted with Gothic foliage, with Gothic versions of classical friezes around the cornice (see fig. 36). Moreover, there is a quantity of oak dining room, library and bedroom furniture original to the house and perhaps designed by Dobson himself. The great staircase is lit by an enormous mullioned and transomed window with excellent stained glass. The formality of the plan leads to few architectural surprises, but within a few years Dobson was to begin to exploit the picturesque possibilities of the Gothic style and in the next ten years made a series of designs in which he rapidly achieved a

Fig. 43 Benwell Tower, Newcastle upon Tyne, 1830-31. An early proposal.
Laing Art Gallery, Newcastle upon Tyne.

confident Gothic manner.

At Benwell Tower, just outside Newcastle, Dobson proposed in 1830 substantial castellated Gothic additions to replace a decayed medieval house while retaining its substantial Georgian service wing. Early designs (see fig. 43) illustrate how Dobson studiously avoided any symmetry in his additions.[7] The composition is composed of several blocks carefully arranged to provide an irregular silhouette from every angle. The Tudor-Gothic style was particularly suited to the creation of picturesque compositions. Its admirers saw in venerable manor houses such as Compton Wynyates and Haddon Hall an ideal of domestic architecture. The style was picturesque, in that it 'looked good in a picture'; it was also traditionally English and free from foreign influences, and capable of responding to the demands of efficient interior planning.

Dobson was well aware of these advantages:

"Whilst studying and sketching examples of Tudor architecture, I found that interior convenience was alone the object sought to be accomplished, and that much of the picturesque effect arose from chance. Much might be said of the advantages of Tudor architecture in the construction of buildings for domestic purposes, in producing varied and picturesque outlines, when the forms appear to rise out of necessity; and I do not see that there can be any objection to adopting the decorated style of detail to a Tudor outline, provided it harmonises with the building. When this style is found to be too costly, then I have found what may be called the Manor House style, or irregular outline, a good substitute; and in some cases it will be found more in harmony with the component part of the landscape."[8]

The first master of picturesque architecture was John Nash, whose best compositions arrange the main living rooms around a central hall, but project them into the landscape to take advantage of views and create the necessary irregularity of skyline. This was Dobson's approach at Benwell Tower. The house was built as a much simplified version of the first designs and consequently now has a rather mean appearance, accentuated by the loss of its chimneys. However, considering the subsequent history of the house and its recent use as a public house, the interiors

Fig. 44 Brinkburn Priory and Manor House, Northumberland, the latter enlarged by Dobson, 1830-37.

Newcastle Libraries & Information Service.

Fig. 45 Neasham Hall,
County Durham, additions
made by Dobson 1834-37;
house demolished.
©*Crown copyright NMR.*

are remarkably intact, with much dark-stained oak panelling and heavily ribbed ceilings.

Contemporary with Benwell Tower, and rather more successful, are the additions Dobson made to Brinkburn Priory Manor House, near Rothbury, Northumberland, from 1830 to 1837 for Major William Hodgson-Cadogan. The house, close to the then roofless remains of Brinkburn Priory, had been built over part of the monastic buildings and had been extended in 1810-11 by the Major's father in a plain Georgian 'Gothick' style. Dobson's work involved rebuilding the older part in his newly mastered castellated Gothic manner (see fig. 44). Despite the fact that no attempt was made to conform to the style of the priory church or the existing house, the additions are remarkably successful and contribute to the overall picturesqueness of the group, in their delightfully secluded setting on the River Coquet. The house contains the staircase, probably of c.1600, from Anderson Place in Newcastle, installed by Dobson following the mansion's demolition by Richard Grainger.

Further significant additions made by Dobson in the mid 1830s included a wing at Blenkinsopp Hall (1832-37, for Colonel Coulson), now demolished, and substantial remodelling of Neasham Hall in County Durham for Colonel James Cookson, a brother of Isaac Cookson of Meldon, made in 1834-37. Neasham appears to have been a late Georgian house of about 1800 to which Dobson made additions of the same scale as those at Nunnykirk: enclosing the house in Tudor wings with decorative gables, moving the

Fig. 46 Beaufront Castle,
Northumberland, 1837-39.
The entrance front, from an
oil painting by J.W.
Carmichael.
*Laing Art Gallery, Newcastle
upon Tyne.*

Fig. 47 Beaufront Castle,
Northumberland, 1837-39.
The garden front.
*Photograph: R. Walton,
©University of Northumbria at
Newcastle.*

entrance to the side and incorporating the plainer older portion by running an ornate parapet across the roof line (see fig. 45). Neasham ended up as a very large house and was demolished in 1970.

Dobson's castellated Gothic designs climaxed in the late 1830s with the building of two large and impressive houses. Beaufront Castle,[9] near Hexham in Northumberland (fig. 46), and Holme Eden, near Carlisle, were both begun in 1837 for families with successful manufacturing interests in the North of England.

William Cuthbert was a partner and major investor in the Cooksons' chemical and glass interests on Tyneside. In 1834 he began negotiating for part of the Beaufront estate near Hexham, including the large late 17th- and 18th-century house, over-

looking one of the most spectacular views in the Tyne Valley. The estate was finally purchased in 1836 and the new house begun in 1837. Dobson's design made the most of what he described as the "varied and picturesque outlines" provided by the Tudor-Gothic style and from the east the house successfully evokes the low rambling composition of Haddon Hall,

Fig. 48 Holme Eden,
Warwick Bridge, Cumbria,
1837. The entrance front.
Photograph: R. Walton,
©University of Northumbria at
Newcastle.

Derbyshire. The house spreads out around a central tower and stair turret placed over the main entrance. To its east a family wing was created in part of the remodelled old house; to the south the main block of the new house (fig. 47) ironically reproduces the standard Dobson plan once again. However, it is so heavily disguised externally by a multitude of buttresses, oriels, bay windows and differing window and moulding details that the plan is only apparent internally.

The only significant variation in plan is the arrangement of entrance, hall and staircase. The hall is a Gothic extravagance and, although not a revival of the true medieval Great Hall, as was being made by Pugin and Salvin elsewhere in the country at that time, it is an attempt to create 'instant history'. As Dobson and Carmichael's watercolour (colour plate viii) shows, by decorating it with hunting trophies, portraits of real or imaginary ancestors, suits of armour and displays of medieval arms, an impression of ancient lineage could be easily provided. However, the watercolour also illustrates the difficulty in finding a useful function for such a room. The early Victorians had more use for a billiard room than for displays of medieval pageantry. The staircase, too, is a fine vaulted space and the other reception rooms are well proportioned and lit with large windows. The ceilings are of conventional heavy ribs, those of the library superbly grained to imitate oak. A rare surviving fireplace suggests that these elements too were like those at Lilburn.

South West View.

Fig. 49 Holme Eden, Warwick Bridge, Cumbria. An early proposal for the south-west front. *RIBA Library Drawings Collection.*

Holme Eden at Warwick Bridge, near Carlisle (fig. 48), is one of Dobson's least-known large houses, but one of his most ambitious. In style it is almost identical to Beaufront, except for the use of the occasional gable and a heavier reliance on tall chimneys for vertical emphasis. It was built in a slightly simpler form than is shown in the drawings in the RIBA (see fig. 49),[10] and without the usually essential conservatory. The stone is the beautiful local red sandstone.

The house was built for Peter Dixon of Peter Dixon and Sons, the largest cotton manufacturer in Carlisle, with mills in Manchester, Carlisle and at Warwick Bridge itself. The firm had undergone great expansion in the 1820s and early 1830s and the Dixon family was near the height of their local influence. Peter was a Mayor of Carlisle in 1838-39, while his elder brother John was High Sheriff of Cumberland in 1838 and Mayor of Carlisle in 1840-41. The family was to provide mayors throughout the 19th century.

The plan of Holme Eden is unique for Dobson at this time for being built around courtyards and for linking the various parts of the service accommodation with extensive corridors. The house therefore presents a compact whole in which house and service wing are not readily distinguishable externally. It is possible that the influence of William Burn is at work here; he too used courts and corridors to organise the complexity of the early Victorian country house. Like all Dobson's larger houses, Holme Eden is raised on a terrace, in this case immediately above the River Eden and the surrounding woods and fields. The orientation is conventional: entrance to the west, main rooms along the south front and dining room to the east; service wing and stables around the courtyard to the north. What is unusual is the complete absence of a central hall. Instead there is a lobby leading indirectly to a long, wide corridor lit from the end and from a small court and leading through a door to a magnificent staircase, always a notable feature of these houses. Can this breaking up of the centralised 'Dobson' plan be an attempt to remove still more thoroughly the danger of draughts? If so, the result is aesthetically unsatisfactory; there is no sense of a natural centre of focus of the house, which is such an attractive feature of Dobson's other houses of this period.

However, Beaufront and Holme Eden, both remarkably unaltered, remain the best expressions of Dobson's brand of castellated Gothic domestic architecture. The days of this style were numbered, for the criticisms of Pugin and his followers ridiculed the fortified gatehouses and castellated parapets of houses that also boasted plate glass windows and large conservatories. In the following decades Dobson enters a period of bewildering variety in architectural style in which we seldom find again such commitment or quality.

Later houses

Dobson's undoubted emotional preference for the classical was allowed little opportunity for expression in his later years. Around 1840 he made some distinctly dull suggestions for classical additions to the interesting old house of Little Harle Tower in Northumberland.[11] Thomas Anderson had purchased the estate around 1835, after selling Anderson Place in Newcastle to Richard Grainger, and wished to modernise and extend it. But Dobson's proposals were uninspired and totally unsympathetic to the older house. It is not surprising that they were rejected and that Anderson later designed his own idiosyncratic Gothic additions to the house, which have been recently demolished.

Dobson was able to make minor additions and alterations to classical houses such as Newton Hall near Wylam, Northumberland, where a quite sympathetic bay to the south front and new staircase window of 1851 develop the tripartite window motif familiar from his work of the 1830s. Later, at Holeyn Hall, also near Wylam, in 1858 he made the substantial addition of a tower, tied to the slightly earlier 19th-century house with heavy window surrounds and an elaborate balustrade.

At Wallington Hall Dobson was given an opportunity to work at one of the most beautiful 18th-century houses in Northumberland.[12] In most respects his commission was typical of those earlier in his career when he had been asked to improve the comfort of older houses, but at Wallington we have the additional dimension of the

Fig. 50 Angerton Hall, Northumberland, 1842, before reduction of service wing.

Newcastle Libraries & Information Service.

Fig. 51 Sandhoe House,
Northumberland, 1843-45.

Photograph: R. Walton,
©University of Northumbria at
Newcastle.

Pre-Raphaelite connections of the Trevelyans. Sir Walter Trevelyan inherited Wallington from his father in 1846 and to his friends' amazement chose to live in this "large modern mansion" rather than his Elizabethan house of Nettlecombe in Somerset. But even to the Trevelyans, who seem to have despised modern comforts, the open courtyard of the house was unpleasantly dark, damp and cold.

Dobson was chosen in 1852 to convert the courtyard into useable living space, presumably because of his years of experience with the houses of the Trevelyans' neighbours. His design was in a subdued Italianate style, thoroughly appropriate to the rest of the house, though the hall impinges little on the older rooms with their exceptionally fine mid 18th-century plasterwork. Only the staircase had to be rebuilt to accommodate the hall, which rises, an independent structure, in two tiers of arcades towards a coffered ceiling. The designs had to be shown to the great critic John Ruskin for his approval, as Ruskin had become Pauline Trevelyan's mentor in all things artistic. Ruskin's only suggestion was that the conventional design of the balustrade around the upper gallery be replaced by one copied from an example at Murano (illustrated by Ruskin in his *The Stones of Venice*, volume ii). Dobson's architecture soon became the frame for a remarkable scheme of Pre-Raphaelite decoration by William Bell Scott, Master of the Government School of Design in Newcastle since 1843, Pauline Trevelyan and her friends, and John Ruskin himself. Of the eight large canvases of scenes from Northumbrian history that Scott painted in 1856-60 to fill eight blank ground

floor arcades, one, *Iron and Coal on Tyneside in the Nineteeth Century*, is an acknowledged Pre-Raphaelite masterpiece. Bell Scott was keen that Dobson should not interfere with the proposed decorations.

In the bulk of his remaining domestic work in the 1840s and 1850s Dobson adapted his Gothic skills and experience to the new climate of the early Victorian period. Angerton Hall in Northumberland (fig. 50), a house he had repaired in the late 1820s, was rebuilt in 1842 in a remarkably unfussy Tudor style with plain gables, unemphatic battlements, and tall windows on flat expanses of wall (the substantial service wing was severely curtailed during the 1950s). The comparative, almost elegant, simplicity of the design is a startling contrast to the houses of only five years previously such as Beaufront and Holme Eden. The difference may be partly one of cost, for the Gothic style was necessarily expensive, but it also reflects a change in architectural fashion within the period.

Sandhoe House, near Hexham (fig. 51), of the following year is a more elaborate essay in the same manner, though with Jacobean details, spiky pinnacles on the corners and gables and a delightful porch with scrolly gable and little Jacobean arcades with details that, in their debased classical form, an earlier Georgian architect would not have tolerated. Inside, a heavy 17th-century style stone fireplace in the hall may be original; a more conventional fireplace with its original grate is in the dining room. Both Angerton and Sandhoe are built of attractive stone in Dobson's favourite kind of situation, over a south-facing terrace.

The simplified Tudor style of Angerton was particularly appropriate for vicarages, an area in which Dobson was very active, at least eight being built between 1840 and 1855. Commissions for vicarages would arise naturally from Dobson's employment to build or restore a church or the house of the local landowner. Often church, vicarage and school would be built as a group of related buildings, as at Birtley, near Gateshead, for the Roman Catholic congregation. Dobson's vicarages, for example those at Seghill, Northumberland, Holme Eden and Benfieldside, County Durham, are unexceptional and quite typical of the period, their Tudor elements being confined to mullioned windows, gables with prominent 'kneelers' and tall chimneys.

Among the larger houses of the period were the substantial additions made to Sudbrooke Holme in Lincolnshire, built in a Tudor-Gothic style for Colonel Richard Ellison in 1851, but now demolished, and several houses around Hexham including The Hags, now Hackwood House, of 1843, and The Leazes of 1853. These last two confirm the increasing simplicity and informality of Dobson's Tudor style in this period, but they are small houses for modest clients.

A more ambitious house is Inglethorpe Hall near Wisbech in Norfolk (fig. 52), built for Charles Metcalf, a Wisbech worthy, in 1857. This is a house that at once takes Dobson into the heart of High Victorian country house design. Here qualities of simplicity and informality are applied to a much larger composition, with many gables of different sizes, some partly crow-stepped. Perhaps uniquely for Dobson there is a steep roof over the staircase tower; the roofline is high and decorated, topped with a weathervane. The whole emphasis of the design is a vertical one, quite unlike the horizontal nature of early 19th-century Gothic. The locality of the house demanded red brick, of a pleasantly varied hue, instead of the stone that Dobson would instinctively have preferred. But this material only adds to the modernity of the house, as brick was increasingly preferred by Victorian Gothic architects not only for economy but also for its texture and colour.

Fig. 53 Neues Schloss, Friedelhausen, Germany, 1852-54. *Bildarchiv Foto Marburg.*

Inglethorpe seems to foreshadow George Gilbert Scott's intention, as expressed in his *Remarks on Secular and Domestic Architecture* (1857), to create a Gothic domestic architecture that was spacious and well-lit, with the most modern conveniences, uncluttered by archaic details, materials and planning. The modern and un-Dobsonian characteristics of Inglethorpe

suggest that Dobson, or his patron, had more advanced ideas in mind. It may be significant that at the time it was being designed Dobson had as a pupil E.R. Robson (from 1853 to 1856), who was subsequently to become an assistant to Scott and then a pioneer of the 'Queen Anne' style of the 1870s and 1880s.

It is more typical of Dobson that his last

Fig. 54 Design for a castellated mansion. From a drawing by Dobson, c.1852.
Laing Art Gallery, Newcastle upon Tyne.

major domestic work of architecture, one of the most complex and ambitious of his life, should be a reversion to the by then stale conventions of castellated Gothic. The restoration and enlargement of Lambton Castle in County Durham took up the last five years of Dobson's working life.

However, before looking at Lambton in more detail, a diversion must be made to Germany to note one of the more curious episodes in Dobson's career. Margaret Dobson's biography refers to a request "from a German nobleman … to design a crenellated mansion for him on the Rhine … [Dobson] went and saw the site and partly completed the plans but failing health compelled him to relinquish the task."[13] Angus Fowler has identified the house as the Neues Schloss at Friedelhausen on the River Lahn (a tributary of the Rhine), built between 1852 and 1854 for Adalbeit, Baron von Nordeck zur Rabenau.[14] Dobson had probably met the Baron's English wife, Clara Phillips, in London around 1851 through her guardian's interest in railways. At any rate we know that Dobson was working on designs for the newly-married couple's house in 1852, although they were never completed and the final form of the 'castellated mansion' (fig. 53) was at least partially determined by the Baron's German architect, Martin Unger, who did have, however, the benefit of several books on English Gothic and Tudor architecture.

The resulting building, on a prominent site facing west over the Lahn is a solid and dull rectangular block with tall octagonal corner turrets, with superficial similarities to some of Dobson's designs. However, the design makes no attempt to create a picturesque silhouette and exploit the castle's romantic situation. The closest parallel to a design by Dobson is a previously unidentified drawing[15] of a heavily castellated house (fig. 54) whose symmetry, large turrets, heavy machicolations, *porte-cochère*, and courtyard

70

fountain are shared by the Neues Schloss. The German castle's entrance front is virtually a condensed version of this, surely earlier, design.

Meanwhile, the rescue of Lambton Castle (fig. 55) from mining subsidence and its subsequent massive enlargement is perhaps more notable as an engineering feat than as a significant contribution to architecture.[16] The house has a long and complex history. Originally called Harraton Hall, the earlier 18th-century house was rebuilt by Joseph Bonomi around 1800. The young John Lambton, later 1st Earl of Durham, then employed Ignatius Bonomi, Dobson's Durham contemporary and friend, to transform Harraton into a picturesque Gothic castle suited to its superbly romantic spot above an enormous terrace overlooking the River Wear. Bonomi's work, which took place between 1815 and 1828, included the landscaping of the park, bridges, lodge gates and walks as well as the great house itself.

However, Lambton had been built over old coal workings that, drained of water by subsequent mining operations, led by 1854 to disastrous subsidence under Bonomi's west block. It is perhaps the ultimate compliment to Dobson's talents as an engineer that he should have been called in by the 2nd Earl in 1857 at the age of 69 to underpin the Castle and to design major new extensions to the Castle. Dobson worked with one of Lambton's coal-viewers, Mr. Heccles, to fill the empty coal seams (some 400 feet beneath the ground) with brickwork, and rebuild the foundations with ten-foot wide and eight-foot deep beds of concrete beneath the walls. Most of Bonomi's west block was pulled down and Dobson designed new reception rooms around a Great Hall. In style and plan they followed closely Bonomi's work of 40 years earlier (except for the replacement of large Gothic windows with square headed ones), the result of deference to Bonomi's work and of Dobson's innate stylistic conservatism.

The Great Hall was the most significant addition, but this was essentially a creation of Sydney Smirke, Dobson's son-in-law, who took over the work following the older architect's incapacitating stroke of 1862. Dobson and Smirke's joint additions were largely demolished in the 1930s and Dobson's contribution to the house as it now remains is minimal.

As we have seen, Dobson was inspired to produce some of his finest and most assured work in the field of country house design. His own statement that "My practice is a great deal in the country"[17] suggests that he himself knew this to be the case. With regard to planning, siting and construction Dobson showed exceptional ability, and, in addition, he was able to achieve distinctive and personal expression across a range of styles. The Grecian severity of Mitford, the classical repose of Meldon, and the romantic picturesqueness of Beaufront and Holme Eden are all evidence of this. By contrast, Longhirst is a more dramatic composition, matched only by Dobson's first and second Newcastle Central Station designs (see Chapter 5), and is indicative of the architect's occasional capacity to produce an unexpectedly memorable effect. Not surprisingly, he has been equated with national figures such as Barry, Blore, Burn and Salvin in terms of country house archi- tecture during the 1830s[18] – even though Dobson was more regionally based.

In this context, it is also worth noting that Dobson's practice as a land- scape gardener, hinted at in his early work at Cheeseburn and Bolam (see pp.18-19), may have been far more extensive than we can now ascertain from the limited existing evidence. Thus his highly knowledgeable contem- porary J.C. Loudon wrote that Dobson had had "extensive experience, not only as an architect, but as a landscape-gardener". Loudon went on: "Mr. Dobson's taste in the latter art, it delights us to say, is not inferior to what it is in the former; and of his practice in both arts examples may be seen in almost every part of Northumberland and Durham."[19] He also referred to Dobson as "an architect of genius".[20]

Notes

1 For Mitford Hall see also *CL*, 17 February 1966.

2 'Dobson's Villa' was demolished in 1970. See Faulkner and Lowery, p.27.

3 *CL*, 17 February 1966.

4 *CL*, 24 February 1966.

5 *Ibid.*

6 *CL*, 8 November 1973.

7 Three elevations of "Designs No. I" are in the Laing Art Gallery, Newcastle upon Tyne.

8 J. Dobson, *Presidential Address to the Northern Architectural Association* (April 1859), reprinted in Wilkes, p.107.

9 *CL*, 29 January and 5 February 1976.

10 RIBA Drawings Collection (G6/38/1-3), previously called 'Benwell Tower'; here iden- tified as being early designs for Holme Eden. Some detailed working drawings are in the Laing Art Gallery, Newcastle upon Tyne.

11 Drawings in NCRO (660/18).

12 R. Trevelyan, *A Pre-Raphaelite Circle*, 1978, pp.67-68, 78, 120.

13 Dobson, p.34.

14 Private communication, for which we are most grateful.

15 In the Laing Art Gallery, Newcastle upon Tyne.

16 *CL*, 24, 31 March 1966; perspective drawing in the Laing Art Gallery, Newcastle upon Tyne.

17 *Report of the Cholera Inquiry Commissioners*, 1854, p.312. Dobson went on: "I have built a great many gentlemen's houses in the counties of Northumberland and Durham, in the counties of Lincolnshire and Cheshire too, and even at Windsor."

18 D. Watkin, *The English Vision*, 1982, pp.133-34.

19 J.C. Loudon, *An Encyclopaedia of Cottage, Farm and Villa Architecture and Furniture* (first additional supplement to 1st edn. of 1833), 1842, pp.1185-86.

20 *Ibid.*, p.1185.

Fig. 55 Lambton Castle, County Durham, with additions of 1862 onwards by Dobson and Sydney Smirke; building subsequently reduced.
Newcastle Libraries & Information Service.

Fig. 56 Archibald Reed Monument, Newcastle General Cemetery (Jesmond Old Cemetery), 1843-46.

Photograph: R. Walton, ©University of Northumbria at Newcastle.

4

Churches and Chapels, 1820-1862

At the present time Dobson is justly celebrated as a classicist and particularly for his country house designs. However, his (mainly neo-Gothic) churches and chapels are less wholeheartedly admired. Indeed, the late Sir John Summerson, doyen of British architectural historians, went as far as to say that for ecclesiastical architecture Dobson "had no aptitude whatever".[1] Yet in his own day Dobson was regarded as a pioneer of the Gothic Revival (the principal church style of the 19th century) and as an ecclesiastical architect 'par excellence',[2] who possessed a particular knowledge of English medieval forms.

Our present-day reservations probably stem from the fact that his work in this field – more than in any other – mirrors the aesthetic uncertainties of the period in which he lived. Dobson can be categorised neither as a thoroughly Georgian architect nor as a proper representative of the High Victorian age. Also, he worked at a time of massive urban and population growth, leading to the construction of large numbers of inexpensive new churches which offered little scope for originality of design. Many of Dobson's designs, usually in a rather plain neo-Gothic lancet style, were of this utilitarian type. Similarly, innumerable ancient churches were now being altered and 'improved', a field of work in which Dobson was also much involved. In this his practice is now seen to reflect an insensitive approach, often involving almost complete reconstruction, which seems at variance

Fig. 57 Design for a new chapel at Elswick, Newcastle upon Tyne, 1840. From a drawing by Dobson.

Robinson Library, University of Newcastle; photograph: Philipson Studios.

with his evidently genuine antiquarian interests. Such an approach began to be discredited even in his own lifetime and would certainly be totally unacceptable today. Even so, ecclesiastical architecture must be regarded as an important theme in Dobson's long career, especially in his later years, and represents numerically more than a quarter of his output.

Examples of Dobson's early classical-style churches and chapels were discussed in Chapter 1. This phase reached a climax in 1825-26 with the neo-Greek rectangularity of St. James's Presbyterian Chapel, Blackett Street, Newcastle (demolished 1859). Here Dobson adapted the Greek temple form to Christian worship, although the interior was arranged more like a small theatre, with seating placed in a semicircle and a gallery above. After this, his essays in classicism for church design were extremely rare. However, his unbuilt proposal for a new chapel at Elswick, Newcastle (1840, fig. 57), part of an intended Grainger development, would have been an interesting synthesis of Greek and Roman forms, while his St. Columba's Presbyterian (now United Reformed) church, North Shields (1856-57), is an excellent example of his later Italianate mode (see pp.115-16).

Early interest in the medieval

During the 1820s the heyday of the Gothic Revival was yet to come, but medieval building was being studied more and more. The Gothic was no longer seen as a decorative novelty but as something worthy of the same archaeological attention that Greek architecture had already received. Thus, among the richly illustrated folios published as source material for architects and connoisseurs alike were John Carter's *Ancient Architecture of England* (1807) and two multi-volume works by John Britton, *The Architectural Antiquities of Great Britain* (1807-26) and *Cathedral Antiquities of Great Britain* (1814-35). Even more authoritative was Augustus Charles Pugin's *Specimens of Gothic Architecture* (1821-23). Meanwhile, in the more popular journals such as *The Gentleman's Magazine* articles had begun to appear calling for the more accurate and sensitive restoration of medieval work, and it was with the same purpose that the historian-turned-architect Thomas Rickman published *An Attempt to Discriminate the Styles of English Architecture* in 1817. Like Dobson and many other architects of the time, Rickman seems to have had equal liking for both the Greek and Gothic styles, but wished especially to facilitate modern Gothic church design. He divided English medieval architecture into four main phases – 'Norman', 'Early English', 'Decorated', and 'Perpendicular' – thus providing the terminology still in use today.

From an early age Dobson seems to have developed a similar antiquarian approach; as a youth he made measured drawings of the tower of St. Nicholas's Church, Newcastle, and of mouldings and tracery at Tynemouth Priory. Again, when drawings he had made as a young man (c.1813) of the old Castle Keep, Newcastle, proved useful many years later for restoration work (see p.106), Dobson recalled that "his attention had been early directed to English architecture, and the Norman Style, of which there were some fine specimens in the country, but perhaps none finer than [this] building".[3] As a young architect, if hardly the originator of the Gothic Revival as his daughter Margaret claimed,[4] Dobson developed this more than ordinary interest in medieval architecture by travelling in England, Wales and France, sketching assiduously, and continued over the years to make studies of this kind. He even built up a collection – displayed in his garden in New Bridge Street, Newcastle – of (mainly medieval) architectural fragments from buildings demolished or restored. These included an original pinnacle from the tower of St. Nicholas's Church, Newcastle, which he replaced in 1827, and two stone columns from the medieval Hospital of St. Mary the Virgin, also in Newcastle (demolished in 1844 for the widening of Neville Street). Indeed, Dobson was involved in a personal campaign to save this latter building, which had been occupied by the Grammar School since Elizabethan times and for which the architect drew up a privately financed scheme of restoration, although to no avail.[5]

Meanwhile, Dobson had joined the Newcastle Literary and Philosophical Society in 1811 and the Newcastle Society of Antiquaries in 1815; he was also in 1824 a founder member of the town's Literary, Scientific and Mechanical Institution. By the 1820s he is to be found giving public lectures on the history of architecture to various local groups.[6] Dobson is known to have possessed and consulted treatises on Greek art and design,[7] and by the same token was probably familiar even then with the kind of scholarly publication on medieval architecture mentioned above; later, he subscribed to such works.[8] In any event, opportunities to work in the Gothic style soon came his way.

St. Thomas's, Newcastle

In 1818 Dobson restored the medieval church of St. John Lee, near Hexham (subsequently much remodelled), and a year earlier had received two commissions for restoration work at Hexham Abbey and at Tynemouth Priory, though neither scheme was carried out. In 1824 he made a careful restoration of the ruinous north transept window at St. Nicholas's, Newcastle; here he made a measured drawing of the structure and rebuilt it in a manner closely approximating to its original form. However, the building which really established Dobson's reputation as an ecclesiastical architect was the Anglican church of St. Thomas the Martyr, Newcastle (consecrated 19 October 1830, see colour plate iv). It was built in the busy but then still semi-rural area of Barras Bridge, north of the town centre, close to the site of the ruins of St. Mary Magdalen's Hospital. The church cost £6,000 and was financed partly by the Corporation and partly by subscription; the intention was to provide a more conveniently situated replacement for the medieval chapel of St. Thomas's Hospital, then being demolished to widen the northern entrance from the old Tyne Bridge. Dobson's St. Thomas's is a typically late Georgian lancet-style design with a centrally placed western tower.

As intimated earlier, this was a period when unprecedented numbers of churches and chapels were being built to serve the needs of the expanding cities and towns. Successive governments, anxious to promote social stability after the Napoleonic Wars, encouraged this process with subsidies for the building of Anglican churches. At the same time, Acts of Parliament during the 1820s removed restrictions on Nonconformist sects, while the Catholic Emancipation Act of 1829 now permitted the construction of Roman Catholic churches; generally, the Nonconformists tended to favour classical architecture, the Roman Catholics Gothic.

St. Thomas's is an early example in the North of England of neo-Gothic design and as such has been said to show "the timidity with which architects then ventured upon the English mediaeval style".[9] It also reflects the situation in the 1820s when, in Dobson's own words, "no architect had courage to attempt anything like purity of Gothic",[10] and when also, despite the growing interest in Gothic and medieval forms, there was still no clearly accepted style for Anglican church design. None, indeed, was stipulated by the Commissioners appointed by the important Act of Parliament of 1818 to administer a church building grant of £1,000,000, although for reasons of economy most of the churches built under their auspices were in the Gothic style. Leading architects of the day were invited by the Commissioners to suggest the most spacious and economical means of church design. No less a figure than Sir John Soane, for example, proposed three alternative types: Norman, Classical and Gothic. Like St. Thomas's, they all took the form of a rectangular box with large windows, clearly on the Georgian or 'auditory' plan, with steeple and entrance at the west; the Gothic version had buttresses and pinnacles of a rudimentary kind.

The design for St. Thomas's was selected from another trio of alternative schemes, submitted as models to a Committee of Newcastle Common Council on 24 July 1827. The choice consisted of the preferred design, another by Dobson himself, and a third by the respected local architect John Green (see Chapter 6). The form of the latter two is not known, but may well have been classical; Dobson at least would have been unlikely to offer a second Gothic scheme. The design as executed was said to exemplify "the Gothic style of the thirteenth century",[11] or 'Early English'. While far from authentic, it does represent a definite advance on the kind of Gothic proposed by Soane. Although not actually funded by the Commissioners, St. Thomas's does resemble their more convincing churches of that time, such as St. Peter's, Brighton (1824-28), by Charles Barry, or J. Potter's St. Mary's, Sheffield (1826-29). All have a large, centrally placed tower forming the western entrance to the church, and square, rather Georgian proportions offset by a profusion of buttresses and pinnacles more decorative than structural in effect. Arguably St. Thomas's has more individuality than its counterparts through Dobson's determined, if idiosyncratic, use of Early English details; this is particularly evident in the tower, with its lofty pinnacles and

Fig. 58 St. Cuthbert's,
Greenhead,
Northumberland, 1826-28.

*Photograph: R. Walton,
©University of Northumbria at
Newcastle.*

open belfry, unique in his work. Moreover, there is no certainty that Dobson was aware of the other designs mentioned above. Nevertheless, he does seem to have been influenced by Rickman, who also admired Early English and specifically recommended the kind of coupled lancets, much increased in height,[12] employed in this design.

Similar in style was Dobson's reconstruction of Belford Parish Church, Northumberland (1828-29), where to a basically Norman chancel he added a completely rebuilt and much larger nave with new north aisle and western tower. The nave has buttresses dividing elongated coupled lancets on the south (although the tower is less distinctive, having more conventional small lancets and pinnacles). An earlier but perhaps much more convincing exercise in Early English is St. Cuthbert's, Greenhead, Northumberland (from 1826, fig. 58). This is a small rectangular chapel (the chancel was added much later, in 1900), beautifully sited, and built, of local stone, partly at the expense of the minor poet and then Vicar of Haltwhistle, Nathaniel Hollingsworth. Its single lancets are narrow and more archaeologically correct, and the design has the simplicity of genuine medieval work. Dobson, we are told, made a particular study of Early English forms[13] and in this case was surely inspired by local examples such as Lanercost Priory, Cumbria, and Haltwhistle Parish Church.

St. Thomas's, meanwhile, is a transitional design retaining much of the character of the Georgian auditorium type of church which emphasised the

congregation's convenience in following the service, with the pulpit as the focal point. Thus the interior (fig. 59) has an almost 18th-century elegance, which would have been further enhanced by its original 'Pompeian' colour scheme of red, black and beige.[14] There is some sense of a nave with side aisles, but instead of division by arcades, slender columns culminate in delicate stone-ribbed vaults which seem to emphasise the fact that the aisles are almost as high as the nave. The thinness of the supporting columns derives from the use of iron in their construction, as in other churches of the period. There is no proper chancel (though Dobson is said to have desired one)[15] and the altar occupies a small recess, while the architect must have regretted the addition of the galleries which he was commissioned to insert in 1837. These partially block the windows and detract from the unusually light and spacious effect he first achieved

Fig. 59 St. Thomas's,
Newcastle upon Tyne,
1827-30. The interior.
*Newcastle Libraries &
Information Service.*

(although they may have been anticipated from the start, since they are supported on corbels which form part of the string-course running along the aisle walls). At Belford and Greenhead the galleries, which were integral to the design, are positioned unobtrusively at the west. However, it should also be noted that the church at Belford, although quite large, lacks the attractive vaulting which is such a feature of St. Thomas's. The latter was Evangelical in tone and even had a three-decker pulpit (clerk's desk, reading desk, and pulpit) that Dobson is supposed to have disliked[16] but which, with galleries, was typical of Anglican church arrangements at the time.

Some neo-Norman churches

Equally typical in this respect was Dobson's next major church, that of St. James, Benwell, Newcastle, of 1831-32. It has been subsequently much altered and enlarged, but plans survive[17] (see fig. 60) indicating a rectangular scheme without aisles or chancel and with a centrally placed tower (without spire) providing the western entrance to the church. Inside there were galleries at the west and extending to the fourth bay of the nave on the north and south sides. The ground floor was totally occupied by seating, with pews

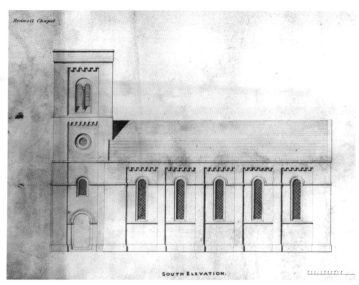

Benwell Chapel

SOUTH ELEVATION.

surrounding even the clerk's desk, reading desk and pulpit – placed well to the west – from which services were conducted. A small altar table was situated directly below the triple windows at the east.

Nevertheless, this church, however Georgian in plan, was quasi-medieval in effect: here Dobson uses for the first time, albeit tentatively, the neo-Norman mode. St. James's had undecorated arches and, with its pediment-like elements, was still rather classical in feel.

Fig. 60 Design for St. James's, Benwell, Newcastle, 1831-32. From a drawing by Dobson.
RIBA Library Drawings Collection.

Fig. 61 St. Cuthbert's, Bensham, Gateshead, 1845-48. The interior in 1987.
Photograph: R. Walton, ©University of Northumbria at Newcastle.

However, Dobson had already made surveys of Norman architecture at Newcastle's Castle Keep[18] (see above) and St. Andrew's church, Newcastle, and, despite the incompatibility of his work at Belford, seems to have developed a substantial interest in the style. The prominently situated St. Cuthbert's, Bensham, Gateshead (1845-48, now disused), is a similar but more advanced design, inspired by a 12th-century church at Barfreston, Kent, which Dobson is known to have examined in 1844.[19] St. Cuthbert's has a five-bay nave, like the Benwell church, but with a substantial apse, reflecting changes in liturgical ideas; there is also a 'transitional' style tower (with spire), at the south west, with the west wall having triple windows under a single arch. Although a north aisle was added later, in 1875, the effect inside

is (or was) still simple and well proportioned, with shafts rising between the side windows to support the timbers of the roof (see fig. 61). The finely carved 'chancel' arch, meanwhile, appears to derive from that of St. Andrew's, Newcastle, which Dobson had restored in 1844 (adding a south transept in similar neo-Norman style). At St. Andrew's, incidentally, he replaced Decorated-style work and even now there remains a disconcerting contrast between the almost metallic precision of Dobson's masonry and the rugged stonework of most of the old church.

Dobson and the Gothic Revival

From about 1830 to 1860, during which time the greater part of Dobson's ecclesiastical work was done, the Gothic Revival developed from a trickle to a flood. It received a tremendous boost through both the architecture and the writings of A.W.N. Pugin (1812-52), a Catholic convert who epitomised a then-current yearning for the Middle Ages, born of a desire for more profound religious observance and a dissatisfaction with the urban and industrial chaos of modern times. Pugin argued that the Protestant Reformation was responsible for a multitude of social ills which could be cured only by a return to medieval concepts of society and design. Thus Gothic, being Christian and 'truthful', was in his view the only style capable of symbolising religious ideas, and in a Christian society the only architecture suitable for the whole range of purposes and forms.

The contemporary explosion in church building gave increasing scope for the implementation of these ideas. New churches were funded, often with difficulty, through a combination of private and ecclesiastical patronage, public subscription, and – in the case of Anglican examples – grants from organisations such as the Incorporated Church Building Society and the Ecclesiastical Commissioners (constituted in 1835). Within the Anglican (and Roman Catholic) world, Gothic now became the accepted style of design. For a short time, during the 1830s and 1840s, a popular alternative was neo-Norman, which Dobson, as we have seen, and even Pugin, sometimes used. But soon the national debate became not whether, but what form of, Gothic should be employed.

The preference for Gothic went hand in hand with the Oxford, or 'Tractarian', Movement, which sought to reform the Church of England by insisting upon the full importance of the Sacraments. It stressed the 'Catholic' tradition of the Church and wished to create a more spiritual outlook through the re-introduction of colour, ritual and symbolism. This approach was popularised and given architectural expression by the 'Ecclesiologists'. In 1839 a group of High Church-inclined undergraduates had formed the Cambridge Camden Society (later re-named the Ecclesiological Society), ostensibly as an antiquarian group, but with the real purpose of promoting clear and definite principles for modern church architecture. This, of course, had to be Gothic. Soon the Society had hundreds of well-connected members, particularly clergymen, and exerted an immense influence through the publication of numerous advisory tracts and their magazine *The Ecclesiologist*, founded in 1841.

The Ecclesiologists' instructions and 'rules', persuasive in their dogmatism, sought to re-introduce ritual and, in effect, adapt the ideas of Pugin to the context of Anglican worship and design. At first they tolerated Early English Gothic, but before long they fixed upon the 'Middle Pointed', their term for Early Decorated, as the only acceptable style. Perpendicular, being 'debased', was as yet utterly taboo. Meanwhile, the famous critic John

Ruskin (1819-1900) was also advocating what he called 'the English earliest decorated', again as opposed to the Perpendicular, or late Gothic style, and had begun to evolve a more general theory of Gothic architecture involving concepts such as colour, nature and truth and the notion that a building was a sacrificial offering to God. Thus his *The Seven Lamps of Architecture* (1849) had an enormous influence during the 'High Victorian' period (c.1850-80), also fostering the growing influence of continental Gothic architecture, although upon Dobson at least Ruskin's more complex ideas seem to have had remarkably little effect.

The Ecclesiologists, again developing the earlier ideas of Pugin, also insisted on the proper incorporation of Christian symbolism into modern church design. Thus a church should be cruciform in shape, or at least make allusions to the Trinity through the use of triple windows or in its general form. It should have a proper altar, preferably of stone, and above all a clearly defined nave and chancel, divided by a chancel arch and screen. Galleries were absolutely forbidden. Dobson is known to have admired some of Pugin's work,[20] and, as we have seen, seems to have been influenced by Ecclesiology, or at least by this general climate of ideas. Certainly most of his later churches are Gothic, and more authoritatively so; some, such as St. John's, Otterburn, Northumberland (see below) are quite Ecclesiologically 'correct'. Also, while favouring Tudor for ancillary buildings such as vicarages (see fig. 62) and schools, he now made increasing use of the preferred Decorated Gothic style, and gradually abandoned the quasi-Georgian notion of symmetrical (western) tower and facade. However, Dobson continued to favour Early English and even neo-Norman modes, and throughout the rest

Fig. 62 The Vicarage, Embleton, Northumberland, remodelled by Dobson 1828.

Authors' photograph.

Fig. 63 St. Paul's, Elswick,
Newcastle upon Tyne,
1857-59.

Photograph: R. Walton,
©University of Northumbria at
Newcastle.

of his career sometimes produced thoroughly non-Ecclesiological church designs.

For example, St. Paul's, Elswick (1857-59, fig. 63) has no proper chancel – for which it was criticised by the Incorporated Church Building Society – and neither has Jesmond Parish Church, Newcastle (1858-61, fig. 64). Built in memory of the celebrated local pastor, Richard Clayton, the latter church has longitudinal galleries as well, perhaps reflecting the ultra-Evangelical persuasion of this parish. These are carefully placed between two tiers of aisle windows, the upper windows set under gables which are at right angles to the axis of the nave. Inside, these galleries (so unusual for their date) flank a well-proportioned nave with stately arcades, from the spandrels of which delicately carved stone shafts rise to support a splendid open timber roof. The five-light east window, upon which lines of sight inexorably converge, is also particularly fine. This is a sturdy, vigorous church of unorthodox design, in a freely adapted Decorated style with considerable variety of window tracery and other forms. The west end, for example, has two large windows surmounted by a rose window and gable cross. The main body of the church – the polygonal vestry was added by R.J. Johnson of Newcastle in 1874 – has a roof of single pitch and the tower, unexpectedly placed at the south east, seems even more massive as a result of not being built as originally designed, i.e. without a spire and not to its intended height; it is pinnacled and at the upper level has pairs of windows on each side.

At Jesmond Parish Church there are also prominent gargoyles and everywhere the hood mouldings terminate in expressively sculpted heads of prophets, kings and saints. This latter feature, incidentally, occurs almost identically in other late churches by or restored by Dobson, for example those at Gilsland, Cumbria (1851), Elswick and Ford, while the sculpture incorporated into his quasi-ecclesiastical Archibald Reed Monument in Jesmond Cemetery of 1843-46 (see fig. 56) is also clearly by the same hand. All this suggests that a specialist carver or team of carvers was regularly employed. The Reed Monument itself was erected by public subscription at a cost of just under £200. It was built by the Newcastle mason William

Fig. 64 Jesmond Parish
Church, Newcastle upon
Tyne, 1858-61.
Authors' photograph.

Brown (also responsible for St. James's, Benwell), although he died during its construction and the work was completed by Ralph Dodds, one of Dobson's most trusted craftsmen (see Chapter 6); the lettering was by William Pearson. Dobson gave his services free. A contemporary description gives a good idea of the architect's intentions:

> "The Monument is placed near the north-west angle of the Cemetery, and is a conspicuous object in approaching the ground from Newcastle. Its beautiful spire rising above the trees, and contrasted with the sarcophagus towers of the entrances, gives a picturesque solemnity to the place, and indicates, at first sight, the sacred object of the inclosure, the walls of which are veiled with ivy, and separated on the north side from the turnpike by a narrow shrubbery. The Design for the Monument ... presents a handsome Gothic structure, partaking of the character of the Monumental Crosses of the fourteenth century. Four vaults for interments are contained within and adjoining its foundations, and in one of these repose the mortal remains of the venerated man whose memory the Monument has been erected to commemorate."[21]

Returning to Dobson's churches, we find that, although designing Jesmond Parish Church with galleries, he nevertheless removed existing galleries from the churches at Embleton, Hexham and Houghton-le-Spring. Yet, again, he actually added them at Hartburn, Northumberland (1835), and at Bishopwearmouth, Sunderland (1849-50); in the latter case his typical scheme of enlargement also provided large galleried transepts (as well as a

further 550 seatings!). Similarly, Dobson's Nonconformist churches had galleries, as one might expect, but at the same time many of his later Anglican schemes, such as St. Cuthbert's, Bensham, and St. Peter's, Oxford Street, Newcastle (1840-43, fig. 65), were designed with them, at the west. The Evangelical tradition died hard in the North, and Dobson was not doctrinaire; also, he was impartial in serving all denominations, and, in offering a wide variety of plans and types, responded to demand.

St. Peter's, meanwhile, was one of Dobson's most important churches.

Curiously positioned side-on within the street, as in the case of the unbuilt Elswick chapel project, it had a western tower, centrally placed, and Dobson incorporated a chancel only after the vicar decided it might improve the original design.[22] Otherwise this church had considerable authenticity, being in a late Decorated style (admired by Sydney Smirke) with aisles and clerestory, and the internal effect (see fig. 66) was spacious, with a substantial chancel arch. Unusually large and rich in form, it was a mature example of Dobson's work (although delays in its completion caused him considerable regret).

Also Decorated and surprisingly ornate – so much so that it was considered somewhat unusual for a dissenting chapel – was the nearby

Church of the Divine Unity in New Bridge Street (1853, fig. 67). Its plan, however, reflected Nonconformist practice in being a simple rectangle with galleries around three sides; these, incidentally, were supported by slender (exposed) iron columns. Occasionally, Dobson's designs actually proved too elaborate for local taste, as with his John Knox Presbyterian Church, Clayton Street West, Newcastle (1851). Although in a comparatively restrained Early English style, this church, also now demolished, was considered 'Papist' and a stone cross capping the building had to be taken down.

Churches on limited budgets

In the main, however, Dobson's urban churches, of all denominations, were usually built on a limited budget of £3,000-£7,000. This was probably a factor in his frequent choice of the simplest Early English forms and the rather routine and utilitarian character of many of the designs – although effective use is made of simple means and Dobson did his best to provide as many adaptations of the style as he could. Most of these churches were of stone, with timber roofs, often having spirelets or simple bell towers, and groups of lancets at the east and west. A good example is All Saints', Monkwearmouth (1846-49); this has a spirelet at the south-west angle of the nave (this combined with a south aisle under a single roof), chancel and south porch. Another was St. Paul's, Hendon, Sunderland (1851-52), a plain and undecorated 'triple-naved' design again situated in a new industrial area.

Trinity Presbyterian Church, New Bridge Street, Newcastle (1846-47), was slightly more elaborate, having twin towers at the west, between which was a group of seven lancets, resembling those at St. Edmund's Chapel,

Gateshead, which Dobson had restored ten years before. Again, the Roman Catholic church of St. Joseph, Birtley, near Gateshead (1842-43), has five lancets at the west, with a modest spirelet above. Lack of money often hampered Dobson's ecclesiastical work. Towers were sometimes not completed as designed, as at Jesmond Parish Church, and on some occasions he had to resort to expedients such as providing roofs of cheaper timber stained to resemble oak. In the case of St. Paul's, Elswick, one of the largest churches he designed, Dobson complained that he had been unable to make the exterior more attractive through want of funds.[23] The church has nave, aisles and clerestory but the internal effect, though spacious, is extremely plain.

Fig. 68 Laygate Presbyterian Church, Frederick Street, South Shields, 1848-49, demolished.
South Shields Library.

On the other hand, a little more could be done if funds – and local taste – allowed. Laygate Presbyterian Church, South Shields (1848-49, fig. 68), although in the familiar Early English style, was paid for by the local industrialist J. Stevenson and probably for this reason had a more than usually impressive tower, with characteristic broach spire (at the south west). This design of tower and spire was also used by Dobson, with only slight modifications, at the approximately contemporary St. Cuthbert's, Bensham, St. Paul's, Warwick Bridge, Cumbria (1845), the latter executed in attractive local red sandstone, and St. Cuthbert's, Benfieldside, Shotley Bridge, County Durham (1848-50, fig. 69). The last-named is one of Dobson's best Anglican churches. Neat and prim, perhaps, rather than soaringly 'medieval', it is nevertheless impressively sited above a hillside and has 'correctly' disposed nave, aisles and chancel.[24]

ST CUTHBERT'S CHURCH, BENFIELDSIDE, SHOTLEY BRIDGE.

Fig. 69 St. Cuthbert's, Benfieldside, Shotley Bridge, County Durham, 1848-50.

Newcastle Libraries & Information Service.

Dobson and church restoration

As mentioned earlier, Dobson carried out numerous church restorations and reconstructions. These were occasioned usually because of the pressing need to provide more accommodation for worshippers; another factor was the typically Victorian desire to 'improve' old buildings. Once again the Ecclesiologists had firm views on the subject. Indeed, church restoration was, they believed, a necessary and Christian duty; its purpose was seen as being to produce a correct Middle Pointed, or at the very least homogeneous effect, even if this meant the destruction of ancient work. The Ecclesiologists also argued that the original form of a building as first conceived, should, as far as possible, be restored.

Dobson, to his credit, was prepared on occasions to go further than many Ecclesiologists in restoring Perpendicular Gothic work, normally thought not worthy of being conserved. Thus in about 1852 he made a comparatively scholarly reconstruction of the Percy Chapel, Tynemouth Priory, delighting in the sculptured bosses of its roof; for his restoration of the circular window above the altar, he used "a common rose window of the period", as the original tracery had disappeared.[25] More typically, however, as early as 1817 Dobson had proposed replacing the late Gothic east window at Hexham Abbey with triple lancets, which in his opinion were more in keeping with the building's basic form (although this scheme was not at this stage carried out), and most of his restorations, though inevitably conditioned by the individual preferences of clergymen and other patrons, were generally in accordance with orthodox Ecclesiological ideas.

Thus at St. Michael's, Houghton-le-Spring, County Durham, Dobson restored the nave roof to what he thought was its original pitch. In a similar spirit, at Embleton Parish Church, Northumberland, he re-built the 'Craster' porch, removed the galleries, and extended the nave aisles westward as far as the west wall of the tower, incorporating the latter into the body of the church; in the lower portion of the tower he inserted a ceiling supported by stone arches, the springers of which were designed to rest in the spaces of some early Norman windows which Dobson had blocked up.[26] All other windows were re-built with 'Middle Pointed' tracery. The effect was to remove what one observer had affectionately described as "the varied ornaments, excrescences and inconveniences"[27] contributed by different generations over the years. Incidentally, Dobson's work here can be contrasted with the thoroughly High Victorian chancel added only 16 years later by F.R. Wilson of Alnwick in 1866-67, inspired by Ruskin with its bands of different coloured stone.

Similarly, when Dobson came to deal with St. Michael's, Ford, also in Northumberland, in 1852, this largely 13th-century church consisted of a single-aisled nave and chancel, the latter entered through a very narrow arch, and externally presented a picturesque appearance with various types of window and a large irregular 'transept' on the south. Dobson kept the unusual bell tower but otherwise swept all irregularity away, blocking up the west door, adding the north aisle and present south porch, and replacing the chancel arch. He re-roofed the nave, raising its pitch by some eight feet. All the windows, except for an ancient lancet in the west wall, were reconstructed in a uniform Early English style. The result was to increase seating accommodation and to 'tidy up', in a manner desired by many clergymen at the time. Much the same effect had also been achieved at St. Mary's, Belford, where only an engraving exists to show the picturesque assemblage that was the old church before Dobson's rather over-enthusiastic reconstruction of 1828-29 (see above). Here, of major original features only the Norman chancel arch and the small south window of the chancel were left untouched.

There is no doubt that Dobson expressed his love of medieval architecture through this kind of work, and believed that he was engaged in the valuable task of preserving buildings for posterity – acting "with judgment and knowledge *where he was not overruled*" (our italics).[28] Yet the effect of these and many other of his restorations was to destroy old work and to produce structures that can seem obtrusively 19th-century in tone.

It will be observed that during the latter part of his career Dobson was becoming ever more involved in restoration work. However, by now the standard 'Ecclesiological' approach to this was coming under attack. In 1849, for example, Ruskin stated that restoration meant "the most total destruction a building can suffer: a destruction out of which no remnants can

Fig. 70 Hexham Abbey, Northumberland, the east elevation reconstructed by Dobson, 1858-60.
Newcastle Libraries & Information Service.

be gathered: a destruction accompanied with false description of the thing destroyed".[29] Ruskin's reverence for old work, shared by his disciple William Morris, underlies a general attitude today that ancient architecture should if at all possible be kept intact. By the 1850s, antiquarians, younger architects and even some of the later Ecclesiologists were beginning to be influenced by these views.

In 1852 the Archaeological Institute of Great Britain and Ireland held its annual meeting in Newcastle; when Dobson took members on a guided tour of the town, he found himself obliged to defend his much earlier reconstruction of the north transept window at St. Nicholas's Church, claiming that departures from its original form had been forced upon him by the church-wardens of the day. Seven years later he rebuilt the east gable of the same church, replacing the old Perpendicular window and circular light above with the present enormous, single Perpendicular design. Taken to task by his fellows at the Newcastle Society of Antiquaries, he managed to explain that at least he had successfully opposed the Church authorities' preference for an even less authentic Decorated scheme.[30]

Even more controversial were Dobson's last major restorations, at Hexham Abbey (1858-60) and St. Gregory's, Kirknewton, Northumberland (1860). At Kirknewton he completely rebuilt the nave and north aisle in Early English style, but the distinguished architect Anthony Salvin, hitherto

91

Sketch of Otterburn Chapel,

Now being erected by Mr Askew and the Misses Davidson.

Fig. 71 St. John's,
Otterburn,
Northumberland, 1855-57.
From an engraving.
Tyne & Wear Museums.

a friend and supporter of Dobson, had vehemently opposed the plan.[31] He argued that Dobson's scheme was structurally unnecessary and incompatible with existing elements such as the 12th-century south chantry and tiny chancel, with their crude but unusual barrel vaults. Salvin feared the demolition of these 'incorrect' portions of the church. Ultimately these latter portions, at least, were spared, it seems largely by default.

At Hexham Dobson finally got the chance to remove the east window of the Abbey which he had examined in 1817 and had been obliged to restore in 1828. Now he replaced this unusual late Gothic five-light structure, with a 'rose' as centrepiece, with two tiers of triple lancets based on those at Whitby Abbey, which he deemed to be contemporary with the building's basic form (see fig. 70). Also he completely removed the Perpendicular Lady Chapel below, though he had drawn up plans to restore this about seven years before. The effect today is hard, neat and academically correct, but

Fig. 72 St. Edward's, Sudbrooke, Lincolnshire, 1860-62.
Authors' photograph.

although approved of by many of his local colleagues, it was censured by some of the journals of the time in the severest terms.[32]

In spite of the controversies of these last years, Dobson achieved great success with two new churches, St. John's, Otterburn (1855-57, fig. 71), and St. Edward's, Sudbrooke, Lincolnshire (1860-62, fig. 72); these are among his most attractive designs. Both were paid for by generous private funds, have rural sites, and are generally similar in plan. St. John's is a small church in the Decorated style, and St. Edward's is equally intimate in scale. The latter has enriched arches with nave, chancel and apse, and is freely based on the 12th-century Steetley Chapel near Chesterfield, Derbyshire; in paying this final homage to the neo-Norman mode Dobson seems also to have drawn upon various other studies he had made at Lanercost Priory and at the little Northumberland church at Rock. In these very late designs Dobson produced a refinement and a delicacy of ornament unprecedented in his work.

In spite of Dobson's interest in medieval architecture, his restorations were frequently insensitive and, more generally, his churches and chapels often lack individuality when compared to his other work. Dobson does not seem to have had the religious fervour of a Pugin or even of later Gothic Revivalists in Newcastle such as R.J. Johnson and W.S. Hicks. Nor, with a few notable exceptions, did Dobson's general approach to design accord with the taste for greater decorativeness which became increasingly manifest as the Victorian period progressed. Similarly, lack of resources coupled with an apparent over-eagerness to meet the varying needs of different denominations, sects and even individual clergymen arguably limited the quality of his achievement in this field. Overall, therefore, ecclesiastical architecture was for the most part a worthy if less distinctive (and even occasionally controversial) element in his career.

Notes

1 J. Summerson, reviewing T.E. Faulkner and A. Greg, *John Dobson: Newcastle Architect, 1787-1865*, 1987, in *Society of Architectural Historians of Great Britain Newsletter*, no. 38, 1988.

2 Obituary of Dobson in *The Building News*, 13 January 1865, pp.25-26.

3 *NJ*, 5 August 1848.

4 Dobson, p.36.

5 See Minutes of the Newcastle Council 1844, Introduction, p.xviii; an illustration of the building is in *AA*, new series, vol. xv, 1892, facing p.198. See also NCRO (ZAN M13/F11, pp.112-45).

6 As late as 1852 we find Dobson guiding a large party of members of the Archaeological Institute of Great Britain and Ireland round the churches, town walls and other antiquities of Newcastle. See J. Bell, *Collection Relative to the Meeting of the Archaeological Institute of Great Britain and Ireland at Newcastle upon Tyne*, 1852 (NCL).

7 Dobson presented a copy of a treatise of this kind by Lewis Vulliamy to the Literary, Scientific and Mechanical Institution; see *NCh*, 12 February 1825. See also A. Greg, 'The Building and its Architect', in *The Literary and Philosophical Society of Newcastle upon Tyne Bicentenary Lectures*, 1994, p.46 n.7.

8 E.g., to H. Lockwood and A. Cates, *The History and Antiquities of the Fortifications to the City of York*, 1834; see E. Jones, *Industrial Architecture in Britain, 1750-1939*, 1985, p.149.

9 Obituary in *The Building News*, *loc. cit.*

10 J. Dobson, *Presidential Address to the Northern Architectural Association* (April 1859), reprinted in Wilkes, p.108.

11 Reported in *NC*, 28 July 1827.

12 See T. Rickman, *An Attempt to Discriminate the Styles of English Architecture*, 1817, p.131.

13 Obituary in *The Building News*, *loc. cit.*

14 Recently discovered via archaeological investigation by the Conservation Architect, Mr. R. Hughes, of Lowe, Rae, Architects, Penrith.

15 Dobson, p.44.

16 *Ibid.*

17 In RIBA (RAN/1/E/4/1-4); the building accounts are in NCRO (ZAN M12/B1), Dobson being paid £70 for his work.

18 See the drawings by Dobson illustrated in Mackenzie 1827, I, facing p.102.

19 See the sketches based on a survey by Dobson in the RIBA Drawings Collection (Smirke Collection Sketch Book vol. 5, pp.84-86).

20 See a sketch attributed to Dobson of a church by Pugin at Warwick Bridge, Cumbria, in the RIBA Drawings Collection (Smirke Collection Sketch Book vol. 5, p.91). Similarly, it has been pointed out that various decorative features at Lilburn Tower (see Chapter 3) are taken directly from some of Pugin's published designs (see *CL*, 8 November 1973, p.1443).

21 *An Account of … the Monument and Tablet Erected to the Memory of the Late Archibald Reed, Esq.*, 1846, p.14; copy in 'Documents connected with Reed's Monument' (NCL file, CR Bio 1808, CL920 R323). It is more than likely that the above description was written by Dobson himself.

22 See correspondence in Lambeth Palace Library (ICBS file no. 2459).

23 ICBS file no. 5050.

24 The original design provided for a north aisle only. A second aisle, porch and organ vestry were added on the south side by J.W. Walton of London, from 1881.

25 Dobson gave a paper on his restoration of the Percy Chapel to the Archaeological Institute of Great Britain and Ireland in Newcastle, 26 August 1852. Copy in Bell, *op. cit.* (see note 6, above).

26 Described by F.R. Wilson in *Proc. Soc. Ant.*, new series, vol. iii, 1887-88, p.176.

27 Archdeacon Singleton, c.1829, quoted in O. Craster, *A History of Embleton Parish Church*, n.d., p.5.

28 *Dictionary of National Biography*, s.v. 'Dobson'.

29 J. Ruskin, *The Seven Lamps of Architecture*, 1849, chapter VI, section XVIII.

30 See *AA*, new series, vol. iv, 1860, pp.152-53.

31 See correspondence in Lambeth Palace Library (ICBS file no. 5529).

32 See, for example, F.R. Wilson, 'Hexham Abbey Church', a paper read before the Architectural and Archaeological Society of Durham and Northumberland, 23 July 1862 (reprinted in its *Transactions*, vol. 1, 1870; see p.26).

Fig. 73 The Central Station, Newcastle upon Tyne, begun 1847, exterior as existing, photographed 1965.
Newcastle Libraries & Information Service.

Colour Plate i The Royal Jubilee School, Newcastle upon Tyne, 1810, demolished. From a watercolour by Dobson. *Laing Art Gallery, Newcastle upon Tyne.*

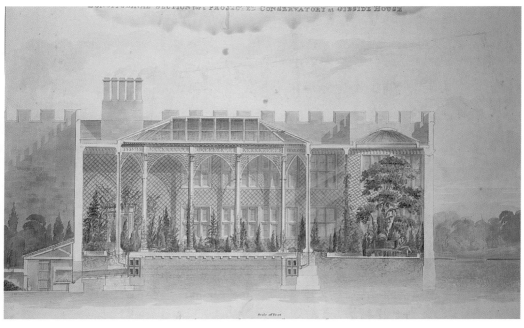

Colour Plate ii Section of the proposed conservatory at Gibside, County Durham. Dobson's drawing of 1814. *DCRO.*

Colour Plate iii The Fishmarket, Newcastle upon Tyne, 1823-26 (interior). From a watercolour by Dobson and J.W. Carmichael. *Laing Art Gallery, Newcastle upon Tyne.*

Colour Plate iv St. Thomas's, Newcastle upon Tyne, 1827-30. From a watercolour by Dobson and J.W. Carmichael. *Laing Art Gallery, Newcastle upon Tyne.*

Colour Plate v The Royal Arcade, Newcastle upon Tyne, 1831-32, demolished. From a watercolour by Dobson and J.W. Carmichael. *Laing Art Gallery, Newcastle upon Tyne.*

Colour Plate vi Meldon Park, Northumberland, from 1832. From a watercolour by Dobson and J.W. Carmichael. *Laing Art Gallery, Newcastle upon Tyne.*

Colour Plate vii Lilburn Tower, Northumberland, from 1828. From a watercolour by Dobson and J.W. Carmichael.
Laing Art Gallery, Newcastle upon Tyne.

Colour Plate viii Beaufront Castle, Northumberland, 1837-39. The billiard room, from a watercolour by Dobson and J.W. Carmichael. *Laing Art Gallery, Newcastle upon Tyne.*

Colour Plate ix Lilburn Tower, Northumberland, from 1828. Detail of library ceiling. *Authors' photograph.*

Colour Plate x Nunnykirk Hall, Northumberland, 1825. Detail of staircase interior. *Authors' photograph.*

Colour Plate xi Grey Street, Newcastle upon Tyne, 1834-37. The lower east side, from a watercolour by Dobson and J.W. Carmichael. *Laing Art Gallery, Newcastle upon Tyne.*

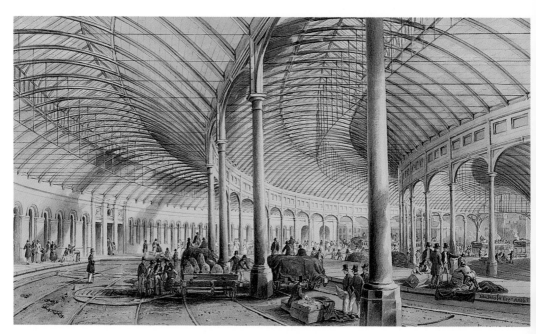

Colour Plate xii The Central Station, Newcastle upon Tyne, begun 1847. The interior, from a watercolour by Dobson and J.W. Carmichael. *Laing Art Gallery, Newcastle upon Tyne.*

Colour Plate xiii The Central Station, Newcastle upon Tyne. The original, unexecuted, design of 1846, from an engraving after Dobson. *Laing Art Gallery, Newcastle upon Tyne.*

Colour Plate xiv The Central Station, Newcastle upon Tyne, the second, unexecuted, design, c.1849-50. From a watercolour by Dobson and J.W. Carmichael. *Laing Art Gallery, Newcastle upon Tyne.*

Colour Plate xv The Vegetable ('Grainger') Market, Newcastle upon Tyne, 1834-35 (interior). From a watercolour by Dobson and J.W. Carmichael. *Laing Art Gallery, Newcastle upon Tyne.*

Colour Plate xvi The 'Grainger' Market, Newcastle upon Tyne, 1834-35. Guests, including Dobson, attend a grand dinner to commemorate its opening, 24 October 1835. From an oil painting by Henry Perlee Parker. *Laing Art Gallery, Newcastle upon Tyne.*

5 Industrial, Railway and Later Public Architecture

The boundary between works of civil engineering and works of architecture is not clear cut, though it was clearer in the 19th century than it is today; at that time architecture was often seen as the application of decoration to structure, rather than as the exploitation of the aesthetic merits of unadorned construction. Today, however, 'functional' works such as bridges, warehouses, docks and piers are better appreciated for their 'architectural' qualities of elegance, proportion and efficient use of materials. Similarly, Georgian and Victorian structures of this kind are now seen as important precursors of 'Modern' architecture.

Industrial and 'engineering' architecture comprised a significant part of Dobson's output (although, unfortunately, much of it does not survive) and he had considerable aptitude for this aspect of design. Indeed, Dobson has been described as "one of the few educated designers who in the early part of the nineteenth century did not shrink from industrial work".[1] Thus his scheme for Seaham Harbour, discussed in Chapter 2, was important as an early example of a planned industrial town (with carefully graded levels of accommodation), while his engineering and constructional skills were often vital, particularly to the larger works of public architecture and to his triumphant underpinning of Lambton Castle at the very end of his career (see p.71). Moreover, his architectural practice reached its climax with the designs for Newcastle's Central Station, in which architectural ambition was matched by engineering invention. The Central Station was also Dobson's most important public building, and this chapter, after discussing the Station, goes on to examine his other later works of public architecture, from c.1840.

Building for industry

Beginning with industrial and other 'functional' structures, we find that docks and their associated buildings (as well as buildings for railways – see below) were obviously essential ingredients in establishing the North East as a major industrial and mercantile centre. Such 'functional' works are scattered through Dobson's career from the earliest years. He built two sets of docks at North Shields for local men in 1813 and 1816, planned improvements and extensions to the Quayside at Newcastle in 1836, 1848 and 1854, designed staithes for Walker, Parker & Co. at the Elswick Lead Works (c.1840) and rebuilt the fishing harbour at Cullercoats in 1846. In the 1840 Newcastle Exhibition of Arts, Manufactures and Practical Science, he even exhibited a "Working model of a Coal Drop, for lowering Waggons loaded

Fig. 74 Grain Warehouses, South Dock, Sunderland. The left by Dobson, 1856-58, the right by T. Meik, 1859, both demolished.
Tyne & Wear Museums.

with Coals to the Deck of the Vessel receiving them – the weights returning the waggon when emptied, to the level of the railway".[2] Again, his Seaham Harbour project had envisaged substantial docks with an important rail link. One of Dobson's few surviving coastal works is his set of two beacons of 1828-29 at Guile Point, Ross Sands, still guarding the harbour entrance of Holy Island, one of the most sacred and romantic places in Northumberland's history. Built of brick on stone bases, and with original timber beacons within, these simple obelisks have a compelling, utilitarian austerity.

Meanwhile, an enormous tobacco warehouse, which narrowly escaped the great 1854 Newcastle Quayside Fire, was built for Benjamin Sorsbie in 1818-19 (its scale illustrated by Dobson's advertisement for 220,000 bricks and 445 dozen flagstones)[3] and there were later railway warehouses at North Shields station (1848) and at the Manors, Newcastle (1849); these structures are all long since demolished. Dobson's only warehouse to survive until recent times was the south Grain Warehouse (1856-58, fig. 74) at the South Dock, Sunderland. This was of brick, with internal floors of timber supported by trussed timber beams on circular cast iron columns, by then, incidentally, a rather old-fashioned constructional technique (used by Dobson at his Manors Warehouse and, even earlier, by Thomas Telford in his St. Katharine's Dock Warehouses, London, of the 1820s). However, the exterior of the south Grain Warehouse, although strangely asymmetrical, with a large elliptical-arched bay off-centre, had a distinctive architectural quality, with a tall ground floor with round arched openings, four lower floors above with segmental-headed windows, and the whole topped with a dentil cornice. Indeed, the design was strong enough to have been imitated by Thomas Meik in 1859 for his adjoining (north) warehouse, although this was a little more up-to-date structurally in having wrought iron lateral girders instead of timber beams. Dobson's warehouse was supported by substantial brick piers, on massive foundations consisting of a four-foot thick concrete raft founded one foot below the surface of rock: a system reflective of the architect's painstaking attention to technical detail and again followed by Meik. Both the Sunderland warehouses were demolished c.1989.

Dobson also made substantial use of concrete for the foundations of his large Manors Station Goods Warehouse, mentioned above. This warehouse, of stone rather than brick, was on a difficult site over a filled-in part of Pandon Dene, a site which, Dobson himself tells us, "was at the time only town deposit, and of a depth of 50 to 60 feet, and that for the most part in a state of fermentation ... the settlement (of the completed warehouse) not exceeding 7in. over the whole".[4] Clearly Dobson was as proud of his engineering skills as he was of his architectural designs.

Manufacturing industry did not play a prominent part in Dobson's career; supposed work for the Cooksons at their South Shields glassworks has not been proved, but he did build a large coach factory in Pilgrim Street, Newcastle, for the important coach-builders Messrs. Atkinson and Philipson (1837, fig. 75). For this he evidently also designed the machinery. Dobson was also responsible for a substantial flax mill on the Ouseburn at Byker, Newcastle (now a complex of craft workshops), for Robert Plummer in 1847-48. Stone-built with bold classical detailing, this still reflects the desire, typical of its period, that utilitarian structures should be monumental and dignified. It is significant that Dobson had designed a house for

Fig. 75 Messrs. Atkinson and Philipson's Coach Manufactory, Pilgrim Street, Newcastle upon Tyne, 1837, demolished. From an engraving.
Laing Art Gallery, Newcastle upon Tyne.

ATKINSON & PHILIPSONS CARRIAGE & HARNESS ESTABLISHMENT.
PILGRIM STREET.

99

Plummer's father, Matthew, at Gateshead Fell in 1823 (the former Sheriff Hill Hall), so in this instance it was a case of a satisfied client of Dobson's domestic work returning to him for a different type of design. (Much the same occurred when Dobson designed a corn mill for R.S. Surtees at Hamsterley, County Durham, in 1819, having worked for Surtees previously at Hamsterley Hall itself.)

Bridges

Dobson also designed an attractive Gothic bridge for Surtees at Hamsterley in 1825, the first of several modest road bridges in the region built at a time of widespread improvements to the country's road system. The state of Britain's roads in the 18th and early 19th centuries was recognised as a national scandal, and was a factor in encouraging the growth of the railways. Thomas Telford and J.L. McAdam were responsible for the major innovations in road construction in the 1810s and 1820s. Telford, also one of the country's greatest bridge engineers, was long thought to have worked with Dobson on the new bridge over the Wansbeck at Morpeth, on the main Newcastle to Edinburgh road, built between 1829 and 1831 to replace the narrow and dilapidated medieval bridge. "Telford chose or approved of the site", the historian Hodgson wrote, "the designs ... are by Mr. Dobson".[5] However, recent research indicates that, while Dobson did submit an unsuccessful design, the present bridge was built by Telford alone.[6] Yet Dobson may have designed the rather similar stone bridge over the Eden at Warwick Bridge, Cumbria (1837), and certainly built several other less important bridges (including some wooden ones), for example on the Mitford Road at High and Low Ford, at Chatton and at Haltwhistle, all in Northumberland.

More significant than any of these road bridges, however, was a proposal Dobson made in 1843 for a high-level bridge at Newcastle,[7] intended to open up the possibility of a direct rail link between London and Edinburgh. There were at least 15 proposals for such bridges in the early 19th century, some to take road or rail traffic alone, the more percipient to combine the two. Dobson provided three alternative, carefully costed designs, a 40-foot wide rail and foot bridge, a 60-foot wide bridge with rail and road on the same level, and a bridge with a road carried beneath the railway, all apparently based on the concept of an iron bridge carried on five 141-foot span stone arches, four over the river and one over the Close. It would have been 110 feet above high water, and sited rather to the west of the present High Level Bridge, joining Neville Street at a position approximating to that of the present Central Station; this location was in order to benefit from the anticipated growth of industry and residential development in Elswick.

Building for the railways

The Newcastle and Carlisle Railway Company, for which Dobson made the above designs, had purchased land west of Forth Banks, where it hoped to provide a station for the shared use of its own line and those of the Newcastle and Darlington Junction Railway and a projected Newcastle to Edinburgh railway. A sketch by Dobson for a proposed railway station for the Newcastle and Carlisle Railway of c.1840 may well relate to this.[8] However, the design has also been identified as being for a station in Carlisle, a town with a wealth of medieval architecture (it is a stretched-out version of Dobson's Tudor-Gothic country houses of the 1830s, such as Beaufront and Holme Eden). In any event, the original Carlisle terminus was a very modest Tudor-style station on London Road. This was built probably to Dobson's design (as perhaps was a temporary station which preceded it) in 1836, but in the same year the line was extended a mile to the north west and from 1863 the Newcastle trains shared the main line Citadel Station of 1848-51, designed by Sir William Tite. In 1844 Dobson also produced an unexecuted design for a station for the Maryport and Carlisle Railway Company, to be situated in Crown Street, Carlisle.[9]

For the all-important Newcastle to Edinburgh line there were by now several possible competing routes. Dobson himself, in partnership with the mining engineer Matthias Dunn and Robert Hawthorn, another engineer, had in 1836 drawn up a prospectus for a Newcastle to Dunbar railway, roughly on the present route, to be carried over the Tweed on another high-level bridge at Berwick.[10] The eminent engineer George Stephenson had at the time preferred this coastal route of Dobson's to the inland alternatives. However, when it came to the siting of a high-level bridge at Newcastle he considered Dobson's proposed location (1843) to be too far west and gave his approval (as did the Newcastle Corporation) to a rival proposal put forward by George Hudson, the Yorkshire-born 'Railway King', also in 1843. A scheme by Grainger (see pp.133-34) was also rejected, not least because of safety issues (his new structure would have been built upon the old Tyne Bridge).[11] The preferred design had been formulated by the architects John and Benjamin Green (see Chapter 6), with Robert Stephenson, Chief Engineer of the York, Newcastle and Berwick, and Newcastle and Darlington Junction Railways, as "consulting engineer";[12] it would have been on the site of the present High Level Bridge.

George Hudson's support was essential for any successful railway development in the North East in the 1840s, for he was single-mindedly devoted to creating a railway route under his control from London to Edinburgh. By this time Hudson was at the height of his powers. He had become Chairman of the York and North Midland Railway, the Newcastle and Darlington Junction Railway, and the York, Newcastle and Berwick Railway, the last-named the successful inheritor of Dobson's 1836 proposal, and was in control of all sections of the potential London to Edinburgh route, except the link across the Tyne. In 1844 he built a terminus station at Gateshead (to designs by the Yorkshire architect G.T. Andrews) and in that year trains first ran from London to the Tyne. In 1845 his economic power persuaded the Newcastle and Carlisle Railway to share with him in the costs of a joint station at his preferred site, south of Neville Street in Newcastle, and in the same year Acts of Parliament were obtained allowing him to build the Newcastle High Level Bridge and Central Station.

The Greens' design for the high-level bridge was now abandoned on the initiative of Robert Stephenson in favour of one by himself detailed by his longstanding collaborator Thomas Harrison (built 1846-49). Meanwhile, Dobson was commissioned to design the Central Station. For this he adopted a Roman classical style, although neither the first nor the second version of the design was fully implemented (see below). Dobson was also responsible at this time for two other stations for the York, Newcastle and Berwick Railway, at Half Moon Lane in Gateshead – a very much smaller building – and the Goods Station at the Manors in Newcastle; both are long since lost.

Suggestions that Dobson was also involved in the designs of the High Level Bridge seem to be unfounded. However, he may well have contributed to the detailing of some of the approach viaducts, including the enormous one over Dean Street (later doubled in width), which helps to create one of the city's most 'sublime' views. Certainly he was paid £490 by the Newcastle and Darlington Junction Railway for 'High Level Bridge' work, although this was at least in part for his work in valuing the property to be demolished, whereby upwards of 800 families lost their homes.[13] With reference to this latter activity, incidentally, a younger contemporary provided an amusing glimpse of one aspect, at least, of Dobson's everyday professional life, recalling that:

> "often, day by day, [Mr. Dobson] might have been seen seated in company with engineers, architects, builders, barristers, and solicitors, and sometimes King Hudson himself, trying to assess the value of some business and business premises … over which the railway trunk line had to pass. These little courts were often held at the Queen's Head, Turf, and other inns famed for their bountiful larders."[14]

Meanwhile, Hudson's power and ambition grew. In 1845 he was elected Conservative M.P. for Sunderland in place of Lord Howick, an opponent of his Northumberland east coast line and recently elevated to the title of Earl Grey. He invested heavily on behalf of the Newcastle and Darlington Junction Railway in the Sunderland Dock Company (for which Dobson was later to build the Grain Warehouse, described above). Another major initiative came in 1847 when Hudson decided to develop Whitby, North Yorkshire, as a fashionable watering-place in order to increase traffic on the Whitby branch of his York and North Midland Railway. To this end he set up the Whitby Building Company, investing in it the huge sum of £10,000 of his own money;[15] the Company acquired fields on West Cliff and began to build crescents and terraces to Dobson's plans (see below, pp.111-12).

However, the bubble suddenly burst. On 31 December 1848 two of Hudson's companies, the York, Newcastle and Berwick Railway (which by then had acquired the Newcastle and Carlisle Railway) and the Newcastle and Darlington Junction Railway, declared unexpectedly low dividends. At the next shareholders' meeting questions began to be asked about the financial management of the companies, about Hudson's part in share dealings within and between his companies and about his personal financial relationship with them. As details of various illegal activities were uncovered during the subsequent investigations, the shares of the companies collapsed in price and the years of 'railway mania' came to a sudden end. Hudson resigned his chairmanships during the year, although for a time he continued to be popular and widely admired for his achievements. (He remained Sunderland's M.P., for example, until 1859, although it has been said that this was to avoid arrest and he certainly ceased to attend Parliament.) In any event, the architectural result of this collapse in public confidence and in the financial powers of the companies was that Dobson's magnificent first design for the Newcastle Central Station (1846) was not carried out.

Newcastle's Central Station

Dobson's first (unbuilt) design for the Station was of great nobility (see fig. 76 and colour plate xiii). It shows two parallel *porte-cochères*, the outer one forming a projecting central portico, the arrangement lying behind 34 pairs of grand Roman Doric columns flanking arched openings on tall plinths. The great central portico carried sculptures of giant seated figures.

Fig. 76 The Central Station, Newcastle upon Tyne. The original design of 1846; a lithograph from a watercolour by Dobson and J.W. Carmichael.

By courtesy of the Literary and Philosophical Society of Newcastle upon Tyne.

These outer arcades were to have had stone groin-vaulted ceilings with a circular light at each intersection; within, the front of the 'station house' (containing the usual offices and facilities) facing the platform formed the segment of a circle of 800 feet radius. The architect himself wrote:

> "The style of the building is Roman, and the most striking feature of the design is the portico in the centre, 200 feet in length by 70 feet in width, flanked on each side by an arcade the same length, by 35 feet in width, allowing sufficient room for carriages to drive in at the end of each arcade, to turn, and go out at each end of the projecting portico. The convenience of this plan in such a climate as ours ... will at once be apparent: and the grandeur of the effect produced by an arcade and portico of this length will readily be comprehended."[16]

It has recently been pointed out that Dobson was probably influenced by the similar, if smaller-scale use of arcades at Cambridge and Heuston (formerly Kingsbridge), Dublin, stations (1845 and 1846 respectively); both were by Sancton Wood, significantly a former pupil of Sydney Smirke.[17] More generally, Dobson's use of arches, vaults and the Roman order is symptomatic of the move in the 1840s from Greek classicism, with its plain walls and strictly rectangular openings, to Roman and Renaissance styles, with their rusticated walls and round-headed windows and arches. Roman classicism was grander, more decorated, more extravagant and carried overtones of luxury and imperial splendour, as opposed to the rather stark intellectual rigour and discipline suggested by the Greek. Indeed, in the 1840s Greek Revival buildings began to be characterised as slightly insipid, as Victorian Imperialism sought its expression in the style of Imperial Rome, flavoured with a wider appreciation of Continental European, particularly French, classical styles. Self-confidence, a notable quality in Victorian architecture, and of the period generally, is also evident in Dobson's initial design, which particularly epitomises the supreme confidence of the men who built Britain's railways. If built, it would have undoubtedly produced the finest railway station outside London, perhaps in the country as a whole.

The design of any railway station facade is crucially dependent on whether the facade lies alongside the tracks, as at Newcastle, or, as in the case of a terminus station like King's Cross in London, is at right angles to the tracks. In the latter instance, as Lewis Cubitt's station of 1851-52 so superbly demonstrates, the opportunity for the facade to reflect the internal forms of the great curved iron and glass train sheds can give rise to an expressive nobility. By contrast, Dobson's facade, 590 feet long, gives no hint of the subtle glories of the train shed behind; this, like Newcastle's Grey Street, makes superb use of the gentle curve on which it lies (see fig. 77 and colour plate xii). No other station, except perhaps the considerably later one at York (by Dobson's former pupil Thomas Prosser, 1877), achieves so much from the combination of largeness of scale, fine detailing in iron, glass and stone, and the interacting curves of the tracks and the roof members.

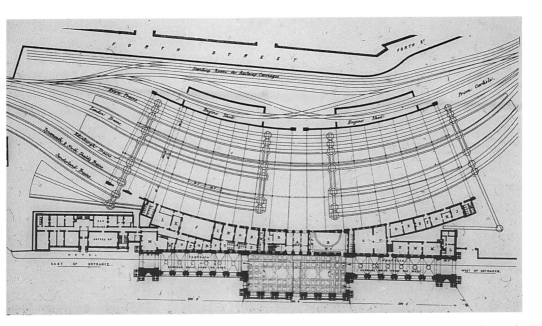

Fig. 77 The Central
Station, Newcastle upon
Tyne, begun 1847.
Original plan, as published
in *The Civil Engineer and
Architect's Journal*.

The use of curved iron principals for the roof, with its three arches each spanning 60 feet, was, as Dobson himself noted, "a new style of roofing".[18] Much imitated subsequently, as at I.K. Brunel's Paddington Station, London (1854), this technique was achieved by rolling the iron out between bevelled rollers. This saved the considerable expense of cutting the iron out of flat plates of iron, a virtue illustrative of the architect's practical approach to engineering and constructional matters. The ironwork at the Central Station was by J. Abbot & Co. of Gateshead.

The station's facilities were to be shared between the Newcastle and Carlisle Railway and the York, Newcastle and Berwick Railway. Each at first had separate platforms, offices and staff. The station was begun in 1847 and opened by Queen Victoria and Prince Albert on 29 August 1850; their busts by David Dunbar the younger still sit inside the entrance to the station. But Dobson must have been greatly disappointed. However fine his train shed was, the Neville Street frontage of the station was a sad testimony to the financial crisis that had hit the railways (the disgraced figure of George Hudson was not present, or indeed mentioned, during the opening speeches).

The station facade as built lacked its *porte-cochères*, which had been abandoned for economy – upwards of £2,000 was saved[19] – and to accommodate a last-minute change in plan necessitated by the provision of a suite of offices for staff transferred from York to Newcastle. Even the central portico, retained in Dobson's second, more attenuated design (colour plate xiv), was still unbuilt. Also abandoned was the Italianate tower at the east end of the station.[20] However, the corner pavilions at the extremities of the facade are still rewarding compositions, reminiscent of the corners of Wren's St. Paul's Cathedral and betraying English and French Baroque influences. The 'wings' between these pavilions and the present portico are, perhaps, less satisfactory designs, unhappily marrying bold semicircular windows on the first floor with pairs of narrow rectangular windows beneath, separated by pilasters and a rather flat and wide entablature. They seem to tell of compromise and last-minute changes.

It was not until 1862-63 that the Central Station was finally completed, when Thomas Prosser, by now architect to what had become the North Eastern Railway, added the present simplified version of the original portico design (see fig. 73). This was based on a revised design by Dobson of 1861 and has pilasters instead of coupled columns as well as lacking the groined vaults proposed in the first, original scheme. Even so, and despite Dobson's continuing disappointment, the portico as built does have something of the scale, dignity and grandeur of the earlier designs. Moreover, the building as a whole (it was later substantially extended to the south and west, mainly from 1892 to 1894) must still be acknowledged as one of the finest of its kind.

Public buildings for the Corporation and others

Although Dobson never again designed anything as important as the Central Station, from the 1840s he continued to be extensively employed on a wide variety of public works. Thus, for example, while the Central Station was first building, Dobson was also engaged in a major restoration of Newcastle's historic Castle Keep. This was carried out under the auspices of the Newcastle Society of Antiquaries as part of their conversion of the building for use as a Museum, the Corporation having granted money and a lease. The Society held a "grand antiquarian banquet" in the Great Hall (this was elaborately decorated with antique banners, tapestries, arms, helmets, armour and the like) on 3 August 1848 to celebrate its reoccupation of "the grand old keep".[21] The restoration, made difficult by serious erosion and defacement, was said to have been greatly facilitated by the fact that Dobson had "when a youth … made drawings of all the principal parts of the building as it then existed".[22] Certainly his characteristic early Victorian approach, involving much recutting and replacement of medieval ornament, is much in evidence, especially in the Chapel and around the entrance to the Great Hall. In any event, the new accommodation soon became inadequate and in 1855 the Society accepted what now seems a rather dubious further plan by Dobson, apparently shelved through lack of funds, to organise more exhibition space. This would have involved placing a new floor over the great hall, thus creating or recreating an upper apartment which was thought to have existed before, and inserting a domed window in the roof above.

By this time the Society of Antiquaries was also engaged in a campaign against the proposed destruction of the adjacent Black Gate, then a rabbit warren of slum dwellings, which the opening out of the roadway from the new High Level Bridge had left exposed. The Corporation was persuaded to offer a prize for the design of a new street frontage involving an approach to

the Black Gate – now rather brutally separated by the railway from the Keep itself. The various designs, never to be carried out, were exhibited at the Newcastle Merchants' Court in 1856. There is a watercolour by Dobson clearly relating to one of these which illustrates a remodelled Black Gate with gables and turrets, flanked by battlemented Gothic ranges having buttresses and blind arches within the bays (see fig. 78). Clearly the architect had lost none of his earlier determination to redesign the castle area, and yet another proposal by him of 1856, to convert the arches of the adjacent railway viaduct to Museum use, may also have been included in this extravagant scheme. The latter no doubt also formed the basis of plans that Dobson submitted to the City Council in 1859 for "the proposed Museum in connection with the castle, so framed as not to hide the keep or St. Nicholas' Church and also to bring in the Black Gate as part of a whole".[23] Nothing, however, came of these schemes, even when the Society later acquired and restored the Black Gate.

A more substantial public work of this period was Dobson's addition to the old Newcastle Infirmary at the Forth, which had become overcrowded and totally unequal to its task. This extension was built at a cost of £10,500, largely through subscriptions and donations, and consisted of a three-storey wing, with basement containing services, dispensary and an outpatients' department; it was sited at right angles to an earlier extension of 1801-03, so as to give the maximum ventilation, space and light. On the ground floor it contained two large, parallel wards. Externally it was a simple, utilitarian classical structure, matching the existing blocks. The Infirmary's centenary in 1851 had led its Committee to decide on a scheme of enlargement incorporating the most modern developments in hospital design, encouraged by their patron the Duke of Northumberland and by their senior surgeons, T.M. Greenhow and C.J. Gibbs.[24]

Dobson seems to have been given the commission virtually as a matter of course and became a member of a Building Committee which inspected hospitals in Manchester, Liverpool, Birmingham and London during the summer of 1851. He even made a separate visit to a new hospital in Brussels and, with characteristic interest in the technical aspects of design, presented plans of all the hospitals visited to accompany the Committee's very thorough Report of 1852. Dobson and his colleagues particularly admired St. Thomas's Hospital, London, the newer parts of which typified the modern 'pavilion' system with large open wards (usually having nurses' rooms and w.c.'s at each end) rather than the old, small, subdivided type of design.[25] This system, believed to reduce infection, was duly introduced in Dobson's Newcastle Infirmary wing – together with the removal of partition walls from the existing wards. However, the new wing, begun in 1852, was obliged to accommodate typhus and cholera patients, as well as victims of the 1854 Quayside Fire (see below), even before its final completion in 1855. Moreover, the operating theatre remained unchanged and the infections which bedevilled hospitals of the time continually reappeared until antiseptic surgery was generally introduced in the 1880s. The old Infirmary was evacuated in 1906 after the opening of the present Royal Victoria Infirmary – itself probably the last large hospital to be built on the 'pavilion' system – and finally demolished in 1954.

Meanwhile, by the 1850s one of Dobson's earlier public works had become a matter of serious concern. Despite, or perhaps because of, its 'advanced' design, the Newcastle Gaol had never been entirely satisfactory in use. With each floor of its radiating blocks accommodating only a single row of cells, it had become overcrowded due to an increase both in population and in crime, and by 1856 had twice as many inmates as originally intended. A Government Inspector had recommended alterations as early as 1838, with the City Council agreeing in principle to enlargement in 1844. But nothing was done and throughout the 1840s and 1850s official reports criticised the prison for both its basic plan and its management; it was referred to, for example, as "ill adapted to its purpose" and "a nursery of crime"[26] (certain re-offending children had been confined in it 50 or 60 times). The main problem was that prisoners could not be separated from each other or kept under efficient control, because they mingled in the communal rooms. Nor could the gaol be enlarged beyond its walls owing to its constricted site, itself condemned as too easily communicating with the outside (it is interesting to note that Dobson's other major prison, at Morpeth, had proved not only more efficient, but also more capable of being updated and enlarged).

Finally in 1857 the Newcastle Council, having considered and rejected the possibility of a completely new gaol, decided to hold a competition "for the best and most economical plan for remedying the existing ... defects".[27] However, nothing came of this and, amid accusations of jobbery, Dobson was invited to submit plans and reports in 1857 and 1858. The ageing but indefatigable architect reminded the Gaol Committee, with much respect, of the omission of one of the radiating buildings from his original scheme of 1822. He recommended at least one new building on what was now known as the 'separate system', rigorously separating classes of prisoner at all times; it was impossible, he said, to extend the prison eastwards at the back of Trafalgar Street. Initially, he was also prepared to demolish one or more of his radiating blocks. However, after visiting the principal prisons in England and conferring with prison governors, he worked out a scheme with the help of Sir John Kincaid (the Senior Government Inspector) which would provide 225 more cells without interfering with the radiating blocks;[28] this was carried out between 1859 and 1861 at a cost of approximately £15,000. Further additions became necessary later in the century; ultimately the prison was closed in 1925 and demolished shortly afterwards.

Rebuilding after the Quayside Fire

Although there is no evidence that Dobson canvassed for support, the complaint that Council Committees had too often favoured him with public works instead of organising competitions for designs had been made before, as with his plan to redevelop the Newcastle Quayside. This had been necessitated by a disastrous explosion and fire in October 1854 which destroyed most of the Quayside's medieval 'chares' and in which, tragically, Dobson's promising son Alexander had been killed (see Chapter 7). At first the Council saw it as a good opportunity to improve a notoriously unhealthy area of the town, and almost immediately Dobson was asked to draw up plans.

Dobson's detailed Report of November 1854 proposed improvements which he claimed to have had in mind for many years – a new street parallel to the Quayside from the Sandhill to Sandgate, with three lateral streets running to the Quay (part of which, innovatively, was to be glass roofed for the conduct of business and exchange) and another new street linking Trafalgar Street with the Quay (see fig. 79). This latter street, he argued (foreshadowing some of the planning schemes for Newcastle of the 1960s), would solve more effectively the longstanding problem of limited access between the upper and lower parts of town, especially now that the Manors Warehouse had been built, than the Council's own idea of extending Pilgrim Street; however, he did include this latter possibility in his plan. The architect also advocated a street continuing the Side to Collingwood Street, passing under the intended High Level Bridge approach, thus providing a link between the Central Station and the Quay.[29]

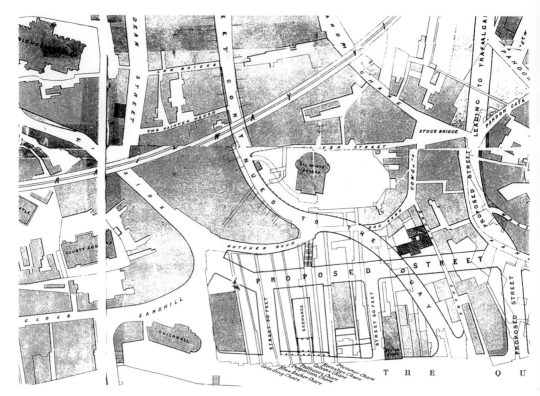

Fig. 79 Plan of proposed
redevelopment of the
Quayside, Newcastle
upon Tyne, after the
Quayside Fire, 1854.
From a lithograph.

*By courtesy of the Literary
and Philosophical Society of
Newcastle upon Tyne.*

Dobson and his former assistant, the Town Surveyor Robert Wallace,
were also employed to value the property involved, arriving at an estimate of
£60,000. Dobson's plans were revised and re-revised. Finally, by May 1856
these were accepted together with a design for street elevations, apparently
selected from alternative schemes by him, which was praised for its variety,
convenience for purchasers, cheapness, and for being "in unison with the
style of buildings in the old part of the town".[30] Thus a drawing by Dobson
(fig. 80) shows a Quayside development with an astonishing mixture of
Tudor, Gothic and Renaissance facades, as though built over a period of several centuries, more or less to a common building line and height but sprout-
ing a profusion of gables, turrets and crests. Presumably Dobson was aiming
for informality, to accord with the remaining medieval buildings of the old
Quayside. Also, there might have been the influence of recent visits the
architect had made to Belgium and probably Germany, where he is said to
have admired the picturesque old towns.[31]

Meanwhile, even by 1857 little progress had been made. The Council
had been completely unable to dispose of the sites, and, amid protests that
the property had been overvalued and that an architectural competition
should have been arranged, it now sold the entire area to the developer Ralph
Walters at a bargain price. Walters, a native of Newcastle but then resident
in London, turned to younger local architects like William Parnell (see
Chapter 6) to design the spacious Italianate streets and buildings of 1858-63

Fig. 80 Proposed elevations of buildings on the site of the Quayside Fire, Newcastle upon Tyne, c.1854. From a drawing by Dobson.

Laing Art Gallery, Newcastle upon Tyne.

which we see today. The final layout at least largely followed Dobson's street plan, but without the implementation of his valuable proposals to link the Quayside with the upper town.

Town planning in the 1850s

Town planning continued to be a significant, if less integrated element during the latter part of Dobson's career. Between 1851 and 1857 he laid out streets in the expanding part of Monkwearmouth, between the Wear bridge and the docks, again for the landowner Sir Hedworth Williamson[32] (see p.49); and as late as 1860 he proposed a new street, possibly in the Gothic style, to continue the line of his earlier St. Mary's Place in Newcastle. At Monkwearmouth, Dame Dorothy, Dock, Ann (later Victor), Barrington, Hardwicke, Bloomfield, Mulgrave and Normanby Streets and Millum Terrace were built in a conventional grid pattern on land which had formerly been a ballast hill; they consisted of neat, two-storey brick terraces with basements (all now demolished) representing an unusually high quality of working-class housing for this time, in line with the developer's usual approach. It is probable that Dobson designed both houses and streets.[33]

Much grander was his plan for the West Cliff development at Whitby (finally drawn up in 1857, although it would appear that building had already been started by Dobson in the early 1850s). As mentioned earlier, it was undertaken for his old patron George Hudson, who had intended to expand his railway system and develop the town as a fashionable resort. The development consists of substantial classical terraces, rather like those at Tynemouth, facing the Abbey ruins and the sea.[34] Although, once again, Hudson's financial problems prevented full implementation of the scheme – there was to have been further development along the cliff top, with a square – East Terrace, with its Royal Hotel, and the adjoining Royal Crescent (fig.

111

81) are particularly fine. The latter (perhaps distantly echoing Dobson's
unbuilt Seaham design) has dignified four-storeyed houses with basements,
and with rusticated ground floors, pedimented windows and balconies.

Some later public buildings

The stylistic plurality characteristic of Dobson's later work is nowhere
more apparent that in his smaller public buildings of this time. For
example, his North Shields Town Hall of 1844-45 (fig. 82), largely financed
by a local benefactor Joseph Laing, is in a very informal Tudor style, with a
double L-shaped plan turning the corner of Howard and Saville Streets and
completing the section between Howard Street and Norfolk Street. It was
built in two separate parts (enclosing J. and B. Green's former Poor Law
Guardians' Hall of 1837), which means that the battlemented ranges with
decorative gables and, at one corner, an oriel window below a plainer gable,
seem slightly disjointed. However, the building was meant to cater for a variety of functions including that of a Mechanics' Institution (added in the second phase) and the emphasis is less on civic monumentality than on fitting
in with the domestic scale of the street.

By contrast, the former Riding School in Northumberland Road,

Newcastle of 1847 (recently converted for use as teaching accommodation for Northumbria University) can be described as classical. Unusually for a Dobson public building it is mainly of brick, but stone is used for some of its over-simplified details such as the surrounds of the three round-arched windows on the street facade – a treatment quite unlike that at the architect's former Sunderland Grain Ware-

Fig. 82 The former Town Hall, North Shields (incorporating an earlier building by John and Benjamin Green), 1844-45.
Authors' photograph.

Fig. 83 The former Barber-Surgeons' Hall, Newcastle upon Tyne, 1851.
Newcastle Libraries & Information Service.

house, a much more convincing utilitarian structure. Meanwhile, two other Dobson public buildings of the same period, both demolished, indicate yet further stylistic diversity: his Bricklayers' Hall, near the Newcastle Castle Garth, was Gothic (1851), while his Northumberland Dock Office, North Shields (1859-61), part of the then general development of the River Tyne, was a block-like neoclassical design, superbly built of ashlar stone, curiously recalling his much earlier work; originally, red brick workers' cottages adjacent to its east side formed a little square.

Dobson's capacity, even willingness, to work in an increasingly eclectic way seems to have proved an asset when he came to execute commissions,

in sharply differing styles, for rival factions of Newcastle's medical fraternity. In 1851 the School of Medicine and Surgery, founded 17 years before, moved into a new Barber-Surgeons' Hall by Dobson in Victoria Street (see fig. 83). This is a major essay in Dobson's now favoured Italian Renaissance style (although later marred by ugly brick extensions). The Barber-Surgeons' Hall was paid for by the York, Newcastle and Berwick

NEWCASTLE-UPON-TYNE COLLEGE OF MEDICINE.
IN CONNECTION WITH THE UNIVERSITY OF DURHAM.

Fig. 84 The College of Medicine, Newcastle upon Tyne, 1852, demolished. From an engraving.
Laing Art Gallery, Newcastle upon Tyne.

Railway Company, whose recent expansion to the Manors had necessitated the demolition of the original early 18th-century Hall. It is a detached rectangular building of two storeys; on the first floor were lecture and dissecting rooms, and a large museum, illuminated partly from above. Its principal or south facade is a symmetrical composition with five bays (the outer two projecting with rusticated quoins) completed by a large cornice, dwarf attic, and (originally) tall rusticated chimneys reminiscent of Vanbrugh's work. The upper windows of the central section form a Renaissance-style arcade with keystones decorated with the 'Aesculapian' snakes, while in the spandrels are the historic armorial emblems of the Barber-Surgeons' Company itself.

No sooner had the Hall been occupied, however, than the profession split. Rather ludicrously, two competing inaugural lectures were given on the same day (1 October 1851), with the majority party defecting to the historic Westmoreland House in Neville Street, to which they now added their new College of Medicine, also by Dobson, in 1852[35] (this was demolished, together with Westmoreland House itself, c.1889, as a result of railway development). No doubt for this rival building (see fig. 84) a completely different image was necessary, and Dobson duly provided a long, low, asymmetrical block (albeit with slightly incongruous plate glass windows) "suggesting collegiate architecture of the Tudor period".[36] It was quaint rather than impressive, but did blend sensitively with Westmoreland House. Meanwhile, the Colleges united in 1857 and the Barber-Surgeons' Hall, hitherto the 'College of Practical Science', became a school in 1863.

The neo-Renaissance style, typified by a design such as the Barber-Surgeons' Hall, was becoming a significant element during the last decade

Fig. 85 Gas Company Office, Neville Street, Newcastle upon Tyne, 1861-62, demolished. From a drawing by Dobson.

Tyne & Wear Archives.

of Dobson's work. This style had been first popularised by Sir Charles Barry, who himself began as a Greek Revivalist, during the 1830s, as the Greek Revival waned; more flexible and potentially ornate, it was developed by architects like C.R. Cockerell, whose own architecture combined Greek, Roman and Renaissance elements (as to some extent did Dobson's Central Station schemes). Cockerell and his followers at the Royal Academy, such as Dobson's friend and son-in-law Sydney Smirke, did much to ensure that classicism remained an important alternative to the now dominant Gothic Revival style.

Thus Renaissance forms became especially favoured during the 1850s and 1860s for what were essentially new forms of public and institutional architecture such as banks, clubs, offices, libraries, museums and town halls. A Newcastle example was one of Dobson's last completed works, the dignified Gas Company Office in Neville Street (1861-62, see fig. 85); this had a rusticated ground floor with arched windows and rectangular windows above, surmounted by a cornice with large brackets, below a balustrade. Further Renaissance-style examples by Dobson include St. Columba's Church, North Shields (1856-57, fig. 86), and his (largely abortive) design for the Warrington Museum and Library, Cheshire, of 1853 (fig. 87). The church, integrated into its setting in Northumberland Square by its plainer wings of brick, has a particularly dignified stone facade. This has five bays with Tuscan half-columns and, at the angles, pilasters supporting an entablature below a balustrade, all standing on a rusticated base.

The Warrington Museum and Library was one of the first rate-maintained municipal institutions of this kind, made possible by the Public Museums Act of 1845. Perhaps as a result of his more widespread renown after the opening of the Central Station, Newcastle, or possibly because of a family connection between patrons, Dobson was commissioned by Warrington Council to prepare plans in 1853; the result was a vigorous and idiosyncratic design which, if executed, would have produced one of his

most ambitious and interesting public works. A site was donated by John
Wilson-Patten, M.P., but sufficient funds could not be raised and the architect was paid off, rather humiliatingly, with a sum less than he had charged;[37]
a local builder was then employed to produce a more economical design
from Dobson's plans.

Dobson himself had proposed a three-storey classical building with
basement, to be built of brick with stone dressings, and having a double
height lecture theatre, library accommodation at ground floor level above an
architectural antiquities room, and the main museum galleries on the top two
floors. It would have had heavily rusticated pilasters, arches and quoins, and
at the upper level panels with relief sculpture instead of windows, the upper
galleries being once again top lit. Strangely, it would have had a cornice
more medieval than classical in form – a solecism, but perhaps intended to
symbolise the range of antiquities displayed. The structure as built (1855-57)
is an almost unrecognisably simplified version of this design.

It will be observed that Dobson's later public works after c.1840, with
the major exception of the Newcastle Central Station, became more piece-
meal, often involving restorations or additions, as well as less coherent stylistically. His designs were no longer conditioned by the severity and discipline of the neoclassical style. Similarly, the days of working for Grainger,
and of grand projects to redesign the whole of central Newcastle, were gone.
Even so, as we have seen, Dobson was still responsible for some interesting
public buildings and planning schemes. However, many of the latter were
not executed and indeed, following the abandonment of his initial Central

Fig. 87 Design for the Warrington Museum and Library, Cheshire, 1853. From a watercolour by Dobson.

Cheshire Libraries and Museums, Warrington Library.

Station design, a surprisingly large number of Dobson's later projects and designs of all kinds also failed to be implemented as he had wished.

Notes

1 E. Jones, *Industrial Architecture in Britain, 1750-1939*, 1985, p.63.

2 Catalogue no. 'Music Room 42'.

3 *NCh*, 2 January 1819.

4 See J. Dobson, *Presidential Address to the Northern Architectural Association* (April 1859), reprinted in Wilkes, p.110. See also T.L. Donaldson, *Handbook of Specifications*, 1860, Part II, pp.831-41. The Manors Goods Station and Warehouse complex is illustrated in W.N. Twelvetrees, *Concrete-Steel Buildings*, 1907, pp.74-75.

5 Hodgson, II 2, p.426.

6 *Ex inf.* Dr. R.W. Rennison.

7 See R.W. Rennison, 'The High Level Bridge, Newcastle; its Evolution, Design and Construction', typescript of paper presented to the Newcomen Society (Transactions, vol. 52, 1980-81), deposited in NCL (Cr 955352A), 46pp., and J. Addyman and B. Fawcett, *The High Level Bridge and Newcastle Central Station: 150 Years Across the Tyne*, 1999, p.22. Dobson's submitted drawings are in TWA (285/290) and DCRO (Q/D/P133).

8 RIBA Drawings Collection (G6/39). See also Addyman and Fawcett, *op. cit.*, p.30.

9 Instead a temporary station was built on the same site, again probably to Dobson's designs, and continued in use until c.1849. See *The Railway Magazine*, August 1963, p.576.

10 W.W. Tomlinson, *The North Eastern Railway, Its Rise and Development*, 1915,

117

p.292.

11 See *Proceedings of the Newcastle Council*, 20 December 1843. It was stated that "the bridge designed by Mr. Dobson, the most western of the bridges, will form an excellent line of communication by railway … and would terminate at a plot of open ground affording ample space for a station; but owing to the distance at which this bridge is placed from the principal streets in the centre of the town, it does not present the facilities and advantages for a carriage-road which the other designs which we have examined afford".

12 *NC*, 29 September 1843.

13 Rennison, *op. cit.*

14 'Old Newcastle Architects and Surveyors', *NWC*, 1 January 1887.

15 C.J. Allen, *The North Eastern Railway*, 1964, p.97.

16 J. Dobson, 'The Central Railway Station, Newcastle upon Tyne', *The Civil Engineer and Architect's Journal*, no. 135, vol xi, December 1848, p.353. See also Donaldson, *op. cit.*, pp.842-66.

17 Addyman and Fawcett, *op. cit.*, pp.86-91.

18 Wilkes, p.109.

19 See *The Builder*, vol. viii, 1850, p.284.

20 A much reduced version of this was later reinstated as part of Thomas Prosser's extension of Dobson's Station Hotel, 1861-63, possibly in consultation with Dobson, only to be now partially hidden by William Bell's subsequent enlargement of 1892-94. See Addyman and Fawcett, *op. cit.*, pp.99-100 and 104-105.

21 See *AA*, new series, vol. xi, 1886, p.177. The decorations were superintended by the artist T.M. Richardson (*NJ*, 5 August 1848).

22 *NJ*, 5 August 1848.

23 *AA*, new series, vol. iv, 1860, p.153.

24 See G.H. Hume, *The History of the Newcastle Infirmary*, 1906, pp.54-55.

25 See *Report of the Deputation of the Building Committee of the Newcastle upon Tyne Infirmary*, 1852 (in the Literary and Philosophical Society of Newcastle upon Tyne, 'Tracts', 8vo series, vol. 135 no.10 and vol. 237 no. 5).

26 See Minutes of the Newcastle Council, 4 August 1858.

27 *Ibid.*, 6 May 1857.

28 *Ibid.*, 1 July 1857 and 7 July 1858, reproducing first and second reports by Dobson.

29 J. Dobson, *Description and Plan of New Streets and Buildings on the Sites of the Late Fires etc.*, 1854. The proposed new street linking Trafalgar Street with the Quay, especially, recalls Dobson's planning ideas of the mid 1820s (see Chapter 2).

30 Minutes of the Newcastle Council, 7 May 1856.

31 Dobson, pp.34 and 70; this is probably the visit supposedly made in connection with the architect's work at Friedelhausen discussed in Chapter 3.

32 For a discussion of Sir Hedworth Williamson's projects see P. Emmerson, 'The Williamson Family of Whitburn, some Aspects of its History', unpublished dissertation for Honours Degree in History and English, Sunderland Polytechnic, 1986.

33 See Fordyce, II, p.480.

34 Dobson's plan of 1857 is with the Whitby Literary and Philosophical Society. A drawing for the elevations of the Royal Crescent, unsigned but evidently by Dobson, is in the North Yorkshire County Record Office, Northallerton (ZW (M) 8/20).

35 See G.G. Turner, *The Newcastle upon Tyne School of Medicine, 1834-1934*, 1934, pp.35ff.

36 *The Builder*, vol. x, 1852, p.658.

37 See Warrington Council Minutes, 1853-54, especially 9 May 1853 and 5 December 1854.

Fig. 88 John Wardle and George Walker, Grey Street, Newcastle upon Tyne, 1834-37, the west side.
Authors' photograph.

6

Dobson's Contemporaries in the North East

obson was an immensely respected and important provincial architect who also enjoyed considerable national renown. However, he was by no means the only figure of significance in the region with regard to planning and architecture. The builder and entrepreneur Richard Grainger, for example, is still accorded an almost mythical status in Newcastle, his name being virtually synonymous with the city's development. Indeed, it is at the present time officially commemorated in the title 'Grainger Town', which is applied to the city centre streets that he laid out (and to part of the surrounding area as well). Other figures, admittedly, were somewhat overshadowed by Dobson and even now are comparatively little known. Yet their contribution was far from insubstantial and Dobson's own status is better appreciated if seen in the light of this. Similarly important is what we know of Dobson's attitude to, and interaction with, his contemporaries (and predecessors) in the North East.

Mention has earlier been made of the burgeoning commercial and industrial development on Tyneside during the late 18th and early 19th centuries, and at this time Newcastle itself was a prosperous and cultivated regional capital. Indeed, long before the Industrial Revolution it had become an important commercial centre, its wealth founded largely on the coal trade. By 1700 Newcastle was the fourth largest English town, and at about this time was described as "a spacious, extended, infinitely populous place".[1] Around the margin of James Corbridge's map of Newcastle of 1723 are illustrations of merchants' houses and public buildings in up-to-date styles. The coal trade actually mitigated Newcastle's geographical remoteness by facilitating contact with the capital and the 18th century saw Newcastle become increasingly culturally sophisticated. Thus from the late 1730s the Newcastle-born composer and impresario Charles Avison started a highly successful series of subscription concerts, while Dr. Robert Thomlinson, a local clergyman, founded in 1741 one of the first libraries in the country open to the public. The Assembly Rooms in Westgate Road opened in 1776, and the town's Literary and Philosophical Society and Society of Antiquaries were founded as early as 1793 and 1813 respectively.

Dobson's predecessors

By this time, too, a comparatively well-informed local architectural profession had begun to emerge. William Newton (1730-98), mentioned in Chapter 1, substantially reinforced the evolving classical tradition in

Newcastle and the North East. He designed not only the Newcastle Assembly Rooms (fig. 89), but also Charlotte Square; the latter was Newcastle's first completed Georgian square, albeit a comparatively modest development (begun 1770). Newton also built a number of country houses for local landowners, industrialists and minor aristocrats (although the more major grandees brought in leading national figures such as Robert Adam, James Paine and, earlier, Sir John Vanbrugh for this kind of work). Newton's houses, as at Backworth (1778) and Acton (1781), both in Northumberland, are mostly in the Palladian style, influenced by Adam and Paine, but his remodelling around 1780 of the now demolished Heaton Hall, near Newcastle, was 'Gothick'. (Heaton, and other present-day suburbs such as Benton, Benwell, Elswick, Fenham, Gosforth and Jesmond, were then villages encircling the still compact town of Newcastle itself.)

Links with national trends are also evident in the work of David Stephenson (see again, Chapter 1) and to a lesser extent that of the Stokoe dynasty of builder-architects. Stephenson was the first Newcastle practitioner to study at the Royal Academy (from 1782 to 1783), as well as being architect to the Duke of Northumberland. It is interesting to note that the design of his church of All Saints, Newcastle, was adapted from an unexecuted scheme by the celebrated metropolitan architect James Gibbs for his church of St. Martin-in-the-Fields, London. Stephenson also designed Newcastle's first Theatre Royal, in Mosley Street (1788, demolished 1836) and in 1789 an interesting Circus or Amphitheatre, on the site of the present

Fig. 90 John Stokoe,
Elswick Hall, Newcastle
upon Tyne, 1803, demol-
ished; photographed in
1967.
*Newcastle Libraries &
Information Service.*

Roman Catholic Cathedral, used for equestrian displays.

Of the Stokoes, John Stokoe (1756-1836) was the son of William
(1722/23-1802) and the father of another William (c.1786-1855). John added
a major extension to the Newcastle Infirmary at the Forth, from 1801, and
designed Elswick Hall (1803, fig. 90). With his son William he was also
responsible for the first Greek Revival building in Newcastle, the Moot Hall
of 1810-12 (see p.15). It may be that William was the main author of this
design, in which case its remarkable competence suggests that he must have
had a training in London or Edinburgh.[2] Certainly William had already
exhibited "two drawings of villas" at the Royal Academy (in 1808).
However, perhaps because of the rise of Dobson, his later career never really took off. He subsequently practised mainly as a speculative developer,
describing himself variously as "architect", "builder" and "architect and
builder".

The emerging profession

Of the local architects mentioned above, Dobson's rather ungenerous
view was that they "were men of talent, whose works might have been
an ornament to the country, had they fortunately been better educated in their
profession".[3] Similarly, Dobson can only have been referring to Newton
when he commented rather scathingly about the design of country houses in

the North East:

"Mr. Payne [*sic*] was unfortunately considered a great authority, and consequently, all the houses built in the north of England were mere copies of Mr. Payne's general plan. An architect, indeed, became a superfluous luxury. When a gentleman wanted a house erected, all he had to do was inform the builder of the size of the rooms required, the plan being a small entrance hall on the south, the staircase opposite, the dining room on one side and the drawing-room on the other, with the library, &c., behind."[4]

As already intimated in Chapter 1, the main problem for Dobson was that his locally-based predecessors and older contemporaries in the North East were not in his view professional architects according to the modern definition of the 'art, profession and business' of architecture (then being promulgated by Sir John Soane and other Royal Academicians). As Soane himself put it:

"The business of the architect is to make the designs and estimates, to direct the works, and to measure and value the different parts, he is the intermediary agent between the employer, whose honour and interests he is to study, and the mechanic whose rights he is to defend. His situation implies great trust ... if these are the duties of an architect, with what propriety can his situation and that of the builder or contractor be united?"[5]

All this accounts for Dobson's later perception that on returning to the North East in 1810, he enjoyed with his friend Ignatius Bonomi of Durham (see below, pp.139-41) "the somewhat barren dignity"[6] of being one of only two professional architects between Edinburgh and York. Dobson was clearly concerned above all to assert his professional status, and involvement in 'the higher branches of the art'.

Fig. 91 Thomas Moore, the former Monkwearmouth Railway Station, Sunderland, 1848.
Authors' photograph.

Locally, however, few adopted such a severe interpretation of events and in fact, possibly because of its geographical – not cultural – remoteness, Newcastle had by the early to mid 19th century an unusually large number of architects and architectural practices,[7] some worthy of comparison with that of Dobson himself. Dobson's closest and most important contemporaries in this regard were Thomas Oliver (1791-1857) and John Green (1787-1852). Meanwhile, in Sunderland there was Thomas Moore (1794-1869), here a rather isolated figure who had started as a joiner, builder and surveyor. In 1848 he designed the Monkwearmouth Railway Station, a finely-crafted Greek Revival structure formerly attributed to Dobson (see fig. 91).

Thomas Oliver

Thomas Oliver was actually Dobson's first pupil and assistant, from 1815 to 1821, after which he began independent practice as a "Land Surveyor and Architect". He was soon employed to undertake surveys for the Newcastle Corporation and between 1824 and 1825 also worked as a surveyor for the Liverpool and Manchester Railway Company. His first significant work was a pair of fashionably stone-fronted houses on the west side of Northumberland Street (1824, demolished) for a Dr. John Baird. Also at about this time he prepared for the Corporation plans for Blackett Street and Eldon Square.

Importantly, however, Richard Grainger had now emerged as someone capable of financing these developments (see Chapter 2). He had set up on his own account in 1816 and was soon building an attractive brick terrace for Alderman William Batson in Higham Place, Newcastle (c.1819-20), followed by houses in such recent streets as New Bridge Street and Carliol Street. At about this time he purchased property for the first time, in Percy Street at the foot of Leazes Lane. As we have seen, Blackett Street and Eldon Square were now built by him, largely to Dobson's designs.

Oliver did design for Grainger the monumental Leazes Terrace (fig. 92,

Fig. 92 Thomas Oliver, Leazes Terrace, Newcastle upon Tyne, 1829-34. *Authors' photograph.*

see also pp.44, 132), which like Eldon Square dramatically aggrandised the established classical tradition of Newcastle street architecture, but the number of other buildings (almost all in Newcastle) which can be ascribed to him is comparatively small. However, his West Clayton Street Congregational Chapel (1851, demolished) was an important work, as was 'Gibson Town', a planned development of streets with neat, two- and three-storey houses "suited to the wants of the humble yet respectable classes of the community".[8] This was laid out between New Bridge Street and the City Road for G.T. Gibson between 1836 and 1848 (largely demolished, 1962-68). It contained the Gibson Street Methodist (New Connection) Chapel of 1837 and the 'Victoria Bazaar' (1836-37), a triangular shopping arcade.

Another major contribution by Oliver was his series of superb engraved maps of Newcastle issued in 1830, 1844, 1849, 1851 and (posthumously) 1858, while his *A New Picture of Newcastle upon Tyne* (1831) is a valuable historical and topographical work. Two of Oliver's sons, Adam and James, became civil engineers. Another, Thomas jnr. (1824-1902, FRIBA 1866), became a noted architect in Sunderland and then in Newcastle. Early in his career he designed the late Greek Revival Londonderry Institute at Seaham Harbour (1853-55). In Newcastle Thomas jnr. founded the partnership of Oliver & Leeson in 1881 (subsequently Oliver, Leeson & Wood). This practice continued with variations in the name (including the addition of W.H. Knowles) and was last recorded in 1947. The Oliver architectural dynasty had lasted 126 years.

The Green family

Fig. 93 John Shaw, Cresswell Hall, Northumberland, 1820-24 (executant architect: John Green), demolished.
Newcastle Libraries & Information Service.

John Green began as a builder in Corbridge, Northumberland, and did not set up in Newcastle (as an architect and civil engineer) until 1820. However, he gained invaluable experience acting as supervisory architect for John Shaw of London at the important, neoclassical Cresswell Hall, Northumberland (1820-24, fig. 93), and soon won a competition in 1822 for the design of the Newcastle Literary and Philosophical Society's building in Westgate Road (see fig. 94). The design as executed seems to be based on elements from several variations put forward by Green and is an interesting synthesis of Grecian and Palladian forms. It would appear that Dobson also

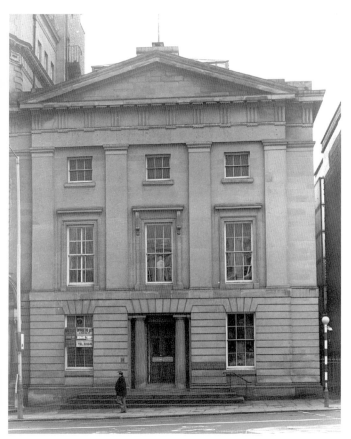

Fig. 94 John Green, premises of the Literary and Philosophical Society of Newcastle upon Tyne, Westgate Road, 1822-25.

Authors' photograph.

offered a proposal, now unfortunately lost, which may have been rejected on grounds of expense. He also appears to have been critical of the completed design.[9]

Green's early and important success with this building had suggested the possibility of rivalry with Dobson himself. Instead, however, Green now began to concentrate on more utilitarian works such as farm buildings (many for the Duke of Northumberland, after his appointment as architect to the Duke in 1829) and, especially, bridges. He designed the first stone bridge over the Tees, at Blackwell, County Durham, in 1832 (widened 1961) and pioneering chain suspension bridges at Warden, Northumberland (1825-26, demolished 1902), Whorlton, County Durham (1829-31, the oldest surviving of its type), and Scotswood, near Newcastle. The Scotswood Bridge, demolished in 1967, opened with great public ceremony in 1831,[10] and it is worth recording that Green exhibited a view of it at the Royal Academy in 1837. In 1841 he was awarded the Telford Medal by the Institute of Civil Engineers (accepted on his behalf by his son) for the innovative laminated timber system used in his impressive Ouseburn (Byker) and Willington (Wallsend) railway viaducts of 1837-39; here in both cases iron later replaced the original wooden construction, in 1867 and 1869 respectively, although this was allowed for by the design.

From about 1837 until his death Green was in partnership with his son Benjamin (1813-58). During this time it is almost impossible to identify any independent work by either architect, although the elder Green was presumably largely responsible for their subsequent engineering work. This included rejected designs for a high-level bridge at Newcastle of 1839 (on the same principle as the aforementioned viaducts) and of 1843 (see p.101). John Green was described as "a plain, practical, shrewd man of business", while his son "was an artistic and dashing sort of a fellow."[11] Indeed, Benjamin Green had been a pupil in London of no less a figure than the distinguished draughtsman and antiquary A.C. Pugin, and was elected a Fellow of the Institute of British Architects (later the RIBA) in 1844. John Green had been

127

elected in 1839 and in both instances their proposers included Benjamin Ferrey, another pupil of A.C. Pugin, and also biographer of the latter's son A.W.N. Pugin.

In the years 1830-31 the name of John Green became involved, with that of Dobson, in a noted controversy which became known as the "Benwell Intrigue".[12] Both architects submitted plans for the design of the proposed new church at Benwell (St. James's), Dobson's being chosen by a Committee majority (23 October 1830) of only seven to six. The Vicar of St. John's, Newcastle, Rev. John Dodd (St. James's being a chapel of ease of this church) was accused of packing the Committee with friends of Dobson in order to secure victory for his favoured architect. With evident embarass-ment, it was resolved "that the thanks of the Meeting be given to Mr. Green, for his designs, with an acknowledgement of Mr. Green's kindness in fur-nishing, and of the talents displayed by him in the same." However, one Committee member, Mr. J.R. Featherston, immediately resigned and before long the affair reached the pages of the satirical magazine *The Northern John Bull* (see fig. 95), amid accusations of copying of plans and of Dobson hav-ing been allowed extra time to prepare his designs because of pressure of work. *The Northern John Bull* went on:

Fig. 95 Handbill advertis-ing issue of *The Northern John Bull* for March 1831, referring to the "Benwell Intrigue".

Northumberland Record Office, and the Society of Antiquaries of Newcastle upon Tyne.

JUST PUBLISHED, THE NUMBER FOR MARCH OF THE NORTHERN

JOHN BULL.

PRICE SIXPENCE.

CONTENTS—LETTER TO THE

Cavalry and Infantry

on their ungentlemanly conduct at the Subscription Concerts, Music Hall.----"The behaviour of the Infantry is common enough, but we did expect something better from the gentlemen of the 3rd."

"You shall no longer have those gay feathers,
That light and gallant hat,
That trim hair and brilliant appearance."

The Vicker's Explanations of his Connections with the

Benwell Intrigue

—Dobson, Green, the Vestry Room—the Names of the Voters, and how they voted.
Brutus Bull—Pitt Clubs—Powdered Pensioners—National Debt, Six hundred Million—Wellington—Wesleyan Methodists—the Laborious Cobbett, with a tender adieu to his brother, the *Northern Lad.*

THEATRE

----the company looked at—Miss Penley the Siddons of the day—Hay, the awkward buffoon, and Hazleton the drawler.
Essay on the Descent of Nobility. Sir James Scarlett, the frontless Lawyer and disappointed Sycophant—Edwards and Oliver the Spy, TheodoreHook, the noted Libeller—

"In various ways men write themselves asses,
This in a newspaper—that in a book;
But the late published tales of the middling classes,
Establish the title of Theodore Hook."

Emma, a Northumbrian Tale. Mathematics, &c., &c.

Printed and Published by W. Fordyce, 48, Dean Street, and may be had of other Booksellers.

"Mr. Green, with great exertion, sent his [plan] in at the proper time, but Mr. Dobson called upon you [Rev. Dodd], and said he had been so occupied, that his was not yet ready – could you put off for a few weeks? To this you agreed, and waited upon Mr. Green to acquaint him with the circumstance. As Mr. Green from politeness, and no doubt partly from fear, to this made no objections, you perhaps concluded there should be none; but we would ask any impartial man, and particularly an artist, if this delay was not a deep injury, as well as a bitter insult?"

The Greens' joint practice was both prolific and eclectic. Their work included many small and conventional neo-Gothic churches, mostly in the counties of Durham and Northumberland (in their restoration work they were even less reverently archaeological than Dobson); attractive Tudor-Gothic stations for the Newcastle and North Shields, and Newcastle and Berwick Railways (from 1835 and 1846 respectively); the neo-Renaissance former Joint Stock Bank, Mosley Street, Newcastle (c.1845); almshouses and other minor public buildings; and public monuments such as the Greek Doric Penshaw Monument, near Sunderland (1844, fig. 96), and Newcastle's famous Grey Monument (for Grainger, 1837-38, the design exhibited at the Royal Academy, 1837). It was said of the Greens that "the North of England has rarely produced men who combined, like [them], refined architectural taste with great engineering skill."[13]

Probably their most important work was the present Theatre Royal, Newcastle (1836-37, fig. 97), also for Grainger; they also designed – originally – its flanking street elevations in Market Street and Shakespeare Street. The Theatre's present character internally is Edwardian rather than Georgian, following reconstruction by Frank Matcham after a disastrous fire

Fig. 96 John and Benjamin Green, the Penshaw Monument, near Sunderland, 1844.
Authors' photograph.

Fig. 97 John and Benjamin Green, the Theatre Royal, Newcastle upon Tyne, 1836-37, photographed c.1930.
Newcastle Libraries & Information Service.

in 1899 (the style has subsequently been maintained during recent remodelling). However, the original design must have been exceptional:

"Upon entering from Grey Street, parties come into the magnificent rotunda ... consisting of two storeys separated by a circular stone gallery supported by richly ornamented stone cantilevers ... A stone staircase leads to the gallery of the rotunda and to the upper circle crowned with deeply sunk panelling. Round both tiers of dress and upper boxes are spacious corridors. The interior of the boxes are lined with red and their front forms the elegant curve of the auditorium. Twelve fluted and gilded columns, of uncommonly slender proportions, support the upper tier of boxes ... pillars of a similar form support the gallery, around the front of which is a gilded scroll."[14]

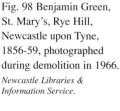

Fig. 98 Benjamin Green, St. Mary's, Rye Hill, Newcastle upon Tyne, 1856-59, photographed during demolition in 1966.
Newcastle Libraries & Information Service.

Benjamin Green did not long outlive his father. He started to show signs of mental illness as early as 1853 (at which time we find him unsuccessfully entering the competition for the Newcastle Town Hall with Matthew Thompson, a former pupil of Thomas Oliver snr.) and died – like the great A.W.N. Pugin himself – in a mental institution. However, the younger Green's developing expertise in his favourite Gothic style was reflected in his late designs for the St. Mary the Virgin Almshouses (1856-58) and Chapel (later St. Mary's Parish Church) at Rye Hill, Newcastle (1856-59, fig. 98). The church, now demolished, was comparatively large and ambitious, while the almshouses, superseding an earlier rejected design by Dobson of 1851, employ a domestic Gothic of which even Pugin would have approved. These works were completed by Benjamin's

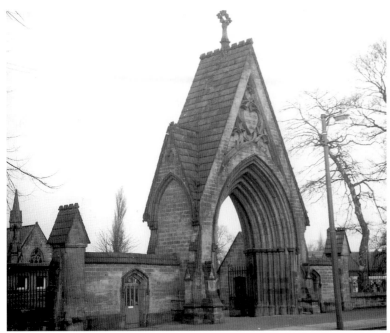

cousin, John Green jnr. (c.1807-68). Green jnr. (who dropped the affix 'jnr. after his uncle's death in 1852) commenced practice around 1832 and worked in Darlington, c.1839-45. He designed in his own right the fine Gothic gateway and chapels of All Saints' Cemetery, Jesmond (1855-56, fig. 99). Also, he succeeded to the Presidency of the Northern Architectural Association (see below) after Dobson's death in 1865.

Fig. 99 John Green jnr.,
All Saints' Cemetery,
Jesmond, Newcastle upon
Tyne, 1855-56.
Authors' photograph.

Richard Grainger and his office

Notwithstanding their very considerable achievements, the practitioners discussed above never quite achieved the status of Dobson in the North East. The only person in the field who did – Richard Grainger – was not an architect at all, although, perhaps ironically in view of Dobson's desire to protect his own professional status, he was frequently described as such.[15] The careers and names of Dobson and Grainger are of course inextricably linked. Some of Dobson's best work was done for Grainger and the two men were at various times both colleagues and competitors before their relationship finally collapsed. Margaret Dobson draws an interesting, if perhaps biased, comparison:

"It is no disparagement to others to remark that Mr. Dobson's artistic hand is ever visible in the new town of Newcastle. And yet it is strange, when we take into consideration the career of these two men – the architect with his genius … throwing all his immense energy into the carrying out of the work, whose name is never remembered in connection with it; the other, the speculator and builder, whose existence can never be forgotten so long as Newcastle stands and Grainger Street retains its name … The diversity of the human intellect is strikingly exemplified here. The curious faculty of succeeding, which some men possess, in contrast to the ability and genius of others, is here discernible. The endowments of Mr. Grainger … seem to have been enterprise and push, and a powerful mathematical brain. Mr. Dobson was the artist, not indeed wanting in mathematical talent (for that he had), but with the fastidiousness of a retiring nature, and without that certain something that

131

brings a man to gain all, to stand first, and to combine success with public *eclat*."[16]

Certainly Grainger was the more powerful figure of the two, his approach being essentially that of a businessman. Thus, for example, his careful division of commissions such as Eldon Square, Leazes Terrace and the Royal Arcade between Dobson and Thomas Oliver probably reflected both his desire for control and an awareness that each architect was evolving plans for the redevelopment of Newcastle which might have competed with his own. Similarly, as we have seen, for the implementation of his central redevelopment Grainger employed his own salaried architects John Wardle and George Walker for most of the street facades (see fig. 88) and buildings like the Central Exchange (fig. 100). He also employed Dobson and the

Fig. 100 John Wardle and George Walker, the Central Exchange, Newcastle upon Tyne, c.1836-37.
Authors' photograph.

Greens (though not, interestingly, Oliver).

Little is known of the earlier careers of Wardle (c.1792-1860) and Walker (fl.1834-63, d.1886) before they worked for Grainger, 1834-41, apart from the fact that Walker had been a pupil of John Green. Of their period with Grainger it was said that "Mr. Wardle was the bustling man outside, putting the designs into execution, while his partner sat pent up in his study, drawing and contriving."[17] After this they set up in partnership, but their subsequent practice was on a modest scale and by 1851 they were working independently. At the "Workhouse, North Elswick" (later the City General Hospital) Walker designed schools, dormitories and an infirmary in 1854-55 (this portion now demolished), while Wardle, who was joined by his son John jnr. in 1850, now concentrated mainly on designing villas and terraces. Also, he too unsuccessfully entered the competition for the Newcastle Town Hall (see below, p.138).

Architects' plans for central Newcastle

Meanwhile, Grainger's all-important 1834 plan for the redevelopment of the central Anderson Place (and adjacent Nuns' Field) site was based on the innovation of a major new street (now Grey Street) running from Dean Street through the area then occupied by the Butcher Market, to the eastern end of Blackett Street. This major street was to have four lateral streets linking eastwards with Pilgrim Street and westwards to what is now upper Grainger Street, the last-named being one of a quadrilateral of streets containing the new Market planned by Grainger. The most northerly of these streets was to become Clayton Street, connecting with Grainger's earlier Eldon Square development.

This arrangement was essentially the scheme as carried out, Grainger himself having planned all or most of the layout, with Dobson's contribution limited at most to an advisory role. Even Dobson himself, not noted for apportioning credit to others, acknowledged "the erection of those magnificent buildings in Newcastle, which owe, in a great measure, their origin to the spirit and enterprise of Mr. Grainger."[18] Nor can any claims that Thomas Oliver snr. was the real author of Grainger's central redevelopment be sustained. Oliver's ideas were concerned mainly with the periphery of the town (see below) and as an architect he played no part in the implementation of the scheme. Moreover, Oliver's published *Plan of Building Ground, together with Proposed and Projected Improvements in Newcastle upon Tyne* of July 1834 is evidence that he was summarising rather than initiating events; this plan shows not only Grainger's proposals but also those of two other developers (one planned by Dobson) and was almost certainly produced for public sale rather than for Grainger himself.

Nevertheless, Grainger was evidently influenced by both Dobson's and Oliver's earlier, unrealised improvement schemes, the latter having been presented to the Corporation in 1830[19] (as well as by the Edinburgh New Town, for his street facades, and by the even more recent 'Metropolitan Improvements' in London by John Nash, of 1811-27). Dobson's plan of c.1825 (see pp.43-44) would have given Newcastle a stately, formal quality more definitively reminiscent of the Edinburgh New Town or even of many Continental cities with their central squares. Oliver adopted a different approach. He was more concerned with the much-needed improvement of communication routes, for which he would have retained Dobson's proposal for extending Blackett Street (minus the classical squares), together with a new lateral route eastwards via Collingwood Street to the New Road and thence to the new industrial areas towards the coast.

Another of Oliver's proposed new streets would have connected the east quayside to Lovaine Place, near the site of the present Civic Centre, linking also with his own Leazes Terrace via Northumberland and Percy Streets. Oliver also suggested the extension of Dobson's earlier proposed street northward from the Castle Garth (an element in Dobson's scheme of c.1820 for the redevelopment of the Castle area, described in Chapter 2), through an innovative connection with a proposed high-level road and railway bridge across the Tyne; this would have been approximately on the site of the present High Level Bridge. (By contrast, Grainger's own later proposal for an elevated bridge of 1843, although linking directly into the newly built Grey Street, included no provision for the railway and therefore stood no chance of being built.)[20] For the central Anderson Place and Nuns' Field site Oliver would have done little more than copy one of Dobson's ideas – a street to run from Newgate Street into Blackett Street opposite Eldon Square, though extended to open up an additional east-west link to the Westgate (West) Road.

Dobson's proposed monumental square may have prompted Grainger's own more commercial idea of a central market within a quadrilateral of intersecting streets. Again, the street connecting Eldon Square with Newgate Street (i.e. Clayton Street, which originally extended to Blackett Street) seems to derive from Dobson's scheme, and the idea of extending it westward from that of Oliver. But Grainger rejected the undue formality of Dobson's classical grid and – unlike Oliver – restricted himself to what was politically and financially possible. Thus his own pragmatic, more informal arrangement connected only with existing routes, its principal street, Grey Street, providing an important link between the upper and the lower town not offered by previous schemes. Moreover, development took place only where an effect of grandeur could be achieved relatively quickly, contrasting with the older areas of town with their quaint if run-down vernacular buildings.

Interestingly, the schemes of Dobson and Oliver could easily have been combined (possibly Oliver allowed for this), in which case Newcastle's slightly enclosed new centre would have been more effectively integrated with the rest of the town. A similar result might also have occurred, incidentally, had Grainger himself built areas of more modest housing around the periphery of his new centre. The attractive stucco-fronted Leazes Crescent of 1829-30, by Oliver, shows what Grainger could do on a rare excursion into this kind of housing development (see fig. 101).

By the late 1830s Grainger was at the zenith of his wealth and prestige. He had successfully exploited his good fortune in being able to employ highly talented local architects, both independent and salaried. With the latter especially he was able to exercise a watching brief over all matters relating to design[21] and again kept control by carefully utilising the services of all these architects for different portions of his scheme.

Fig. 101 Thomas Oliver, Leazes Crescent, Newcastle upon Tyne, 1829-30.
Authors' photograph.

Suddenly, however, he had to withstand the Council's rejection of his important new proposal to build new Law Courts and Civic Offices on a site between Grey and Pilgrim Streets (1838). Grainger did eventually manage to have the fully worked-out design, by Wardle and Walker, adapted for use as a banking-house (now the Lloyds Bank building at the upper end of Grey Street), but after this setback his career began to go downhill amid accusations of financial impropriety, as he increasingly over-reached himself. Thus in 1838-39 he purchased at great cost Elswick Hall, but his proposed redevelopment of its huge estate with housing, factories, a shipping quay and even a railway terminus (impractical because of the remoteness of the site), largely failed to materialise. Meanwhile, Dobson remained in contact with Grainger – his unbuilt chapel proposal of 1840 (see pp.75-76) would have formed part of Grainger's abortive Elswick scheme – but before long their relationship finally broke down over monetary disputes. Dobson wrote: "I cannot longer entertain that feeling of anxiety to serve a person in the manner I have striven and wished to do, that would treat me so shamefully if he could."[22]

Dobson's pupils and assistants

By this time Dobson was at the height of his career, his practice being very considerable. His later assistants included: James Craig (who had begun as a joiner); Martin Greener (who subsequently practised in Sunderland); Johnson Hogg; Gibson Kyle; James Moffat; Thomas Prosser; George Ridley (for many years his chief draughtsman, before taking up a similar position in London with Sydney Smirke, c.1840-70); and E.R. Robson. There exists an interesting near-contemporary account of Dobson's procedures:

> "The whole of these [assistants] he would place at work suitable to their bent and acquirements. Mr. Dobson did not trouble himself much about articled pupils or apprentices. He was always too full of business to give either room or time for the 'purely' elementary education of beginners. Mr. Dobson insisted on some proficiency and fitness in those whom he employed. He was always approachable to his assistants, or, indeed, to any young professional man seeking his advice. He often said, 'If you err, err on the side of strength.' He had a horror of shams, and warned young men of the dangers attending flimsy and cheap construction."[23]

Many of Dobson's assistants did significant later independent work. Johnson Hogg was originally a stonemason and had succeeded to Ridley's position in Dobson's office. He designed the neo-Gothic Northern Counties Institution Asylum, Moor Edge (c.1860), and was also responsible for the Grammar School in Rye Hill (1866, now demolished), although this provoked controversy for being a copy of a design already used in London and for the commission not having been open to competition. Gibson Kyle (1820-1903) designed the Ruskinian 'Italian-Gothic' United Free Methodist

Chapel in Prudhoe Street, Newcastle (1861-62, now demolished). Thomas Prosser (fl.1835-84, FRIBA 1876), who also worked for a time for Ignatius Bonomi of Durham, went on, as we have seen, to become architect to the North Eastern Railway and complete Dobson's Newcastle Central Station design. The career of E.R. Robson (1835-1917) has already been alluded to in Chapter 3. After going on to work for George Gilbert Scott, 1857-60, he became a nationally known School Board architect, publishing the influential *School Architecture* in 1874. He was in partnership, from 1870 to 1875, with J.J. Stevenson, also from the North East and another former pupil of Scott.

Meanwhile, most of Dobson's former pupils and assistants remaining on Tyneside were responsible, with older independents like John Green jnr., George Walker and John Wardle, for founding the Northern Architectural Association (now incorporated within the RIBA) in 1858. Thomas Austin and R.J. Johnson (see below) were also involved. Its aims were to promote union amongst its members, the elevation of the architectural profession, the establishment of a uniformity of practice, and the general advancement of 'the art and science of architecture'. Not surprisingly, Dobson gave his blessing and was elected its first President, delivering his important inaugural Address in April 1859.

Dobson's younger contemporaries

Younger independent contemporaries of Dobson in Newcastle included Septimus Oswald (1823-94), who set up practice in 1855 after working for Andrew Oliver. (Oliver was another local architect, apparently unrelated to Thomas Oliver, who had begun as a joiner and carpenter; he was an assistant to John Green, 1822-35, before designing much of Neville Street and building numerous houses and terraces around Westgate and Elswick up to the 1850s.) Oswald, whose practice was continued well into the 20th century by his son Joseph (b.1851), was responsible for a range of fairly conventional commercial and ecclesiastical work, the latter including his United Methodist Free Church in Byker Lane (from 1875) and a church for the same denomination in the High Street, Gosforth (1876-77). Also in Newcastle, from c.1850, having earlier trained in London under Edward I'Anson, was William Parnell (d.c.1886). His works include St. Nicholas's Buildings (c.1850), Exchange Buildings, Quayside (c.1861-62), 'Phoenix House', Sandhill (c.1869, fig. 102), and

Fig. 102 William Parnell, 'Phoenix House' (formerly 'Queen's Buildings'), Sandhill, Newcastle upon Tyne, c.1869.
Authors' photograph.

the Tyne Theatre and Opera House (now the New Tyne Theatre), Westgate Road, opened in 1867.

There was also the scholarly Thomas Austin (1822-67), who set up in Newcastle in 1852 after articles with the important Lancaster practice of Sharpe and Paley. In 1862 he joined up with his friend R.J. Johnson (1832-92), who had returned to the North East after working under George Gilbert Scott (with Robson and Stevenson) following an earlier spell in Newcastle. Austin and Johnson purchased Dobson's practice following his death in 1865 and completed some of the older architect's works, for example St. Nicholas's Church, Cramlington, Northumberland. However, following Austin's own death soon after this (on his way home from a convalescent trip to Australia), Johnson was left to continue the practice alone.

Earlier, Austin had been responsible for a remarkably sensitive reconstruction of Brinkburn Priory (1858-59), and it is significant that both Austin and Johnson were already adopting a more reverently archaeological approach to restoration work. Johnson's influential *Specimens of Early French Architecture* (1864) illustrated unrestored medieval examples in the hope that lessons could be learnt and he must surely have been thinking of Dobson's recent work at Hexham Abbey (see pp.92-93) when in 1861 he addressed the Northern Architectural Association as follows: "I cannot forbear remarking how destructive and bad most modern restoration has been; we in our pride, set up for ourselves a notion of what a building should be and at once ruthlessly sweep away the work of six centuries of men."[24] Examples of Johnson's own practice in this field include his restoration of Mitford Parish Church, Northumberland (1874-79), and – for the Society of Antiquaries – that of the Black Gate, Newcastle (1883). In fact, Johnson, a devout Anglican, went on to become Newcastle's premier late Victorian architect. Like Dobson before him he achieved both a regional and a national reputation, practising successfully in a range of styles.

Finally among Dobson's younger contemporaries there was the eclectic, even eccentric, John Johnstone (c.1814-84), who had been a clerk of works for George Gilbert Scott and his early partner Moffat around 1845; later, in 1875, he became President of the Northern Architectural Association. He designed the neo-Gothic Masonic Hall in Maple Street, Elswick (1870-72), and then, more typically, a series of increasingly decorative Renaissance-style commercial buildings in Newcastle including the County Hotel, Neville and Grainger Streets (1874, later much altered and enlarged), the Royal Court Yard and 11-15 Bigg Market (c.1882) and the former Newcastle and Gateshead Gas Company Offices, Grainger Street (later Wengers' Department Store), of 1884-86.

Johnstone's principal work in Newcastle was the Town Hall, situated in the Groat Market area opposite St. Nicholas's church (see fig. 103). Johnstone was also responsible for the impressive Gateshead Town Hall (1868-70), like its Newcastle counterpart in Italian Renaissance style. For

Fig. 103 John Johnstone and W.A. Knowles, the Town Hall, Newcastle upon Tyne, 1855-63, demolished; photographed c.1900.
Newcastle Libraries & Information Service.

the Newcastle commission he won a competition in 1853 with his then partner W.A. Knowles, although their plans were modified the following year in consultation with the Town Surveyor Robert Wallace and it was also necessary to incorporate within the structure the Greens' earlier uncompleted Corn Exchange (see p.45). Johnstone and Knowles exhibited drawings of their (comparatively restrained) design at the Newcastle Fine Art Exhibition in 1855.[25]

The Newcastle Town Hall was finally built with many further modifications and in two main phases, from 1855 to 1857 and from 1861 to 1863, to contain Council Chamber, committee rooms, office accommodation for the Mayor, Town Clerk, Treasurer, Surveyor and River Commissioners, and shops, further offices, and public rooms including (on the first floor) a large concert hall. However, the building went grossly over budget and was severely censured by Councillors (and by Dobson) for poor design. Dobson had been opposed to the project from the start, presumably the reason why he did not compete for such an important commission.[26] In his view the structure was dangerously inaccessible and, moreover, "dwarfed our noble cathedral".[27] He believed that the Groat Market should have been kept open as an approach to St. Nicholas's and there is a watercolour by him,[28] illustrating a plan to Gothicise the area, which seems to relate to what his daughter described as his last improvement scheme:

"A grand architectural effect might have been gained by putting the old houses back a little, and making handsome facades. The vista from end to end would have been most imposing. It would have embraced St. Nicholas', with its unique lantern tower, the Old Castle, the Black Gate, the High Level Bridge, and the opposite hills, and we should have had a fine open square, where a monument could have been erected in a conspicuous position. All must regret that his opinion was not received."[29]

Ultimately the Town Hall was demolished as Dobson had desired, but more than a century later (c.1969) and then only to be replaced by the present undistinguished office block.

Ignatius Bonomi, Dobson's friend and rival

It seems appropriate to conclude this chapter by examining the career of Ignatius Bonomi (1787-1870), the one contemporary of Dobson's in the North East he acknowledged as being of similar professional status and an old friend. In contrast to Dobson, Bonomi came from an illustrious architectural and artistic family. He trained under his father, Joseph (1739-1808), while his younger brother, also Joseph (1796-1878), was a noted sculptor and Egyptologist, as well as Curator of Sir John Soane's Museum. Bonomi the elder, an Italian, had met Robert and James Adam in Rome and was recruited to work for them as a draughtsman, at first in Italy and then (from 1767 to 1781) in London; so talented was he that there was even a clause in his contract forbidding him to work on his own account. After this he himself became a fashionable neoclassical architect in London and was a frequent exhibitor at the Royal Academy between 1783 and 1806, being elected ARA in 1789.

Bonomi the elder's death in 1808 meant that Ignatius Bonomi could not complete his training with an intended Grand Tour and instead had to commence practice almost immediately. One of his first works was to complete the improvements begun by his father at Skelton Castle, North Yorkshire (from 1810). However, Bonomi seems to have been too inexperienced to sustain his father's London practice and in 1813 returned north to take up the post of Durham County Bridge Surveyor; this carried a more than useful salary of £200 a year. One of Bonomi's first public duties was to complete the Durham Gaol and Assize Courts (from 1813). He retired from his official post in 1850 but remained in Durham until 1856.

Bonomi scrupulously followed his father's Soanian model of professionalism but, curiously, declined membership of the newly formed Institute of British Architects in 1835; nor did he ever exhibit at the Royal Academy. His plans and estimates were always clear and workmanlike but were never presented in the elaborate and attractive way that Dobson's often were. Bonomi's pupil and assistant, from 1831 to 1842, was J.L. Pearson, later a distinguished Gothic Revivalist. Unlike Dobson, Bonomi entered into partnership (with J.A. Cory – who also had a considerable aptitude for Gothic – from 1842 to 1856). Also unlike Dobson, Bonomi was twice subjected to major complaints from clients. Lord Durham of Lambton Castle, earlier rebuilt by Bonomi, complained about structural failure caused by undermining after 1855 and brought in Dobson to report and ultimately rebuild (see p.71). Earlier, in 1844, Lord Londonderry, of nearby Wynyard Park, actually took the issue of structural failure following Bonomi's rebuilding of 1841-42 to arbitration (Dobson again being involved, with A. Salvin and T.L. Donaldson). Bonomi on this occasion was largely, if not completely, exonerated.

Bonomi's practice, mostly in County Durham, Yorkshire and occasionally Northumberland, was extensive but not as substantial as Dobson's. Perhaps because of working in a smaller town, he did not receive as many opportunities as his Newcastle contemporary for major public and monumental works. Also, in spite of his advantageous background, Bonomi had perhaps been obliged to commence practice a little prematurely and in any case may have lacked the necessary ambition.

Like Dobson, he practised in both the neoclassical and the Gothic styles. His (mainly neo-Gothic) churches are mostly neat and unremarkable, though he was capable of sensitive restoration work, as at St. Lawrence's, Pittington, County Durham (1845-46). His stone bridges, as at Shincliffe, near Durham (1824-26), have a typically late Georgian simplicity and elegance, while he has some claims to be regarded as the first railway architect, since he designed the Skerne railway bridge, near Darlington (1824-25), for the pioneering Stockton and Darlington Railway; this latter bridge is of stone (a modification from the Railway Company's original proposal for a central span of iron) and although somewhat altered still retains the original effect of a triumphal arch.

Fig. 104 Ignatius Bonomi, Windlestone Hall, County Durham, 1830-34.
Authors' photograph.

Less talented than his father, Bonomi has been described as competent, his output being "less impressive either in quality or in quantity"[30] than that of Dobson. Arguably it is also less distinctive. However, his better classical works are comparable with most of Dobson's and indeed the finest of these, Burn Hall and Windlestone Hall (fig. 104) (see p.58), show, as mentioned earlier, a sophisticated awareness of contemporary French architectural trends.

Notes

1 D. Defoe, *A Tour through the Whole Island of Great Britain,* 1724-26 (ed. with an introduction by G.D.H. Cole, 1927), vol. 2, p.659.

2 H. Colvin, *A Biographical Dictionary of British Architects, 1600-1840,* 3rd edn., 1995, p.928.

3 J. Dobson, *Presidential Address to the Northern Architectural Association* (April 1859), reprinted in Wilkes, p.103.

4 *Ibid.,* p.106.

5 Quoted in A.T. Bolton, *Life and Work a Century Ago: An Outline of the Career of Sir John Soane,* 1926, p.5.

6 Wilkes, p.104.

7 Ward's *Northumberland and Durham Directory,* 1850, p.130, lists 17, a figure which, incidentally, rose to nearly 70 by 1900 (see Ward's *Directory of Newcastle-on-Tyne,* 1899-1900, pp.560-61).

8 J. Collingwood Bruce, *Handbook to Newcastle upon Tyne,* 1863, p.116. For more on Oliver and 'Gibson Town' see R.D. Giddings, 'Thomas Oliver, 1791-1857' (unpublished dissertation for the degree of B.Arch., University of Newcastle upon Tyne, 1981).

9 For more on this building see A. Greg, 'The Society's Building and its Architect', *The Literary and Philosophical Society of Newcastle upon Tyne Bicentenary Lectures,* 1994, pp.27-47.

10 See *NCh,* 16 April 1831.

11 'Old Newcastle Architects and Surveyors', *NWC,* 1 January, 1887. For more on the Greens see Colvin, *op. cit.,* Greg, *op. cit.* and D. Lovie, *The Buildings of Grainger Town,* 1997.

12 See the material in NCRO (ZAN M12/B1).

13 Letter to *NWC,* 8 January 1887 by P. L. Addison, regarding 'Old Newcastle Architects and Surveyors', cited above, note 11.

14 Contemporary description quoted in H. Oswald, *The Theatres Royal in Newcastle upon Tyne,* 1936, p.86.

15 For example, he is referred to as an architect in *The Dictionary of National Biography* and in contemporary local Directories. See also Wilkes and Dodds, pp.142-43 and I. Ayris, *A City of Palaces: Richard Grainger and the Making of Newcastle upon Tyne,* 1997. In addition, see the *Report of the Cholera Inquiry Commissioners,* 1854, p.302. Giving evidence to the Commission, Grainger was

asked "Are you a builder and an architect?" He replied: "Yes."

16 Dobson, pp. 64-65.

17 'Old Newcastle Architects and Surveyors' (Part 2), *NWC*, 8 January 1887. However, *NJ*, 3 June 1837, recorded that the west side of Grey Street, the west half of Market Street, the south side of Shakespeare Street, and Grainger Street were "entirely designed in Mr. Grainger's office by Mr. Wardle under Mr. Grainger's immediate directions".

18 Wilkes, p.103.

19 They are indicated on Oliver's 1830 *Plan of Newcastle upon Tyne* and further explained in Oliver.

20 See *Proceedings of the Newcastle Council*, 20 December 1843, and Wilkes and Dodds, p.142.

21 See note 17 above.

22 Quoted in Wilkes, p.72.

23 'Old Newcastle Architects and Surveyors', *NWC*, 1 January 1887.

24 R.J. Johnson, 'Early French Architecture', address given to the Northern Architectural Association, 25 April 1861; reprinted in Proceedings of the Northern Architectural Association, 1861. For more on Johnson see T.E. Faulkner, 'Robert James Johnson, Architect and Antiquary', in *The Durham University Journal*, new series vol. lxi, no. 1 (January 1995), pp.3-10 + xii.

25 See *The Builder*, vol. xiii, 1855, p.553.

26 See *Proceedings of the Newcastle Council*, December 1854, p.39.

27 Dobson, p.71.

28 Now in a private collection. It was included in the bicentenary exhibition 'John Dobson: Newcastle Architect, 1787-1865' at the Laing Art Gallery, Newcastle upon Tyne (October-December, 1987).

29 Dobson, p.71. Also, this proposal develops aspects of Dobson's earlier scheme for a Corn Exchange, in the area of Middle Street, of c.1825 (see Chapter 2).

30 Colvin, *op. cit.*, p.137. For more on the Bonomis see J.H. Crosby, *Ignatius Bonomi of Durham, Architect*, 1987, and P. Meadows, *Joseph Bonomi, Architect 1739-1808* (exh. cat., 1988).

7 The Achievement and Legacy of John Dobson

Dobson's severe stroke of 1862, at the age of 74, brought his long career to a sudden end. He retired briefly to Ryton, County Durham, but returned to his New Bridge Street house in Newcastle shortly before his death on 8 January 1865. In his will Dobson left his "household furniture and stores, plate, linen and pictures" to his daughter Margaret (named after Dobson's mother, née Clark), who in turn bequeathed a number of framed architectural perspectives and several fine pieces of furniture to the Laing Art Gallery, Newcastle, at her death in 1905. He left all his "plans, drawing office furniture, and drawing and other instruments" to his son John and all his "books, prints, and sketches" to his son-in-law Sydney Smirke.

Smirke, a decade younger than Dobson, was also Dobson's closest friend and confidant among contemporary architects. He had won the Royal Academy Gold Medal in 1819 and was Professor of Architecture at the Academy, 1861-65; he was also the father of Sydney jnr. (1841/2-1912), architect and watercolourist. The present locations of most of Dobson's plans and sketches remain sadly unknown. Nor does any trace remain of what must have been Dobson's very numerous office papers and accounts. Even in 1885 Margaret Dobson, compiling her *Memoir of John Dobson*, bemoaned the paucity of relevant documentary material, especially the loss of what she described as the very extensive correspondence between her father and Sydney Smirke.

Dobson was the most eminent architect to have been born and have worked in the North East. He was also the first from the region to achieve a measure of national status – even though he did not enter any of the great national architectural competitions and exhibited only rarely at the Royal Academy. He produced over 400 works and projects of virtually every building type, most of them in Northumberland, County Durham and what is now Tyne and Wear, some in Yorkshire and the modern county of Cumbria, and a few further afield, but he is especially linked with Newcastle, where he practised for over 50 years. Here, as indicated earlier, he had been determined to establish himself as an architect alone, as opposed to the builder-architects practising in Newcastle at that time. His ungenerous remark about his predecessor David Stephenson (that he was not an accomplished architect)[1] must be explained by the fact that Dobson wanted to emphasise his own role in the development of the architectural profession.

We have already noted some of the early influences on Dobson as he became immersed in the London architectural scene around 1809-10, including the fashionable neoclassicism of his slightly older contemporary Robert Smirke. The castle style architecture of Smirke and others was also influential. Then, on his return to the North East, Dobson was evidently inspired by the Graecophile Sir Charles Monck of Belsay Hall, both in terms of neoclassicism and the perfection of fine ashlar construction (see Chapter 1 and below); later he commented: "I consider that the North of England is much indebted to the worthy baronet's enterprise and cultivated taste."[2] This statement contrasts with Dobson's highly critical attitude towards what he saw as the inconveniences created by the rigid symmetry of earlier country house architecture in the North East, including that of such major figures as Vanbrugh and Paine.

However, Dobson does seem to have had some admiration for the 'picturesque outline' characteristic of Vanbrugh's work, and not surprisingly the Picturesque Movement current during Dobson's early years was another major influence. The Picturesque permeated painting and engraving of the period, as in the work of Dobson's master Varley, and above all led to new ways of thinking about the relationship of buildings to landscape that were particularly relevant to Dobson's work (here the ideas of Repton seem to have been particularly influential). With regard to the legacy of Gothic and medieval architecture, so strongly associated with the Picturesque during the early 19th century, Dobson was much influenced by the prevailing mood of antiquarianism and later by the ideas of Pugin and the Ecclesiologists (see Chapter 4). Of the latter he noted: "we are much indebted to the societies of Oxford and Cambridge, who introduced the custom of clerical gentlemen devoting a portion of their time to the study of ecclesiastical architecture."[3]

Dobson's career spanned parts of both the Georgian and Victorian epochs. As we have observed, this general period reflected not only changes in architectural fashion but also the major social and economic developments of the time, and Dobson worked substantially for the new entrepreneurial middle classes, establishing themselves through commerce and industry on Tyneside and elsewhere. A sense of tradition, a feeling for the relationship of a building to its site, and engineering skill underlined his facility in working within the numerous styles then considered appropriate, and in designing the vast range of building types which he undertook. Indeed, it is the quantity and variety of Dobson's architecture which strikes an observer reviewing his career, rather than any single stylistic theme (this applies especially to his later years). Thus, while probably most highly regarded as a neoclassicist, he was also, as we have seen, a highly competent exponent of the popular Tudor-Gothic style and in the ecclesiastical field a pioneer of the Gothic Revival in the North East. The majority of Dobson's urban buildings have been demolished, but many of his numerous villas and country houses in the region do survive (see Chapter 8, Catalogue of Works, pp.160-80).

Builders and craftsmen

Themes in Dobson's work are generally less to do with style than with the excellence of his buildings in terms of their felicitous siting, sound construction and functional efficiency. The only known example of a subsequent structural failure involving one of his buildings was that of the restored tower of Lymm Parish Church, Cheshire, and even this was caused by his praiseworthy desire to incorporate part of the old 1521 tower into his ultimately too elevated reconstruction of 1851.

Dobson's constructional talents are particularly evident in his handling of dressed ashlar; the masonry of his finest works could hardly be surpassed. In this respect he followed the tradition set by Sir Charles Monck, to whom, as already mentioned, he gave credit for having upgraded the standard of masonry in the North East (but his view of building construction in the region at the outset of his career as "rude and unmechanical"[4] was somewhat unfair). Dobson used local stone wherever possible, noting that "the county of Northumberland affords such an abundant supply of the finest freestone, that this material becomes there not only by far the most durable, but really the least expensive."[5]

Dobson employed a variety of building contractors, including Thomas Marsh of Blaydon, Thompson & Hunter and (for St. Peter's Church, Newcastle) Richard Cail, a prominent Gateshead builder, railway contractor and owner of brickworks and quarries. In addition, he favoured on several occasions a few particularly expert men, such as the builder and plasterer Ralph Dodds (who became a friend and was one of the pall-bearers at his funeral), the carpenters Thomas Hall and Thomas Wallace, the builder and plasterer Robert Robson (who also made Dobson's architectural models), and Gibson Kyle. Robert Wallace, initially a builder and joiner, was employed by Dobson as his clerk of works at Lilburn Tower, and, as we have seen, later became the Town Surveyor of Newcastle. Dobson's terms and specifications for building contractors were recognised nationally as models of their kind,[6] while to have worked for Dobson became a qualification in itself, and masons who had done so sometimes advertised in this way. Dobson, we are told, "never exceeded an estimate, and never had a legal dispute with a contractor".[7] Another commentator recalled that:

> "Perhaps there was never an architect more trusted alike by employer and employed ... 'His word was law'; and as he generally set his foot against letting his works to those whose estimate or tender appeared to him inadequate – certainly a most just and honourable trait in his character – he could 'with a good grace' insist upon the work being well done, knowing that the contractor would be well paid for his labour."[8]

While the architect used several different building firms, a specialist carver or team of carvers seems to have been recurrently employed (see p.84). In addition, the notable stained glass designer William Wailes of Newcastle (1808-81) was also closely associated with Dobson's work. Examples of this are at St. Cuthbert's, Benfieldside, St. Cuthbert's, Bensham (where Wailes worshipped), Lymm Parish Church (see above) and at the restored Percy Chapel, Tynemouth Priory. Dobson was not himself a craftsman (although he was adept at modelling in clay)[9], but he may well have designed chimney-pieces and other integral items such as bookcases in some of his country houses (e.g., Lilburn, Holme Eden) and, as at Lilburn also, may have sometimes turned his hand to furniture design.

Fig. 106 Chair from the 'Nunnykirk Suite', c.1825-28.

James A. Johnson and Associates, Vermont, Victoria, Australia.

Probably the most celebrated example in this field is the 'Nunnykirk Suite', which consists of a dining table (24 feet in length), 16 chairs, wine coolers, a console sideboard and two side cabinets, all in a richly-carved Graeco-Roman style (see fig. 106). It was designed in about 1825 for William Orde of Nunnykirk, at the time of Dobson's reconstruction of the house, and was made by John Humble of Kelso (as was the furniture at Lilburn), using oak, mahogany and burr elm. The suite came on the market in the early 1990s but its present whereabouts is unknown.

Technical aspects of design

Dobson's work is noteworthy for its emphasis upon the technical and functional aspects of design. We have already examined his meticulous researches into hospital and prison types, for example, and the importance of his industrial and 'engineering' architecture. Similarly, the main topics of his inaugural Presidential Address to the Northern Architectural

Association in 1859, apart from that of the growth of the profession itself, are his improvement in the comfort of country houses, his practical adaptation of castellated forms for prison architecture, and his discovery (while excavating some Roman remains) of a method of eradicating dry rot. Dobson also alluded to his ingenious and economical design for the Newcastle Central Station roof. One can imagine the zeal with which he must have worked on this, with his technical collaborators, and it is significant that at the Great Exhibition in London of 1851 he exhibited not only models of the station itself, but also an innovative rolling machine used in rolling iron for the principals of the roof. (This was designed by Thomas Charlton, an engineer with Hawks, Crawshay & Sons, of Gateshead, the company who had earlier fabricated the ironwork of the Newcastle High Level Bridge.)[10]

The design of the Central Station roof was a considerable feat given Dobson's lack of experience in metallic construction, so much so that a modern commentator has even questioned his authorship in favour of a claim for the engineer Robert Stephenson.[11] No doubt Dobson owed much to advice from Stephenson and Thomas Harrison (see Chapter 5) and to the assistance of the technicians at Abbot & Co.; in addition, he must have almost certainly consulted the firm of Hawks, Crawshay (see above). However, it seems inconceivable that a respected figure like Dobson, who prided himself on his professionalism, would have wanted to take the credit for something he did not design, or even take the risk of doing so. Moreover, it is significant that his authorship of the roof was never challenged at the time or later; indeed, his achievement was handsomely acknowledged at an inaugural dinner at the new station on 30 July 1850, at which he was applauded for "the glorious roof that he had projected".[12] This was in the happy presence of both Harrison and Stephenson.[13]

It is true that Stephenson (in 1844), and not Dobson as stated by his daughter Margaret, determined the idea of the Central Station's curved platforms. However, Dobson himself never claimed to have done this; nor did he make any claim to be the inventor of the rolling machine, mentioned above. Meanwhile, his model of the Station roof concurrently exhibited at the Great Exhibition won him an Honourable Mention, the jury being chaired by no less a figure than I.K. Brunel.[14] (One would also like to know more about his "roof for Messrs. Smiths' shipbuilding yard", a model of which Dobson also exhibited with the above.) Finally with reference to the Station, it should be noted that before designing it Dobson spent much time in stations studying the conduct of business and the departure and arrival of trains, and successfully planned for the inevitable increase in traffic.

Patrons and clients

Dobson may have been too unambitious to set up in London at the start, despite the apparent encouragement of well-connected friends.[15] However, the capital was well provided with architects in about 1810 and so it was probably an astute move to go into practice in the North East. Early in his career commissions were few, admittedly, but he soon had the beginnings of a useful country house and villa practice for the local gentry and before long a situation underpinned by the expanding commerce and industry of the region led to his being prolifically employed.

Dobson's patrons can be divided into four interconnected groups. First, there were the aristocrats such as Sir Jacob Astley, Lord Londonderry, and the Earl of Strathmore, all of whom had industrial interests too. The favour of the Duke of Northumberland helped provide the indirect patronage of County public works, although for major work at Alnwick Castle during the 1850s, the Duke employed the more nationally known Anthony Salvin. Secondly, there were the landed gentry, including the Blacketts, the Collingwoods, the Ordes, the Riddells, and William Lawson of Longhirst who made money from coal as well. Thirdly, there was an established Newcastle oligarchy for whom Dobson worked regularly over the years; this consisted of men like the reformer Sir Thomas Burdon, the solicitor Armorer Donkin, Sir John Fife and T.E. Headlam of the medical establishment, and the M.P. John Hodgson Hinde – all private patrons and useful also in the choice of his designs for civic works. (Burdon was Mayor of Newcastle in 1810 and 1816, Fife in 1838 and 1843 and Headlam in 1837 and 1845.) Similarly valuable in this regard was the patronage of his friend Archibald Reed (see p.84-85), Mayor on no fewer than six occasions between 1800 and 1831. Fourthly, and most importantly, Dobson's largest group of clients were the middle-class bankers, merchants and industrialists (who married into the other categories whenever possible). Sir William (later Lord) Armstrong and George Hudson are the best known of these, but also important were the Carlisle cotton manufacturer Peter Dixon, the Newcastle banker Thomas Fenwick, and the Cookson family of glass and chemical manufacturers on Tyneside. Minor figures of this kind included Robert Plummer (flax), Michael Robson (docks), and the tobacco merchant Benjamin Sorsbie (although Sorsbie was important enough to be Mayor of Newcastle in 1814 and 1827 and Plummer was another influential Councillor).

Most of Dobson's work outside the region was gained through family connections with such clients, but he did achieve a more national reputation after the opening of the Newcastle Central Station. For this Dobson presented drawings to Queen Victoria and despite, or perhaps because of, the setbacks associated with the commission, he continued to exhibit models and drawings of his first and finest design; for example at the Great Exhibition in London in 1851 (see above), and at the Manchester Art Treasures Exhibition of 1857 (as well as locally at the Newcastle Fine Art Exhibition of 1855). He also exhibited a view of the Station's proposed "arcades and portico" at the Royal Academy in 1850. Otherwise Dobson hardly ever exhibited his designs outside Newcastle and seems to have made little effort to seek work outside the North East.

Personal and professional matters

Dobson (in later years) "was of middle height, fairly stout, of dark complexion, with sloe black eyes and jet black hair (see fig. 105). He had a quick, observant look, and never seemed absent-minded."[16] There are two oil portraits of him in the Laing Art Gallery, Newcastle, one of which is reproduced on the cover of this book;[17] also reproduced as the book's frontispiece is a 'photographic portrait' of Dobson published at the time of his death by Messrs. W. & D. Downey of Eldon Square. A bust of the architect is reproduced in his daughter Margaret Dobson's *Memoir of John Dobson*, but the whereabouts of the original of this is unfortunately not known.

Although a sensible, and genial man, and robust and vigorous in physique – he enjoyed boxing and fencing in his youth – Dobson was not a businessman and seems to have lacked the ultimate degree of ambition necessary to fully promote himself. Thus he failed to push through his early plans for the rebuilding of central Newcastle, leaving the entrepreneur Richard Grainger to implement a different scheme. However, as we have seen, in later years Dobson enjoyed a favoured position with the Newcastle Corporation, for which he also frequently acted as an arbitrator, and built up a substantial practice with clerks, draughtsmen and pupils who assisted with design. (In addition he had a large and lucrative practice as a surveyor.)

At this point it is worth noting that two of Dobson's sons were among his assistants. John jnr. (b.1827) was employed from 1854 after his brother Alexander's death, although probably only in an administrative capacity, since he had begun his career as a master mariner and seems to have made no effort to continue the practice after his father's death; while Alexander (b.1828) worked for his father, before and after a pupillage in London with Sydney Smirke from 1849 to 1852; he was elected ARIBA in 1850. Alexander Dobson had also studied under Prof. Donaldson at King's College, London, winning prizes for both theory and practice[18] and had already travelled widely in England examining historic architecture. He was about to go on a Continental Gothic study tour when he lost his life in the disastrous Quayside fire of 6 October 1854. This highly talented young man had clearly been destined to take over his father's practice; possible hopes of an architectural dynasty were not to be. The Quayside fire had started at a factory in Gateshead, causing a catastrophic explosion which spread the fire across the river to Newcastle. It is worth quoting a contemporary account of the calamity:

"The long and narrow street in Gateshead where the fire broke out was filled with people from end to end at the time of the explosion, the firemen, the police, and various assistants being within a dozen yards of the burning pile. A number of influential inhabitants were also present, rendering every assistance in their power, and among them were … Mr. Alex. Dobson, son of John Dobson, Esq., architect, of this town; and several others. In this narrow gorge the burning rubbish fell in tons together, burying the gentlemen we have named ... Of course their death, under such circumstances, must have been instantaneous."[19]

Dobson suffered a further bereavement in 1857 with the death of his grandson John (the only son of John jnr.) at the age of 14. Dobson had married in 1816 Isabella (1794-1846), daughter of Alexander, a master mariner, and Isabella Rutherford of Gateshead. His wife, a talented amateur artist, bore him eight children (three sons and five daughters). Four survived to adulthood: their two eldest sons and two eldest daughters. The latter were Isabella, who married the architect Sydney Smirke, and Margaret Jane, best known for her useful, if not entirely reliable biography of her father, mentioned above. Dobson himself came from a large family, being the second of twelve children. Little is known of his siblings, although his sisters Mary (b.1789) and Harriet (b.1805) both married mineworkers; his elder brother Alexander (1786-1867) outlived him by two years and was present at his funeral. Dobson's mother Margaret died in 1828 and his father John about a year earlier.

Obviously Dobson must have been an exceptionally dedicated man. "His hours of rising were four or five in the morning, and his remarkable power of doing without sleep enabled him constantly to work till twelve at night."[20] He himself tells us how in his youth he gained inspiration from the aged Royal Academician Benjamin West, still working a few days before he died,[21] and Dobson himself retired only after his stroke in 1862. There was a lighter side. Early in his career, when pressure of business was less, he enjoyed designing for the stage; similarly, in 1814 he was responsible for many of "the various embellishments throughout the town [of Newcastle]" commemorating the peace with France, including a 'transparency' of "Britannia seated with the British Lion pacing the shore in attitude of defiance, shipping in the background – motto 'Prosperity to Britain'".[22] In January 1826 we find him attending a fancy-dress ball as a "Colonel in the Egyptian Service".[23] He loved music and indeed "all that was beautiful in art and nature"[24] and is said to have enjoyed his limited leisure time.

But only a few weeks after the death of his son in the Quayside explosion, a blow from which he never really recovered, and with his wife also dead, he was planning the redevelopment of the very locality near where the unfortunate young man had been killed. "I still can feel the same anxiety to improve, and the same pleasure and delight in my profession that I felt when I was but a boy" he told his younger colleagues, many of whom he helped and encouraged, in 1859.[25]

Characteristics of Dobson's work

Like many early 19th-century architects, and for that matter more than most, Dobson avoided specialising in a single style, believing that a range of styles could be used, according to the building specimen or type. In this he resembled or followed C.R. Cockerell, who took over from Soane as the intellectual leader of the profession and, like his predecessor, became

Professor of Architecture at the Royal Academy. Cockerell recommended in his Royal Academy Lectures "a latitudinarian spirit, rather than one of bigotry", based on the principle that "each peculiarity of architecture had its application in time and place".[26] Dobson, similarly, held "that to every building of importance, there ought to belong a special character, based upon the purpose for which the building was designed, and that it was the part of the architect fully to develop this character in his work".[27] Accordingly, he continued or even advanced the stylistic plurality seen to a lesser extent in the work of his regional predecessors such as Newton, the Stokoes and even David Stephenson.

The general characteristics of Dobson's architecture were, according to a 19th-century authority, "adaptability, ingenuity, patience, constructive imagination, and an instinctive intelligence of the *genius loci*".[28] Similarly, a younger contemporary referred to "that wonderful grasp which appears in all his designs, revealing at a glance the several uses for which the buildings are intended".[29] Dobson achieved a remarkable level of competence through his long career. He was not so much an innovator as a consolidator of current styles and was always too pragmatic to get involved in controversies such as the 'Battle of the Styles' between the Victorian Goths and Classicists, or become immersed in the complex architectural theories of the day.

Even Dobson's most modest works usually made something of their site. When engaged to make a design, it was his custom, we are told, to "make himself thoroughly acquainted with the *genius loci* from every point of view".[30] His love of nature, and early training as a gardener, may give some truth to the claim that he almost preferred the landscape and 'dressed gardens' surrounding his works to the buildings themselves.[31] Similarly, Dobson's thorough assimilation of the Picturesque (see above), is particularly evident in his Tudor-Gothic designs, and is also reflected in his determination from an early age to produce the most attractive, even glamorous presentations of his designs (hence his pupillage with Varley).

Dobson evolved a meticulous, fine-lined style of draughtsmanship, while in many of his presentation watercolours the buildings drawn by him were effectively combined with landscape and figures by his collaborators, such as T.M. Richardson or, more usually, J.W. Carmichael. Indeed, with Richardson, in 1831, he helped set up the Northern Society of Painters in Watercolours. However, although Dobson was an early exponent of the form, Margaret Dobson's belief that he was the first to exhibit coloured architectural perspectives at the Royal Academy or elsewhere, is incorrect. Indeed, these perspectives had begun to be fashionable from the 1780s and 90s, Robert Adam, Sir William Chambers, James Wyatt and Joseph Bonomi snr. being noted practitioners.

Dobson's architecture has a certain distinctive solidity and strength which is invariably recognisable, at least in the case of work done before the bewildering eclecticism of his final phase. The work of his last years seems

to betray a slight loss of confidence, perhaps occasioned by bereavement and rapidly changing architectural trends. Yet, as we have seen, during this period Dobson showed some aptitude in his belated use of the Italian Renaissance style. He even achieved an unexpected late flowering in church design, although for the most part his neo-Gothic architecture, while important to him, seems to lack the passion of his better classical work. A colleague recalled of Dobson at his death in 1865 that "studying his profession when Greek architecture was the ephemeral fashion … his mind appears to have been imbued with a preference for classic architecture, which the 'revival' or growth of an appreciation of mediaeval art could not supplant".[32]

Fig. 107 West entrance gates to Gosforth Park (formerly House), Newcastle upon Tyne, 1830.

©Crown copyright NMR.

Fig. 108 Newcastle General Cemetery (Jesmond Old Cemetery), 1834-36, south gates.

Authors' photograph.

Generally Dobson's ability lay less in forming delicate details (with some noteworthy exceptions) than in the composition of mass, particularly when expressed in block-like forms. Good examples include his west entrance gates for Ralph Brandling at the former Gosforth House (1830, fig. 107), his Jesmond Cemetery Chapels and Gates of 1834-36 (see figs 24, 108 and 115) and his imposing Collingwood Monument at Tynemouth (fig. 109), designed in 1842. Thus the Greek Revival and neoclassical styles provided opportunities for his talent at its best. In this he may be compared to the slightly earlier Thomas Harrison of Chester and Manchester, and John Foster jnr. of Liverpool; similarly, these were also major regional figures who achieved some national recognition as well.

There are peaks of achievement in Dobson's long career. Longhirst is as fine or finer than anything of that

Fig. 109 The Collingwood
Monument, Tynemouth,
from 1842.
*Newcastle Libraries &
Information Service.*

time, while the Newcastle Central Station as
first proposed was a magnificent design – in
the spirit of Vanbrugh according to several
critics of the day.[33] This latter design also
reflected the strong views Dobson had now
evolved on the subject of railway station
architecture. "Being quite a new class of
structures erected for purposes unknown until
the present age", he argued, "they [railway
stations] ... ought to suggest, a character of
their own, and fresh combinations in design
... They are, moreover, especially public
works – structures constantly seen by thousands and tens of thousands of persons; and
might, therefore, do much towards improving
the taste of the public."[34] Also – perhaps curiously in view of his earlier Carlisle project
(see p.101) – he had now decided that the
Gothic style was unsuitable for this kind of
architecture, being "very ill adapted to buildings totally different in purpose, and therefore
requiring to be differently constituted from
those in which such modes are exemplified
... what class of mediaeval structures are there that have aught in common
with railway stations and termini?"[35] Dobson's first design for the Central
Station was praised for its convenience, expressiveness of purpose, unity yet
variety, picturesqueness of outline, and handling of light and shade,[36]
although of his second, truncated proposal (see p.105) a contemporary critic
wrote, perhaps rather unfairly, that it "verges close on the faults so common
in the Renaissance styles. It is neither quite truthful nor quite appropriate...
the ornamentation has too much the character of being put there for ornament's sake alone."[37] However, the failure of either to be built typifies the
many disappointments and frustrations of Dobson's professional life, sto-
ically endured.

Dobson and his contemporaries and successors

Architects contemporary with Dobson on Tyneside have been discussed
in Chapter 6. As we have seen, the best work of some of these, such as
Thomas Oliver snr., the Greens (of whom it must be acknowledged that John
Green snr. had exceptional engineering skills), and perhaps even William
Stokoe jnr., is comparable with his own. However, Oliver and Stokoe built
little and Benjamin Green's career ended prematurely. In any case Dobson
was certainly pre-eminent as a designer of villas and country houses.
Probably more in touch with the national scene than the others (with the pos-
sible exception of Benjamin Green), Dobson can perhaps be more appropri-

Fig. 110 John Wardle jnr.,
the Hancock Museum,
Newcastle upon Tyne,
1880-84.
Authors' photograph.

Fig. 111 R.J. Johnson,
Bank, formerly of
Hodgkin, Barnett, Spence,
Pease & Co., Collingwood
Street, Newcastle upon
Tyne, 1888-91.
Authors' photograph.

ately related to London-trained provincial contemporaries like R.D. Chantrell of Leeds or J. Foulston of Plymouth.

In 1845 Dobson became a Fellow of the Institute of British Architects in London, proposed by Donaldson, Salvin and Sydney Smirke; how he must have approved of the declaration he was obliged to sign: "I will not have any interest or participation in any trade contract or materials, supplied at any works, the execution of which I may be engaged to superintend." Locally, it was said of Dobson that "to no one has the revival of architecture in the north been so largely indebted",[38] while his election in Newcastle as first President of the newly formed Northern Architectural Association in 1859 indicated the esteem in which he was held. At his death, the Association's Hon. Secretary, Thomas Oliver jnr., wrote that Dobson "not only laid the foundation of local practice, but, for many years was the head corner stone thereof".[39]

As mentioned in the preceding chapter Dobson's practice was carried on for a short while by Thomas Austin in partnership with R.J. Johnson. Johnson later took into partnership his own former pupil W.S. Hicks (1849-1902). Hicks then set up on his own in 1882 before being joined by his brother-in-law H.C. Charlewood in 1888 to form the firm of Hicks & Charlewood. This practice survived in the hands of their successors until the 1940s and, with different personnel, later still. Thus a line of succession – almost a 'family tree' – can be traced within the Newcastle architectural profession from Dobson to at least the mid 20th century. Indeed, it was essentially a legacy of professionalism, rather than any narrowly defined stylistic influence that Dobson left.

However, the long survival of classicism in the North East can be partially attributed to him. A good example of this is John Wardle jnr.'s still remarkably Dobsonian Hancock Museum, Newcastle, of 1880-84 (fig. 110), and the trend was still evident as Newcastle's business district migrated to Mosley and Collingwood Streets north of the Central Station later in the century. Here massive Renaissance-style banks and offices were designed by distinguished local architects such as R.J. Johnson, Oliver, Leeson & Wood, and F.W. Rich (see fig. 111).

Later still, Robert Burns Dick (1868-1954), a tal-

ented exponent of the 'stripped classical' style fashionable after the First World War, further developed the Dobson (and Grainger) tradition of monumentalist architecture and planning in Newcastle. His works include the architectural treatment of the Tyne Bridge (1924-28), the Magistrates' Courts, Police and Fire Stations, Pilgrim Street (1931-32, fig. 112), the former Northumberland County Council Offices (completed 1934) and the church of the Divine Unity, Ellison Place (1938-40).

Fig. 112 Robert Burns Dick, Magistrates' Courts, Police and Fire Stations, Pilgrim Street, Newcastle upon Tyne, 1931-32.
Authors' photograph.

Fig. 113 John Dobson Street, Newcastle upon Tyne, just prior to partial demolition of high level concrete walkway, c.1995.
Authors' photograph.

Epilogue

At the time of writing, there is still no permanent display relating to Dobson in any local art gallery or museum, although the major bicentennial exhibition at the Laing Art Gallery, Newcastle, of 1987, organised by the present authors, raised public awareness of his work. Moreover, time has not treated Dobson's buildings well. The period of greatest destruction was that of the 1960s and 1970s, when cities like Newcastle were being extensively redeveloped. It is perhaps ironic that at this time was constructed the only street commemorating Dobson, as part of the then current central redevelopment plan. Thus, with sublime incongruity, 'John Dobson Street' passes under a high-rise block of flats and was at one time spanned by an equally bleak concrete walkway (see fig. 113), now largely removed. However

paradoxically, Dobson seems to have been perceived as a precursor of the 'comprehensive redevelopment' policies fashionable at the time, his name (and that of Grainger) being repeatedly invoked to justify the substantial replanning in Newcastle then taking place.

The period of the 1960s and 1970s was also blighted by the loss of two of Dobson's finest works in Newcastle – and indeed anywhere – the Royal Arcade and Eldon Square. The Royal Arcade was doomed by

Fig. 114 Model of scheme of c.1963 to incorporate part of Dobson's Royal Arcade within 'Swan House', Pilgrim Street, Newcastle upon Tyne.

Newcastle Document Services.

its location at the eastern entrance to Mosley Street, the site of proposed traffic improvements, and had been in decline for many years. It was demolished to make way for the new Swan House office development (see Chapter 2), but only in stages (1963-69) as various schemes to conserve all or part of it (see fig. 114) were considered but ultimately abandoned. In the end, a rather unsatisfactory compromise was reached whereby a slightly shortened facsimile of the Arcade's interior was incorporated into the new complex as a (little used) pedestrian thoroughfare.

Meanwhile, the crucial 1963 *Development Plan* for Newcastle also proposed the comprehensive redevelopment of Eldon Square; Dobson's ranges were to be replaced by a prestigious new shopping complex and high-rise hotel. This scheme was abandoned in 1971, because of cost, but redevelopment went ahead in modified form with Dobson's eastern wing surviving, rather forlornly, by default. The official view seemed to be that structures like the Royal Arcade and Eldon Square were expendable because of their dilapidation and because the city possessed a superfluity of Grainger and Dobson architecture.[40]

However, still surviving despite numerous demolition threats over the years, and singularly expressive of Dobson, are his Jesmond Cemetery Chapels and Gates (figs. 24, 108 and 115). Dobson himself must have been particularly proud of these buildings, for he continued to exhibit his original designs long after the Cemetery was laid out.[41] For the 19th-century theorist

156

Fig. 115 Newcastle
General Cemetery
(Jesmond Old Cemetery),
1834-36, showing chapels
and north entrance. From
an engraving.
Tyne & Wear Museums.

J.C. Loudon the composition was the most appropriate he had seen,[42] while
to a modern critic it is "grandly original, severely noble and uncompromisingly stark".[43] Sir Albert Richardson found "superlative merit"[44] in its
design, while more recently Sir John Summerson described it as a masterpiece.[45] Dobson was buried here on 14 January 1865:

> "the relatives of the deceased were anxious for as much privacy as
> possible, in connection with the proceedings ... to a great extent, the
> wish was complied with, however much the fellow townsmen of Mr.
> Dobson might have desired to pay their last respects to his private worth
> and great professional reputation."[46]

No more appropriate resting place for the architect could be imagined
than the cemetery he had designed himself.

Notes

1 J. Dobson, *Presidential Address to the Northern Architectural Association* (April
1859), reprinted in Wilkes, p.103.

2 *Ibid.*, p.108.

3 *Ibid.*

4 *Ibid.*

5 J. Dobson, 'The Central Railway Station, Newcastle upon Tyne', *The Civil
Engineer and Architect's Journal*, vol. xi, no. 135, December 1848, p.354. Dobson
made this comment in connection with his use of Prudhoe stone for Newcastle Central
Station.

6 Those for his extensions to the Newcastle Quayside, the Manors Warehouse and associated buildings, and the Newcastle Central Station were included in Prof. T.L. Donaldson's influential text book *Handbook of Specifications*, 1860, Part II, pp.824-66.

7 Dobson, p.35.

8 'Old Newcastle Architects and Surveyors', *NWC*, 1 January 1887.

9 Thus for example a younger contemporary recalled that the honeysuckle ornament on Dobson's own house in New Bridge Street was carved "from a design modelled in clay by Mr. Dobson with a silver spoon, after breakfasting with his friend Mr. Ralph Dodds, who at once made a safe mould and cast of the design in plaster for him." (*Ibid.*).

10 See *Official Descriptive and Illustrated Catalogue* of the Great Exhibition of 1851, p.323; Charlton had been Hawks, Crawshay's engineering foreman for the High Level Bridge.

11 V. Haworth, 'Robert Stephenson in Newcastle', unpublished paper given to the Victorian Society (North East Group), 1989.

12 From a toast to Dobson proposed by Mr. (William) Lockey Harle; see *NCh*, 2 August 1850.

13 Mrs. Haworth (see note 11 above) made much of the fact that at this inaugural dinner in the Station Stephenson stated that "Beyond drawing the outline, he [Mr. S] had no right to claim any credit for the works above where they now sat. Upon Mr. Harrison the whole responsibility of their execution had fallen." However, it is important to note that the dinner took place in an area "partitioned off with a skeleton framing of wood, covered with canvas and lined with calico". Thus Stephenson was referring not to the Station roof, but to his great engineering works the Newcastle High Level Bridge, the Berwick Viaduct and the Menai Tubular Bridge, painted 'cartoons' of which had been placed on one side of the dining 'room'. See *NJ*, 3 August 1850 and *NCh*, 2 August 1850. In addition, Stephenson went on to describe the event as the proudest of his life (*NC*, 2 August 1850).

14 *Reports by the Juries* (of the Great Exhibition of 1851), 1852, p.208.

15 Dobson, p.15.

16 'Old Newcastle Architects and Surveyors', *NWC*, 1 January 1887.

17 Also in the Laing Art Gallery, Newcastle, is a pencil drawing of Dobson by Thomas Heathfield Carrick.

18 *The Newcastle Daily Chronicle*, 9 January 1865.

19 *Proceedings of the Newcastle Council*, 1853-54, Introduction, p.100 (*c*).

20 Dobson, pp.16-17.

21 Wilkes, p.102.

22 *NA*, 17 May 1814.

23 Sykes, II, p.191.

24 Dobson, p.20.

25 Wilkes, p.102.

26 C.R. Cockerell, Fifth Royal Academy Lecture on Architecture, reported in *The Builder*, vol. vii, 1849, p.86.

27 Dobson, p.19. Again, Humphry Repton (see main text, above) had also very similarly stressed the importance of 'character' in architecture. See his *An Enquiry into the Changes of Taste in Landscape Gardening, etc.*, 1806, p.174.

28 *Dictionary of National Biography*, s.v. 'Dobson'.

29 'Old Newcastle Architects and Surveyors', *NWC*, 1 January 1887.

30 Dobson, p.14.

31 See obituary of Dobson in *NDJ*, 9 January 1865.

32 F.R. Wilson, Vice-Presidential Address to the Northern Architectural Association, Proceedings of the Northern Architectural Association, 1865, p.4.

33 See obituary of Dobson in *The Building News*, 13 January 1865, quoting a review in *The Athenaeum* of Dobson's designs earlier exhibited at the Royal Academy.

34 J. Dobson, *op. cit.*, p.353.

35 *Ibid*.

36 *The Civil Engineer and Architect's Journal*, vol. xii, no. 139, April 1849, p.14.

37 J. Fergusson, *History of the Modern Styles of Architecture*, 2nd edn., 1873, p.554.

38 Fordyce, II, p.589.

39 From letter of commiseration to Margaret Dobson; text in account of 6th Annual Meeting, 24 January 1865, in Minute Book of the Northern Architectural Association, 1858-1884 (with the Literary and Philosophical Society of Newcastle upon Tyne).

40 For more on the post-1945 redevelopment of Newcastle, including the demolition of Eldon Square and the Royal Arcade, see T.E. Faulkner, 'Conservation and Renewal in Newcastle upon Tyne', in Faulkner (ed.), *Northumbrian Panorama: Studies in the History and Culture of North East England*, 1996, pp.138-44.

41 As at the Newcastle Fine Art Exhibition of 1855; see *The Builder*, vol. xiii, 1855, p.553. These designs were presumably versions of that illustrated in the Prospectus of 29 January 1834 in TWA (DT/NGC/5).

42 Quoted in J.S. Curl, 'Northern Cemetery under Threat', *CL*, 2 July 1981, p.68.

43 *Ibid.*, J.S. Curl.

44 A.E. Richardson, *Monumental Classic Architecture in Great Britain and Ireland in the Nineteenth Century*, 1914, p.87.

45 J. Summerson, reviewing T.E. Faulkner & A. Greg, *John Dobson: Newcastle Architect, 1787-1865*, 1987, *Society of Architectural Historians of Great Britain Newsletter*, no. 38, 1988.

46 *NDJ*, 16 January 1865.

8 Catalogue of Works by John Dobson

This chronological list of Dobson's works, which includes unexecuted as well as executed designs, has been compiled mainly from contemporary and near-contemporary sources. It makes particular use of local newspapers and also draws on archival evidence, obituaries of Dobson, the list of works published in the *Newcastle Daily Journal* shortly after Dobson's death, Margaret Dobson's *Memoir of John Dobson* (1885) and various other sources, published and unpublished. The reference quoted (or initial reference when more than one is given) is the earliest evidence of Dobson's authorship. Those works which bear only a reference to the *Memoir* (e.g. "Dobson, p.119") may require further substantiation, although in these and other instances observable errors of dating in the *Memoir* have been corrected.

The catalogue does not include most of the numerous surveys, valuations and arbitrations that Dobson undertook, nor does it mention the frequent occasions on which he acted as agent for the sale of building land, etc. (other than in those cases where he also supplied designs for buildings or streets).

Note: in addition to the abbreviations cited on page 6, (D) = formerly County Durham (for buildings now in Cleveland or Tyne and Wear); (N) = formerly Northumberland (for buildings now in Tyne and Wear); dem. = demolished (although the absence of this notation is no guarantee that the building in question is still in existence). Under each year, buildings and designs are listed in alphabetical sequence. Most of these works are assigned on documentary evidence to a single specific year, but sometimes the dating is approximate or a building is known to have been constructed over a period of several years (or constructed later after a delay). In instances where these different types of dating are found under the same year, works documented to that year alone are given first, followed by works dating approximately to that year, followed by works begun or designed in that year but known to have been finished later. Thus a representative sequence goes: 1852, c.1852, 1852-53, 1852-55, 1853.

The authors would be very pleased to hear of any corrections or additions to the catalogue, preferably supported by contemporary evidence.

1810-14

ROYAL JUBILEE SCHOOL, CITY ROAD, NEWCASTLE UPON TYNE, classical, 1810, dem. (see also entry for 1854) [Mackenzie 1827, II, p.452; drawing in Laing Art Gallery, Newcastle upon Tyne]

NORTH SHIELDS, TYNE AND WEAR (N), house and shop "on an extensive scale", 1811 [*NC*, 20 Jul 1811]

SCOTTISH PRESBYTERIAN CHURCH, HOWARD STREET, NORTH SHIELDS, TYNE AND WEAR (N), classical, 1811, now Salvation Army Chapel [*NC*, 3 Aug 1811]

WESLEYAN METHODIST CHAPEL, NEW ROAD, NEWCASTLE UPON TYNE, classical, 1812 [*NC*, 25 Jul 1812]

EARSDON, NORTHUMBERLAND, unidentified house for Mr. Nicholson, 1813 [*NDJ*, 16 Jan 1865]

FIELD HOUSE, GATESHEAD, TYNE AND WEAR (D), classical house for George Barras, 1813, dem. 1931 [Dobson, p.73; Manders, p.133]

PRIORY, TYNEMOUTH, TYNE AND WEAR (N), speculative scheme of restoration, 1813, not carried out (see also entries for 1817, 1852) [Dobson, p.99]

BRADLEY HALL, NR. RYTON, TYNE AND WEAR (D), alterations to mid 18th-century house, including moving of entrance, for 1st Lord Ravensworth, c.1813 [*NDJ*, 16 Jan 1865]

CHEESEBURN GRANGE, NORTHUMBERLAND, substantial Gothic remodelling of 18th-century house for Ralph Riddell, c.1813, additions by J.A. Hansom, c.1860, the latter dem. (see also entries for 1818, 1841) [*NDJ*, 16 Jan 1865; drawings in Collection Major Philip Riddell]

BROAD CHARE, NEWCASTLE UPON TYNE, warehouse, 1814 [Dobson, p.125]

GIBSIDE, TYNE AND WEAR (D), proposed minor alterations, including addition of battlements to servants' quarters at east, addition of billiard room, and addition of conservatory, to Jacobean house, for 10th Earl of Strathmore, 1814; house now ruinous (see also entries for c.1818, 1856) [drawings in DCRO (D/St/X46A,81A and D/St/P6/2/6,7)]

HOUSE OF CORRECTION, TYNEMOUTH, TYNE AND WEAR (N), additions, 1814 [Dobson, p.118]

HOWDON DOCKS, WALLSEND, TYNE AND WEAR (N), 1814 [Dobson, p.127]

THEATRE ROYAL, MOSLEY STREET, NEWCASTLE UPON TYNE, embellishments and illuminations, 1814, dem. 1836 (see also entry for 1817) [*NA*, 17 May 1814]

WALLSEND, TYNE AND WEAR (N), staithes, 1814 [Dobson, p.125]

SEATON DELAVAL HALL, NORTHUMBERLAND, proposed alterations and additions to Sir John Vanbrugh's 18th-century house, for Sir Jacob Henry Astley, 1814-17 (see also entry for 1860) [drawings at Seaton Delaval Hall]

1815-19

BACKWORTH HALL, NORTHUMBERLAND, alterations to William Newton's late 18th-century house, for R. Grey, 1815 [*NDJ*, 16 Jan 1865]

BLACKETT STREET, NEWCASTLE UPON TYNE, survey and valuation, for Blackett family, 1815 (see also entry for 1824) [drawing in NCRO (ZBL 62/4)]

FALLODON HALL, EMBLETON, NORTHUMBERLAND, additions, evidently including service wing and stable block, for Sir George Grey, Bt., 1815, partially rebuilt early 20th century [*NDJ*, 16 Jan 1865]

HAMSTERLEY HALL, COUNTY DURHAM, alterations, for R.S. Surtees, 1815 [*NDJ*, 16 Jan 1865]

MANOR OFFICE, HEXHAM, NORTHUMBERLAND, conversion, for Col. Beaumont, 1815 [*NDJ*, 16 Jan 1865]

PRESTWICK LODGE, PONTELAND, NORTHUMBERLAND, small classical house for Percival Fenwick, 1815 [*NC*, 9 Jun 1815]

UNTHANK HALL, NORTHUMBERLAND, additions, for Robert Pearson, 1815, rebuilt 1862, reduced 1965 (see also entry for 1860) [*NDJ*, 16 Jan 1865]

WATERVILLE HOUSE, NORTH SHIELDS, TYNE AND WEAR (N), house for R. Rippon, 1815, destroyed by bombing, 1941 [*NDJ*, 16 Jan 1865; illustrated in Faulkner and Lowery, p.68]

CRAMLINGTON HOUSE, NORTHUMBERLAND, classical house for A.M. de C. Lawson, c.1815, dem. c.1969 [*NDJ*, 16 Jan 1865]

ALL SAINTS' CHURCH, NEWCASTLE UPON TYNE, repairs to David Stephenson's 1786-96 church, 1816 [Mackenzie 1827, I, p.305]

BENWELL GROVE, NEWCASTLE UPON TYNE, house for Charles Cook, 1816, dem. c.1914 [*NDJ*, 16 Jan 1865]

ELAND HALL, PONTELAND, NORTHUMBERLAND, alterations, including insertion of south doorway, to 18th-century house, for William Barkley (?), 1816 [Dobson, p.76]

MINSTERACRES HALL, NORTHUMBERLAND, additions to late 18th-century house for George Silvertop, probably including classical bay window and colonnaded porch, 1816 (see also entry for 1843) [*NDJ*, 16 Jan 1865]

NORTH SHIELDS, TYNE AND WEAR (N), dock for Michael Robson, 1816 [*NDJ*, 16 Jan 1865]

NORTH SHIELDS, TYNE AND WEAR (N), docks for Mr. Blackburn, 1816 [Dobson, p.127]

PERCY TENANTRY COLUMN, ALNWICK, NORTHUMBERLAND, unexecuted design, 1816 [press cutting 4 June 1816 in Alnwick Castle Collection (DWS, Northum. 187A/151)]

TYNE BREWERY, ST. MARY'S STREET, SANDGATE, NEWCASTLE UPON TYNE, 1816, dem. [Dobson, p.127]

WHICKHAM, TYNE AND WEAR (D), house for J. Errington, 1816 [Dobson, p.76]

STRAWBERRY PLACE, NEWCASTLE UPON TYNE, house for J. Harvey, c.1816, dem. [*NDJ*, 16 Jan 1865]

BOLAM, NORTHUMBERLAND, laying out of gardens and lake for Hon. W.H. Beresford, 1816-18 [affidavit in NCRO (ZMI B13/X11)]

AXWELL PARK, TYNE AND WEAR (D), alterations to James Paine's 18th-century house, including construction of a garden temple, for Sir John Clavering, 1817 [*NDJ*, 16 Jan 1865]

BELFORD HALL, NORTHUMBERLAND, alterations and additions, including north entrance, wings and south lodge, to James Paine's 18th-century house, for William Clark, 1817 [*NDJ*, 16 Jan 1865; *NCRO* (692/40)]

CUSTOMS HOUSE, GLASGOW, alterations, 1817, dem. [*NDJ*, 16 Jan 1865]

CUSTOMS HOUSE, LIVERPOOL, alterations, 1817, dem. [*NDJ*, 16 Jan 1865]

CUSTOMS HOUSE, NEWCASTLE UPON TYNE, alterations, 1817, dem. c.1840 [*NDJ*, 16 Jan 1865]

JESMOND GROVE, NEWCASTLE UPON TYNE, alterations to, or reconstruction of, house for James Losh, 1817, later Gothicised, dem. 1927 [Dobson, p.77; illustrated in Faulkner and Lowery, p.22]

PERCY STREET, NEWCASTLE UPON TYNE, proposed crescent off Percy Street, not carried out, 1817 [*NDJ*, 29 Mar 1817]

PRIORY CHURCH OF ST. ANDREW, HEXHAM, NORTHUMBERLAND, proposed restoration of east window, 1817, not carried out (see also entries for 1828, 1858-60) [*NDJ*, 16 Jan 1865]

PRIORY, TYNEMOUTH, TYNE AND WEAR (N), proposed restoration (of Lady Chapel?) as a "Chapel of Ease", 1817, not carried out (see also entries for 1813, 1852) [*NDJ*, 16 Jan 1865]

ST. NICHOLAS'S, NEWCASTLE UPON TYNE, installation of heating by stoves, 1817 (see also entries for 1823-24, 1827, 1832-34, 1859, 1862) [*NDJ*, 16 Jan 1865]

ST. NICHOLAS'S, NEWCASTLE UPON TYNE, repairs to steeple, 1817 (see also entries for 1823-24, 1827, 1832-34, 1859, 1862) [*NDJ*, 16 Jan 1865]

SCHOOL, PONTELAND, NORTHUMBERLAND, 1817 [Dobson, p.115]

SOUTH SHIELDS, TYNE AND WEAR (D), glassworks for Isaac Cookson, 1817 [Dobson, p.127]

THEATRE ROYAL, NEWCASTLE UPON TYNE, remodelling of entrance hall of David Stephenson's 1788 building, 1817, dem. 1836 (see also entry for 1814) [*Durham County Advertiser*, 9 Jan 1818]

TYNEMOUTH CASTLE, TYNE AND WEAR (N), "planned fortifications", 1817 [Dobson, p.128]

VILLA REALE, SANDYFORD, NEWCASTLE UPON TYNE, classical villa for Capt. John Dutton, 1817 [*NDJ*, 16 Jan 1865]

WEST JESMOND HOUSE, NEWCASTLE UPON TYNE, Gothic villa for Sir Thomas Burdon, 1817 (see also entry for 1823-27) [*NDJ*, 16 Jan 1865]

DOXFORD HALL, NORTHUMBERLAND, classical house for William Taylor, 1817-18 [*NDJ*, 16 Jan 1865]

BLACK DENE HOUSE, NEWCASTLE UPON TYNE Gothic house for Dr. Thomas Emerson Headlam, 1818, rebuilt by Dobson for Thomas (?) Cruddas, 1851; again rebuilt, in stages, by R. Norman Shaw, 1870-85, and F.W. Rich, 1896-97 (see also entry for 'Dene House', 1851) [*NDJ*, 16 Jan 1865]

CHEESEBURN GRANGE, NORTHUMBERLAND, restoration of chapel (RC) for Ralph Riddell, 1818, additions by J.A. Hansom, c.1860, the latter dem. (see also entries for c.1813, 1841) [*NDJ*, 16 Jan 1865]

JESMOND VILLA (or HOUSE), NEWCASTLE UPON TYNE, additions to classical house for Armorer Donkin, 1818 [Dobson, p.77; illustrated in NCRO (ZAN/M13/F11, p.91)]

ST. NICHOLAS'S, GOSFORTH, NEWCASTLE UPON TYNE, additions, classical, 1818, subsequently further enlarged [*NC*, 18 Jul 1818; drawing in NCRO (1875/A/50)]

ST. NICHOLAS'S, GOSFORTH, NEWCASTLE UPON TYNE, sexton's cottage, Tudor, 1818, dem. [drawing at St. Nicholas's Church]

'SANDYFORD BRIDGE', NEWCASTLE UPON TYNE, 1818 [Dobson, p.128]

WALLINGTON HALL, NORTHUMBERLAND, "Large additions to Museum" for John Trevelyan, 1818 (see also entry for 1853-54) [*NDJ*, 16 Jan 1865]

GIBSIDE, TYNE AND WEAR (D), unknown work, c.1818, for which Dobson was paid £50, house now ruinous (see also entries for 1814, 1856) [account in DCRO (D/St/V1513 pp.14, 15)]

TOBACCO WAREHOUSE, NEWCASTLE UPON TYNE, for Benjamin Sorsbie, 1818-19, dem. [*NC*, 13 Jun 1818; *NCh*, 2 Jan 1819]

CHIPCHASE CASTLE, NORTHUMBERLAND, alterations, including some refenestration and addition of south-west Doric doorcase (?), to 17th-century house, for John Reed, 1819 [*NDJ*, 16 Jan 1865]

CLERGY JUBILEE SCHOOL, CARLIOL SQUARE, NEWCASTLE UPON TYNE, classical, 1819, dem. [*NC*, 22 May 1819]

HAMSTERLEY, COUNTY DURHAM, corn mill for R.S. Surtees, 1819 [*NC*, 1 May 1819]

HEBBURN HALL, TYNE AND WEAR (D), alterations, including bay windows (?), to 17th- and 18th-century house, for Cuthbert Ellison, 1819 [Dobson, p.80]

HEXHAM ABBEY HOUSE, NORTHUMBERLAND, alterations, including south porch (?), for T.R. Beaumont, 1819 [Dobson, p.79]

PRESTON VILLA, NORTH SHIELDS, TYNE AND WEAR (N), house for John Fenwick, 1819, dem. 1967 [Dobson, p.79]

ROCK TOWER (HALL), NORTHUMBERLAND, restoration of 16th- and 17th-century house, and Gothic additions (including two hexagonal wings on south front of old 'pele tower', stables and coach house), for Charles Bosanquet, 1819 [Dobson, p.91]

ST. ANDREW'S, WHITBURN, TYNE AND WEAR (D), restoration, 1819 [Dobson, p.100]

ST. JOHN'S, ST. JOHN LEE, NORTHUMBERLAND, restoration, 1819, substantially altered 1885 [*NCh*, 13 Feb 1819]

ST. MARY'S, WHICKHAM, TYNE AND WEAR (D), restoration, 1819, subsequently rebuilt by A. Salvin, 1860-62 [Dobson, p.101]

WEST CHIRTON HOUSE, NORTH SHIELDS, TYNE AND WEAR (N), house for Michael Robson, 1819, dem. c.1937 [Dobson, p.80]

ST. NICHOLAS'S CHARITY SCHOOL, NEWCASTLE UPON TYNE, 1819-20 [Mackenzie 1827, II, p.446]

1820-24

AYDON CASTLE, NORTHUMBERLAND, restorations, for Sir Edward Blackett, 1820 [Dobson, p.81]

BIDDLESTONE HALL, NORTHUMBERLAND, major alterations to late18th-century house (possibly by John Carr of York), for W. Selby, 1820, Gothic chapel added later in 19th century; dem. 1957 except for chapel [*NDJ*, 16 Jan 1865; NCRO (CLA 49/50); *History of Northumberland*, XV, 1940, pp.427-28; Pevsner 1992, p.186; illustrated in Faulkner and Lowery, p.37]

BROOME PARK, NORTHUMBERLAND, alterations and additions to late 18th-century house for William Burrell, 1820 (or 1829?), dem. 1953 [*NDJ*, 16 Jan 1865; NCRO (ZAN M.13/F.13, p.25); illustrated in Faulkner and Lowery, p.38]

NEWCASTLE UPON TYNE, "projected town towards Ponteland Road", not carried out, 1820 [Dobson, p.128]

BELFORD, NORTHUMBERLAND, houses in Church St., Market St., etc. for William Clark, c.1820 [stylistic attribution]

BLAGDON HALL, NORTHUMBERLAND, addition of plain classical north wing, for Sir Matthew White Ridley, c.1820 [Pevsner 1992, p.189]

CASTLE, NEWCASTLE UPON TYNE, proposed conversion to prison and magistrates' courts, c.1820 [Mackenzie 1827, I, p.202]

PONTELAND RECTORY, NORTHUMBERLAND, alterations, c.1820 (?) [*NDJ*, 16 Jan 1865]

THIRSTON HOUSE, FELTON, NORTHUMBERLAND, classical house for Newton family, incorporating some earlier work, c.1820 [stylistic attribution, DoE list]

BOLTON HALL, WEST BOLTON, NORTHUMBERLAND, additions, possibly the south and north-west ranges, probably for William Burrell, 1820s [*NDJ*, 16 Jan 1865; Pevsner 1992, p.197]

CHESTER HILL, BELFORD, NORTHUMBERLAND, plain classical farmhouse for/on estate of William Clark, 1820s [*NDJ*, 16 Jan 1865]

HAWTHORN DENE HOUSE (ORIGINALLY HAWTHORN HIVE COTTAGE), COUNTY DURHAM, Gothic house for Major George Anderson, 1821, remodelled by Thomas Moore, c.1850, ruinous [*NDJ*, 16 Jan 1865; illustrated in Meadows and Waterson, p.58]

SOUTH HILL HOUSE, PLAWSWORTH, COUNTY DURHAM, classical house rebuilt for Thomas Fenwick, 1821, altered [Dobson, p.82]

NEWBROUGH HALL, NORTHUMBERLAND, classical house for Rev. Henry Wastell, c.1821 [*NDJ*, 16 Jan 1865]

GAOL AND SESSIONS HOUSE, MORPETH, NORTHUMBERLAND, castellated, for County of Northumberland, 1821-28, partly dem. [*NC*, 10 Aug 1822; NCRO (ZAL 89/37); drawing in Laing Art Gallery, Newcastle upon Tyne]

GAOL, CARLISLE, CUMBRIA, unbuilt design, probably castellated, 1822 [*Carlisle Patriot*, 3 Mar and 17 Aug 1822]

HOUSE OF CORRECTION, HEXHAM, NORTHUMBERLAND, alterations and additions, 1822, dem. [*NC*, 17

Aug 1822]

ARCOT HALL, CRAMLINGTON, NORTHUMBERLAND, additions to 18th-century house, for George Shum Storey, c.1822 [*NDJ*, 16 Jan 1865]

GAOL, CARLIOL SQUARE, NEWCASTLE UPON TYNE, castellated, 1822-28, dem. c.1929 (see also entries for 1839, 1859-61) [*NC*, 26 Oct 1822; NCRO (NRO (93) Catalogue 16, B3); NCRO (ZAN M13/F11, p.90); plans and specifications in TWA (No. 279/1)]

ACTON HOUSE, NORTHUMBERLAND, minor alterations to late 18th-century house, for Major de Lisle, 1823 [*NDJ*, 16 Jan 1865]

FLOTTERTON HOUSE (HALL), THROPTON, NORTHUMBERLAND, classical house for Christopher Weallands, 1823 [Mackenzie 1827, II, p.485]

NEW BRIDGE STREET, NEWCASTLE UPON TYNE, Dobson's own house, 1823, and other classical "detached villas" on the north side of the street, including Ridley Villas (?) 1823-24, some dem. [*NCh*, 29 Mar 1823; *NC*, 7 Feb 1824; Mackenzie 1827, I, p.189]

NEWTON-ON-THE-MOOR, NORTHUMBERLAND, house ('Newton Villa'/'Villa Farm'?) for Thomas Jamieson, 1823 [*NDJ*, 16 Jan 1865]

PRISON, BELFORD, NORTHUMBERLAND, Tudor, for County of Northumberland, 1823 [*NC*, 22 Nov 1823]

PRISON, WOOLER, NORTHUMBERLAND, Tudor, for County of Northumberland, 1823 [*NCh*, 22 Nov 1823]

SWANSFIELD HOUSE, ALNWICK, NORTHUMBERLAND, plain classical house for Henry Collingwood Selby, 1823, dem. 1975 [Dobson, p.83, Pevsner 1992, p.144]

ST. NICHOLAS'S, NEWCASTLE UPON TYNE, restoration of north transept window, 1823-24 (see also entries for 1817, 1827, 1832-34, 1859, 1862) [Mackenzie 1827, I, p.248]

SHERIFF HILL HALL (HOUSE), GATESHEAD, TYNE AND WEAR (D), classical house for Matthew Plummer, 1823-24, dem. except for service wing c.1967 [*NDJ*, 16 Jan 1865; illustrated in Meadows and Waterson, p.33]

FISHMARKET etc., NEWCASTLE UPON TYNE, classical addition to Guildhall, 1823-26 [Mackenzie, 1827, I, p.217]

WEST JESMOND HOUSE, NEWCASTLE UPON TYNE, Gothic additions to Dobson's house of 1817, for Richard Burdon Sanderson, 1823-27; house, later known as Jesmond Towers, now La Sagesse School, has received substantial additions by Thomas Oliver jnr. (1869) and T.R. Spence (1885) (see also entry for 1817) [Dobson, p.83]

SEAHAM, COUNTY DURHAM, town planned for 3rd Marquess of Londonderry, 1823-28 [*NC*, 6 Dec 1828; drawings in DCRO (D/Lo/P596/1-8), later plan in DCRO (D/SHD/181), correspondence in DCRO (D/Lo/E610)]

MITFORD HALL, NORTHUMBERLAND, classical house for Bertram Osbaldeston Mitford, designed 1823, built 1828-29 [*NDJ*, 16 Jan 1865; Hodgson, II.2., p.67; NCRO (2024/3)]

BLACKETT STREET, NEWCASTLE UPON TYNE, for Richard Grainger, 1824, redeveloped 1960s and later (see also entry for 1815) [Mackenzie 1827, I, pp.188-89]

BOW VILLA, MORPETH, NORTHUMBERLAND, for Dr. John Robb, 1824 [stylistic attribution; *ex inf.* A.H. Tweddle]

HOUSE OF CORRECTION, ALNWICK, NORTHUMBERLAND, additions, for County of Northumberland, 1824 [*NCh*, 8 May 1824]

LUNATIC ASYLUM, BATH LANE, NEWCASTLE UPON TYNE, additions, 1824, dem. [Mackenzie 1827, II, pp.525-26]

NEWTON-ON-THE-MOOR, NORTHUMBERLAND, "Farm Offices" for Thomas Cook, 1824 [*NC*, 20 Mar 1824]

RIVER TYNE, NEWCASTLE UPON TYNE, "plans and sections" for the Corporation, 1824 [*NDJ*, 16 Jan 1865]

ROTHBURY, NORTHUMBERLAND, "mansion house with offices", 1824 [*NC*, 3 Apr 1824]

LONGHIRST HALL, NORTHUMBERLAND, classical house for William Lawson, 1824-25 [Hodgson, II.2, p.159]

SCOTTISH PRESBYTERIAN CHURCH, BISHOPWEARMOUTH, TYNE AND WEAR (D), 1824-25 [*Durham Advertiser*, 18 Sep 1824, 1 Oct 1825]

NEWCASTLE UPON TYNE, proposal for redevelopment of central Newcastle, c.1824-25 [Mackenzie 1827, I, p.200]

1825-29

HAMSTERLEY, COUNTY DURHAM, simple Gothic bridge (identifiable with the one now called Handley Cross Bridge?), 1825 [Dobson, p.129]

HARBOTTLE, NORTHUMBERLAND, bridge, 1825 [Dobson, p.129]

INDEPENDENT CHAPEL, SUNDERLAND, TYNE AND WEAR (D), 1825 [*NDJ*, 16 Jan 1865]

LYING-IN HOSPITAL, NEW BRIDGE STREET, NEWCASTLE UPON TYNE, Gothic, 1825; later, until mid 1990s, Broadcasting House, now retained as centrepiece of new commercial development [Mackenzie 1827, II, p.518]

NUNNYKIRK HALL, NORTHUMBERLAND, substantial classical remodelling of 18th-century house, for William Orde, 1825 [Hodgson, II.1., p.330; *NDJ*, 16 Jan 1865]

ST. MICHAEL'S, ALNWICK, NORTHUMBERLAND, restoration, 1825 [Dobson p.101]

SHAWDON HALL, NORTHUMBERLAND, alterations and additions, for William Hargrave Pawson, 1825 (see also entry for 1858) [*NDJ*, 16 Jan 1865; NCRO (530/20/478)]

CORN EXCHANGE, MIDDLE STREET, NEWCASTLE UPON TYNE, unexecuted Gothic (?) design, c.1825 [Mackenzie 1827, I, pp.199-200]

ELLISON PLACE, NEWCASTLE UPON TYNE, house for David Cram, c.1825, dem. [Mackenzie 1827, I, p.190]

NEWCASTLE UPON TYNE, proposed new road, squares, etc. from Blackett Street to West Road, c.1825 [Mackenzie 1827, I, p.201]

TRAFALGAR STREET, NEWCASTLE UPON TYNE, proposed extension to Quayside, c.1825 [Mackenzie 1827, I, p.202]

ELDON SQUARE, NEWCASTLE UPON TYNE (including Northern Counties Club), classical facades to a plan by Thomas Oliver, for Richard Grainger, 1825-31, mostly dem. c.1970 [Mackenzie 1827, I, p.189; Oliver, p.97]

PICTON PLACE, NEWCASTLE UPON TYNE, classical villas, including 'Picton House' and one for William Todd, c.1825-30, all dem. [Dobson, p.97]

BROOME PARK, NORTHUMBERLAND, "Dwelling house near Broome Park", 1826 [*NC*, 22 Apr 1826]

GORTANLOISK, DUNOON, ARGYLL AND BUTE, shooting lodge for Sir John Fife, 1826 [*NDJ*, 16 Jan 1865]

HALTWHISTLE, NORTHUMBERLAND, bridge, 1826 (identifiable with the one referred to in the entry for 1828?) [*NC*, 29 Apr 1826]

HALTWHISTLE OLD VICARAGE, NORTHUMBERLAND, improvements, for Rev. N.J. Hollingsworth, 1826, now converted into three dwelling-houses [*NDJ*, 16 Jan 1865]

ST. JAMES'S PRESBYTERIAN CHAPEL, BLACKETT STREET, NEWCASTLE UPON TYNE, classical, 1826, dem. 1859 [Mackenzie 1827, I, p.386; NCRO (ZAN M13/F12, pp.94, 96]

SUMMERHILL PLACE, NEWCASTLE UPON TYNE, house, 1826 [*NC*, 11 Nov 1826]

COXLODGE, NEWCASTLE UPON TYNE, undetermined work for John Walker (?), possibly at Coxlodge Hall (dem.), c.1826 [*The Builder*, vol. xxiii, 1865, p.27; *NDJ*, 16 Jan 1865]

SCOTTISH PRESBYTERIAN CHURCH, MONKWEARMOUTH, TYNE AND WEAR (D), classical, 1826-27, replaced by larger building 1892 [*NC*, 21 Jul 1827]

ST. CUTHBERT'S, GREENHEAD, NORTHUMBERLAND, Gothic, 1826-28, chancel added 1900 [*NDJ*, 16 Jan 1865; plans in ICBS (No. 766)]

ST. MARY'S, BELFORD, NORTHUMBERLAND, restoration and rebuilding, 1826-29 [*NDJ*, 16 Jan 1865; ground plan in ICBS (No. 756)]

BELLISTER CASTLE, NORTHUMBERLAND, alterations, for John Kirsopp, 1827, altered c.1890 and restored after a fire, 1902-05 [*NDJ*, 16 Jan 1865]

BOROUGHBRIDGE, NORTH YORKSHIRE, wooden bridge, 1827 [Dobson, p.129]

CHAPEL, HEWORTH, TYNE AND WEAR (D), for "Mr. Hall, viewer", 1827 [*NDJ*, 16 Jan 1865]

GRAMMAR SCHOOL, MORPETH, NORTHUMBERLAND (i.e., either The Chantry or Harle House), restoration, 1827 [*NC*, 24 Feb 1827]

QUAKERS' MEETING HOUSE, NEWCASTLE UPON TYNE (off Pilgrim Street), alterations (?), 1827, dem. [Dobson, p.102]

ST. NICHOLAS'S, NEWCASTLE UPON TYNE, restoration of steeple, 1827 (see also entries for 1817, 1823-24, 1832-34, 1859, 1862) [Sykes, II, p.213]

WALBOTTLE, NEWCASTLE UPON TYNE, bridge, 1827 [Dobson, p.130]

NORTHERN ACADEMY OF ARTS, NEWCASTLE UPON TYNE, classical, 1827-28, dem. 1960s [*Newcastle Magazine*, vi, 12, p.570]

ST. THOMAS THE MARTYR, NEWCASTLE UPON TYNE, Gothic, 1827-30, galleries added by Dobson, 1837 [*NC*, 26 Jul 1827; perspective in Laing Art Gallery, Newcastle upon Tyne]

ARTHUR'S HILL, NEWCASTLE UPON TYNE, streets and elevations planned for Isaac Cookson, 1827-33 (John Street, Edward Street, William Street, etc.), dem. [TWA (1512)]

ANGERTON, NORTHUMBERLAND, repairs to "Mansion House", including new chapel (?), 1828, dem. c.1840 (see also entries for 1828, 1842) [*NC*, 16 Aug 1828]

CHURCH AT GLOUCESTER, for J. Cargill, 1828 [*NDJ*, 16 Jan 1865]

EARSDON, NORTHUMBERLAND, repairs to farm, 1828 [*NC*, 16 Aug 1828]

EDINBURGH, house for Charles Bruce, 1828 [Dobson, p.85]

EMBLETON VICARAGE, NORTHUMBERLAND, substantial Tudor-Gothic additions to 'pele tower', including re-facing of the tower and a large new wing facing the garden, for Rev. George Dixwell Grimes, 1828 [*NDJ*, 16 Jan 1865]

HALTWHISTLE, NORTHUMBERLAND, bridge, 1828 (see also entry for 1826) [*NCh*, 5 Apr 1828]

HARTBURN, NORTHUMBERLAND, repairs to farms, including Angerton (see also entries for 1828, 1842), 1828 [*NDJ*, 16 Jan 1865]

LONG BARTON, NORTHUMBERLAND, repairs to farms, 1828 [*NC*, 16 Aug 1828]

MATFEN HALL, NORTHUMBERLAND, alterations (to the Dower House?), for Sir Edward Blackett, 1828 [Dobson, p.84]

MORPETH, NORTHUMBERLAND, bridge at High Ford, 1828 [*NC*, 6 Apr 1828]

PRIORY CHURCH OF ST. ANDREW, HEXHAM, NORTHUMBERLAND, repair of east window, 1828 (see also entries for 1817, 1858-60) [Sykes, II, p.225]

WOOLSINGTON HALL, TYNE AND WEAR (N), alterations, for Matthew Bell, 1828 [Dobson, p.85]

BONNYRIGG HALL, NR. MATFEN, NORTHUMBERLAND, shooting-lodge, for Sir Edward Blackett, before 1828, dem. [*ex. inf.* J. Rees]

LILBURN TOWER, NORTHUMBERLAND, Tudor-Gothic house for Henry John Collingwood, 1828-29 (see also entry for c.1843-44) [*NC*, 10 Jan 1829; perspective in Laing Art Gallery, Newcastle upon Tyne]

NEVILLE STREET, NEWCASTLE UPON TYNE, planned 1828, built c.1835 [*NDJ*, 16 Jan 1865]

TREWHITT HOUSE (HALL), NETHERTON, NORTHUMBERLAND, alterations, including refacing (?), to classical house, for John Smart, c.1828-1830 [*NDJ*, 16 Jan 1865; Dobson, p.86]

CASTLE HOUSE (HARBOTTLE CASTLE), HARBOTTLE, NORTHUMBERLAND, remodelling, for Thomas Fenwick Clennell, 1829 [Dobson, p.86]

CROSS, MARKET PLACE, HOLY ISLAND, NORTHUMBERLAND, reconstruction, for Henry Collingwood Selby, 1829 [*NDJ*, 16 Jan 1865; *Proc. Soc. Ant.*, 3rd series, vol. iii, 1907-08, p.286]

GLANTON PIKE, WHITTINGHAM, NORTHUMBERLAND, additions, including porch, for Henry Collingwood, 1829 [*NDJ*, 16 Jan 1865; NCRO (ZSI 119/144)]

MORPETH, NORTHUMBERLAND, unexecuted design for the 'New Bridge', near Bridge Street, 1829, bridge eventually built by Thomas Telford, 1829-31 [Hodgson II.2, p.426; *NCh*, 18 Jul 1829; *The Gentleman's Magazine*, 1832, iii, p.505]

RIDLEY HALL, NR. BARDON MILL, NORTHUMBERLAND, alterations, for John Davidson, 1829, rebuilt by H. Adamson, 1891 [*NDJ*, 16 Jan 1865; C. Hardy, *John Bowes and the Bowes Museum*, 1970, p.213; NCRO (404/420)]

ST. JOHN'S, NEWCASTLE UPON TYNE, restoration, 1829 (see also entries for 1830, 1848, 1855, 1859) [Dobson, p.104; NCRO (ZAN M12/B1, p.14)]

BEACONS, GUILE POINT, HOLY ISLAND, NORTHUMBERLAND, for Trinity House, Newcastle, 1829-30 [TWA (GU/TH/21/32)]

ST. MARY'S PLACE, NEWCASTLE UPON TYNE, Tudor-style terrace, from 1829 [*NCh*, 6 Jun 1829; *NC*, 20 Mar 1830]

1830-34

GOSFORTH PARK (HOUSE), NEWCASTLE UPON TYNE, additions, including entrance gates, to James Paine's 18th-century house, for Ralph Brandling, 1830; house altered 1881 and, following a fire, after 1921 [*NDJ*, 16 Jan 1865]

ST. ANDREW'S, BYWELL, NORTHUMBERLAND, alterations, 1830 (see also entry for 1850) [Pevsner 1992, p.204]

ST. JOHN'S, NEWCASTLE UPON TYNE, repairs or restoration, 1830 (see also entries for 1829, 1848, 1855, 1859) [NCRO (ZAN M12/B1, pp.26,34)]

ST. MARY'S, STAMFORDHAM, NORTHUMBERLAND, restoration, 1830, largely rebuilt by B. Ferrey, 1848-49 (see also entry for 1848) [Dobson, p.104]

ST. NICHOLAS'S, WEST BOLDON, TYNE AND WEAR (D), addition of gallery, 1830 [*NC*, 31 Jul 1830]

THE HERMITAGE, ACOMB, NORTHUMBERLAND, additions or alterations to 17th- and 18th-century house, for Robert Allgood, 1830 [plans and elevations in NCRO (ZALM/6)]

WATERGATE BUILDING, SANDHILL, NEWCASTLE UPON TYNE, 1830 [*NC*, 19 Jun 1830]

BURNHOPESIDE HALL, LANCHESTER, COUNTY DURHAM, classical house, c.1830 [stylistic attribution, N. Pevsner and E. Williamson, *The Buildings of England: County Durham*, 1983, p.352]

GALLOWSHAW RIGG, NORTHUMBERLAND, house for Sir Edward Blackett, Bt., c.1830 (?) [*NDJ*, 16 Jan 1865; drawing in NCRO (ZBL 269/72)]

HIGH CROSS HOUSE, BENWELL, NEWCASTLE UPON TYNE, house for Mr. Buddle, c.1830, dem. c.1907 [*NDJ*, 16 Jan 1865]

TOLL HOUSE, BARRAS BRIDGE, NEWCASTLE UPON TYNE, Tudor, c.1830, dem. [*NDJ*, 16 Jan 1865]

BENWELL TOWER, NEWCASTLE UPON TYNE, rebuilt as castellated Tudor-Gothic house for Thomas Crawhall, 1830-31; chapel added 1881, house becoming Bishop's Residence, now a public house [*NDJ*, 16 Jan 1865; *AA*, 3rd series, vol. xix, 1922, pp.89-98; drawings in Laing Art Gallery, Newcastle upon Tyne]

BRINKBURN PRIORY HOUSE, NORTHUMBERLAND, large additions to house of c.1800, including west range, and bow window on east side, for Major William Hodgson-Cadogan, 1830-37 [*NDJ*, 16 Jan 1865; drawing in Laing Art Gallery, Newcastle upon Tyne]

BRINKBURN PRIORY, NORTHUMBERLAND, minor repairs to ruined priory for Major William Hodgson-Cadogan, 1830s, building fully restored by Thomas Austin, 1858-59 [A.B.E. Clark, *Brinkburn Priory, Northumberland* (English Heritage Guide), 2nd edn., 1992, p.21]

NORTH ELSWICK HALL, NEWCASTLE UPON TYNE, house for B. Johnson, 1830s (?) [*NDJ*, 16 Jan 1865]

NORTH SEATON HALL, NORTHUMBERLAND, estate buildings, probably for William Watson jnr., 1831, evidently including Gothic workers' cottages and perhaps a Gothic lodge, all dem. c.1960 [*NC*, 21 May 1831]

SCHOOL, HENDON, SUNDERLAND, TYNE AND WEAR (D), 1831, dem. [Fordyce, II, p.466]

CASTLETOWN HOUSE, ROCKCLIFFE, CUMBRIA, alterations, for R. Mounsey, 1831 (?) (see also entry for 1847) [*NDJ*, 16 Jan 1865; *CL*, 7 Sep 1989, pp.134-39]

WYNYARD PARK, CLEVELAND (D), unspecified work (alterations?), for Lord Londonderry, c.1831 (see also entry for 1838) [*NDJ*, 16 Jan 1865; *CL*, 4 Sep 1986, p.666]

ROYAL ARCADE, NEWCASTLE UPON TYNE, classical, for Richard Grainger, 1831-32, dem. 1963-69 [Dobson, p.119; drawings in Laing Art Gallery, Newcastle upon Tyne, and Private Collection]

ST. JAMES'S, BENWELL, NEWCASTLE UPON TYNE, neo-Norman, 1831-32, much enlarged 1864, 1879-80, 1895 [*NC*, 16 Apr 1831; ICBS (No. 1328); NCRO (ZAN M12/B1); drawings in RIBA (RAN/1/E/4/1-4)]

CHESTERS, NORTHUMBERLAND, additions, including arcade to north entrance and perhaps central doorway on south side, to John Carr's 18th-century house, for John Clayton, 1832 (and 1837), remodelled and enlarged by R. Norman Shaw, 1891-93 [Dobson, p.87; *AA*, 4th series, vol. xxxvi, 1958, pp.221-26]

DARLINGTON, COUNTY DURHAM, house for J. Wilson, 1832 [*NDJ*, 16 Jan 1865]

MELDON PARK, NORTHUMBERLAND, classical house for Isaac Cookson, 1832 [*NDJ*, 16 Jan 1865; drawings in Laing Art Gallery, Newcastle upon Tyne]

SCHOOL, STAMFORDHAM, NORTHUMBERLAND, Tudor, 1832 [Dobson, p.115]

WHITBURN HALL, TYNE AND WEAR (D), alterations and additions to 17th- and 18th-century house, for Sir Hedworth Williamson, Bt., 1832 (and 1856), dem. 1980 [*NDJ*, 16 Jan 1865; illustrated in Meadows and Waterson, p.38]

BLENKINSOPP CASTLE, NORTHUMBERLAND, addition of mine agent's house, castellated, c.1832, rebuilt by W. Glover, 1877-80 [Pevsner 1992, pp.192-93]

ST. NICHOLAS'S, NEWCASTLE UPON TYNE, underpinning of tower, also addition with J. Green of north-west and south-west porches, 1832-34 (see also entries for 1817, 1823-24, 1827, 1859, 1862) [Sykes, II, p.345; *The Builder*, vol. i, p.229; *AA*, 4th series, vol. ix, 1932, pp.142-44]

CULLERCOATS, TYNE AND WEAR (N), building sites for sale to elevations by Dobson, 1833 [*NCh*, 16 Nov 1833]

BAPTIST CHAPEL, TUTHILL STAIRS, NEWCASTLE UPON TYNE, repairs and alterations to Elizabethan dwelling used as chapel, 1834, dem. [*NDJ*, 16 Jan 1865]

CHAPEL AT HOWDON DENE, TYNE AND WEAR (N), 1834 [*NDJ*, 16 Jan 1865]

GENERAL CEMETERY, GATESHEAD, TYNE AND WEAR (D), 1834 [*NC*, 11 Oct 1834]

HIGH WARDEN, HEXHAM, NORTHUMBERLAND, additions, for John Errington, 1834, house recently reduced in size [Dobson, p.89]

ST. CUTHBERT'S (RC), COWPEN, NR. BLYTH, NORTHUMBERLAND, Gothic, 1834 [*NDJ*, 16 Jan 1865]

STAMFORDHAM (OLD) VICARAGE, NORTHUMBERLAND, additions, c.1834 and/or 1847 [Dobson, p.115; Pevsner 1992, p.576]

MARKETS, NEWCASTLE UPON TYNE, Vegetable and Butcher Market, including street frontages (?), for Richard Grainger, 1834-35 [drawings in Laing Art Gallery, Newcastle upon Tyne]

GENERAL CEMETERY, NEWCASTLE UPON TYNE, classical lodges, gates, etc. 1834-36 [*NC*, 29 Mar 1834; Prospectus with engraving of initial proposal in TWA (DT/NGC/5)]

GREY STREET, NEWCASTLE UPON TYNE, east side between Shakespeare Street and Mosley Street, for Richard Grainger, 1834-37 [drawings in Laing Art Gallery, Newcastle upon Tyne, Getty Museum, California, and Private Collection]

NEASHAM HALL, COUNTY DURHAM, large Elizabethan-style additions to 18th-century house, for Col. James Cookson, 1834-37, further extended 1904, dem. 1970 [*NDJ*, 16 Jan 1865; illustrated in Meadows and Waterson, p.66]

1835-39

HOUSE OF CORRECTION, TYNEMOUTH, TYNE AND WEAR (N), additions, 1835 [*NC*, 31 Jan 1835]

MONKWEARMOUTH, TYNE AND WEAR (D), planning development of Monkwearmouth Shore and new road from bridge to North Quay, for Sir Hedworth Williamson, Bt., 1835 [*NJ*, 3 Oct 1835]

MORPETH, NORTHUMBERLAND, bridge at Low Ford, 1835 [*NC*, 2 May 1835]

ST. ANDREW'S, HARTBURN, NORTHUMBERLAND, addition of west gallery for an organ, 1835 [*NDJ*, 16 Jan 1865]

BLENKINSOPP HALL, NORTHUMBERLAND, large additions, including south-east tower, to early 19th-century house, for Col. J.B. Coulson, c.1835, substantial later additions c.1877-80; partly removed mid 20th century [*NDJ*, 16 Jan 1865; NCRO (ZAN M.13/F.13, pp.26-27)]

GREY MONUMENT, NEWCASTLE UPON TYNE, unsuccessful proposal, 1836 [*NC*, 20 Feb 1836]

POLICE OFFICES etc., MANOR CHARE, NEWCASTLE UPON TYNE, 1836 [*NC*, 23 Apr 1836]

RAILWAY STATION, LONDON ROAD, CARLISLE, CUMBRIA, Tudor, for the Newcastle and Carlisle Railway, 1836, dem. [Dobson, p.118]

SUNDERLAND AND DURHAM JOINT STOCK BANK, MOSLEY STREET, NEWCASTLE UPON TYNE, 1836 [Dobson, p.120]

TYNE TO DUNBAR RAILWAY, prospectus issued by Dobson, Matthias Dunn and Robert Hawthorn, 1836 [W.W. Tomlinson, *The North Eastern Railway, its Rise and Development*, 1915, p.292.]

ELLISON SCHOOLS, GATESHEAD, TYNE AND WEAR (D), Tudor, 1836-37, dem. [*NCh*, 15 Oct 1836]

HOLY TRINITY, GATESHEAD, TYNE AND WEAR (D), formerly St. Edmund's Chapel, restoration, 1836-37, greatly enlarged by S. Piper 1893 [*NCh*, 15 Oct 1836; ICBS (No. 1969)]

COACHMAKERS' MANUFACTORY, NEWCASTLE UPON TYNE, for Messrs. Atkinson and Philipson, 1837, dem. c.1920 [*NDJ*, 16 Jan 1865]

HOLME EDEN, WARWICK BRIDGE, CUMBRIA, Tudor-Gothic house for Peter Dixon jnr., 1837 [*NDJ*, 16 Jan 1865; drawings in Private Collection, and RIBA (G6/38/1-3)]

QUAYSIDE, NEWCASTLE UPON TYNE, new quay of 1000 feet from Broad Chare to the Swirle, 1837 [*NC*, 25 Aug 1837; T.L. Donaldson, *Handbook of Specifications*, 1860, Part II, pp.824-30]

SAVINGS BANK, HEXHAM, NORTHUMBERLAND, classical, 1837 [*NC*, 7 Jul 1837]

WILLIAMSON MONUMENT, ST. NICHOLAS'S, NEWCASTLE UPON TYNE, monument to R.H. Williamson, classical, 1837 [*NC*, 23 Jun 1837]

MONKWEARMOUTH, TYNE AND WEAR (D), dock office, North Dock, for Sir Hedworth Williamson, Bt., c.1837, dem. [T. Corfe (ed.), *The Buildings of Sunderland 1814-1914*, 1983, p.18]

BEAUFRONT CASTLE, HEXHAM, NORTHUMBERLAND, Tudor-Gothic house for William Cuthbert, incorporating an earlier house, 1837-39; [*NC*, 11 Mar 1837; drawings in Laing Art Gallery, Newcastle upon Tyne]

PUBLIC BATHS, NORTHUMBERLAND ROAD, NEWCASTLE UPON TYNE, 1837-39, dem. [*NJ*, 25 May 1839]

ST. MICHAEL'S, ALWINTON, NORTHUMBERLAND, restoration, 1838 [*NDJ*, 16 Jan 1865]

SOUTH SHIELDS, TYNE AND WEAR (D), steam ferry stations and approaches, with Robert Wilson, engineer, 1838 [DCRO (G/D/P43)]

TYNEMOUTH, TYNE AND WEAR, "CROWN HOTEL, BATHS, ETC.", 1838 [*NC*, 2 Nov 1830]

WYNYARD PARK, CLEVELAND (D), unidentified work (alterations?), following final dismissal of Philip Wyatt by Lord Londonderry, 1838 (see also entry for c.1831) [*NDJ*, 16 Jan 1865; correspondence and accounts in DCRO (D/Lo/C331)]

CRASTER TOWER, NORTHUMBERLAND, minor alterations to medieval and 18th-century house, including bay window on east side, for Thomas Wood-Craster, 1839 [*NDJ*, 16 Jan 1865; drawings in NCRO (ZCR Maps 55)]

DISPENSARY, NELSON STREET, NEWCASTLE UPON TYNE, classical, 1839 [*NDJ*, 16 Jan 1865]

GAOL, CARLIOL SQUARE, NEWCASTLE UPON TYNE, minor additions, 1839, dem. c.1929 (see also entries for 1822-28, 1859-61) [*NC*, 24 May 1839]

TYNEMOUTH, TYNE AND WEAR (N), crescent and villas, for Messrs. Dawson and Bowes, 1839 [*NA*, 2 Feb, 1 Jun 1839]

WILLIAM CLARK MONUMENT, ST. AIDAN'S, BAMBURGH, NORTHUMBERLAND, Gothic, 1839 [*Durham Chronicle*, 21 Sep 1839]

MARKET HOUSE, NEVILLE STREET, NEWCASTLE UPON TYNE, classical cattle market office and toll house, 1839-40, internally much altered after occupation by Barclay's Bank later in the 19th century, now part of the Centre for Life [*NDJ*, 16 Jan 1865; *AA*, 5th series, vol. xxv, 1997, pp.125-40]

1840-44

ASYLUM FOR THE BLIND, NORTHUMBERLAND STREET, NEWCASTLE UPON TYNE, classical, 1840, dem. [*NDJ*, 16 Jan 1865]

CARLISLE, CUMBRIA, house for H. Bendle, perhaps in Victoria Place, 1840 [*NDJ*, 16 Jan 1865]

CHAPEL, ELSWICK, NEWCASTLE UPON TYNE, unbuilt design for Richard Grainger, classical, 1840 [ICBS (No. 2421, referring to what appears to have been an earlier version of the scheme, of 1838); drawings dated 1840 in Library, University of Newcastle upon Tyne]

EAST BOLDON HOUSE (FRONT STREET), TYNE AND WEAR (D), minor alterations, for William Gray, 1840 [*NDJ*, 16 Jan 1865]

GATESHEAD, TYNE AND WEAR (D), viaduct for Brandling Junction Railway Co., 1840 [*NDJ*, 16 Jan 1865]

LINETHWAITE, BEDALE, CUMBRIA, house for H. Harrison, 1840 [*NDJ*, 16 Jan 1865]

MOOR HOUSE, RAINTON, COUNTY DURHAM, classical house for George Roper (?), 1840, dem. [Dobson, p.89]

SWINBURNE CASTLE, NORTHUMBERLAND, alterations (?), for Thomas Riddell, 1840, largely dem. c.1966 [Dobson, p.89; illustrated in Faulkner and Lowery, pp.61-62]

CARLISLE, CUMBRIA (?), proposed Tudor-Gothic railway station for the Newcastle and Carlisle Railway Co., c.1840, not carried out [RIBA Drawings Collection (G6/39)]

ELSWICK, NEWCASTLE UPON TYNE, staithe for Elswick Lead Works, c.1840 [*NDJ*, 16 Jan 1865]

JESMOND HIGH TERRACE, NEWCASTLE UPON TYNE, classical terrace, c.1840, dem. 1960s [Dobson, p.124]

LITTLE HARLE TOWER, NORTHUMBERLAND, unexecuted designs for classical additions to earlier house, for Thomas Anderson, c.1840 [drawings in NCRO (660/18)]

ST. MARY'S TERRACE, NEWCASTLE UPON TYNE, c.1840 [Dobson, p.124]

ST. THOMAS'S PLACE, NEWCASTLE UPON TYNE, classical terrace, c.1840, dem. 1960s [*NDJ*, 16 Jan 1865]

SUDBROOKE HOLME, LINCOLNSHIRE, Tudor-style estate cottage, for Richard Ellison, c.1840 (?) [J.C. Loudon, *An Encylopaedia of Cottage, Farm and Villa Architecture and Furniture* (first additional supplement to 1st edn. of 1833), 1842, pp.1185-86]

BATHS, TERRACE AND HOTEL, ROKER TERRACE, MONKWEARMOUTH, TYNE AND WEAR (D), classical, 1840-41 [*NC*, 17 Apr 1840; Fordyce, II, p.422]

ST. PETER'S, OXFORD STREET, NEWCASTLE UPON TYNE, Gothic, 1840-43, dem. c.1936 (see also entry for 1860) [*NC*, 11 Mar 1842; ground plan in ICBS (No. 2459)]

JESMOND ROAD, NEWCASTLE UPON TYNE, houses, including Carlton Terrace (nos. 29-49) for "Mr. Grey and Mr. Maughan" and others c.1840-45; some dem. [*NC*, 16 Aug 1839; *NCh*, 7 Aug 1841; *NDJ*, 16 Jan 1865]

BROAD CHARE, NEWCASTLE UPON TYNE, warehouses for Trinity House, possibly in conjunction with Thomas or Andrew Oliver, or merely acting as agent, 1841 (see also entry for 1841-42) [*NC*, 26 Mar 1841; TWA (GU/TH/21/22); *AA*, 5th series, vol. xiii, 1985, p.180]

CHEESEBURN GRANGE, NORTHUMBERLAND, addition (?) of chapel (RC), for Ralph Riddell, 1841; additions by J.A. Hansom, c.1860, the latter, and the chapel, dem. (see also entries for c.1813, 1818) [Dobson, p.106; Pevsner 1992, p.218]

ST. OSWALD'S, ARNCLIFFE, WEST YORKSHIRE, alterations, 1841 [Dobson, p.107; but work also attributed to A. Salvin in N. Pevsner (revised E. Ratcliffe), *The Buildings of England: Yorkshire, the West Riding*, 1967, p.614]

ST. PATRICK'S (RC), FELLING, TYNE AND WEAR (D), Gothic, 1841, rebuilt by C. Walker, 1893-95 [*NCh*, 5 Jun 1841]

ST. THOMAS OF CANTERBURY (RC), LONGHORSLEY, NORTHUMBERLAND, Gothic, 1841, [Dobson, p.106]

SCHOOL, BARRASFORD, NORTHUMBERLAND, Tudor, 1841 (now a private residence) [Dobson, p.115; F. Atkinson, *Victorian Britain: The North East*, 1989, p.215]

TRINITY HOUSE, BROAD CHARE, NEWCASTLE UPON TYNE, alterations, 1841-42 (see also entry for 1841) [TWA (GU/TH/21/22); *AA*, 5th series, vol. xiii, 1985, p.180]

ANGERTON HALL, NORTHUMBERLAND, Tudor house for Ralph Atkinson, 1842 (see also two entries for 1828); house substantially reduced 1957 [*NJ*, 15 Jan 1842]

COLLINGWOOD MONUMENT, TYNEMOUTH, TYNE AND WEAR (N), classical, 1842, statue by J.G. Lough (see also entry for 1849) [*NC*, 28 Jan 1842]

ST. NICHOLAS'S, WEST BOLDON, TYNE AND WEAR (D), restoration, 1842 [*NDJ*, 16 Jan 1865]

ST. MARY AND ST. JOSEPH'S (RC), BIRTLEY, TYNE AND WEAR (D), Gothic, 1842-43 [*NC*, 20 May 1842]

ST. MARY AND ST. JOSEPH'S PRESBYTERY AND SCHOOL, BIRTLEY, TYNE AND WEAR (D), Tudor, 1842-43, school largely dem. [*NC*, 20 May 1842]

BAMBURGH CASTLE, NORTHUMBERLAND, restoration, for Lord Crewe's Trustees, 1843, castle substantially remodelled 1894-1904 [Dobson, p.90]

BIRTLEY HALL, TYNE AND WEAR (D), house for J. Warwick, 1843, dem. c.1916 except for lodge on Durham Road [*NDJ*, 16 Jan 1865; illustrated in Meadows and Waterson, p.29]

CHAPEL (RC), MINSTERACRES, NORTHUMBERLAND, for George Silvertop, 1843, replaced by new chapel by J.A. Hansom, 1852-54 (see also entry for 1816) [Dobson, p.107; Pevsner 1992, p.390]

HARTBURN VICARAGE, NORTHUMBERLAND, alterations, for Rev. J. Hodgson, 1843 [Dobson, p.115]

HIGH LEVEL BRIDGE, NEWCASTLE UPON TYNE, unexecuted proposal, 1843 [*NC*, 22 Dec 1843; *Proceedings of the Newcastle Council*, 20 Dec 1843, p.20; submitted drawings in TWA (285/290) and DCRO (Q/D/P133)]

ST. MARY'S, MORPETH, NORTHUMBERLAND, restoration of nave, 1843 [*NDJ*, 16 Jan 1865]

THE HAGS, HEXHAM, NORTHUMBERLAND, Tudor-style house for Charles Head, 1843 [*NDJ*, 16 Jan 1865]

SANDHOE HOUSE, HEXHAM, NORTHUMBERLAND, Tudor-style house for Sir R.S. Errington, Bt., 1843-45 [*NC*, 14 Feb 1845; *NDJ*, 16 Jan 1865]

REED MONUMENT, JESMOND CEMETERY, NEWCASTLE UPON TYNE, Gothic, 1843-46 [*NC*, 23 Jun 1837]

LILBURN TOWER, NORTHUMBERLAND, alterations to Dobson's 1828-29 house, for Edward John Collingwood, c.1843-44 (see also entry for 1828-29) [*CL*, 8 Nov 1973, p.1442]

CARLISLE, CUMBRIA, proposed railway station for the Maryport and Carlisle Railway Company in Crown Street, 1844, not carried out [*The Railway Magazine*, Aug 1963, p.576]

HOSPITAL OF ST. MARY THE VIRGIN, NEWCASTLE UPON TYNE, proposed restoration, 1844, not carried out [Minutes of the Newcastle Council, 1844, Introduction, p.xviii]

ST. ANDREW'S, NEWCASTLE UPON TYNE, addition of south transept, neo-Norman, 1844 [*NDJ*, 16 Jan 1865; NCRO (ZAN M13/F12, p.82)]

HAUGHTON CASTLE, NORTHUMBERLAND, restorations, probably including the bay windows in the centre of the north and south fronts, for William Smith, 1844-45; further restorations and additions by A. Salvin, 1876 [*NDJ*, 16 Jan 1865; *History of Northumberland*, XV, 1940, p.214]

TOWN HALL, NORTH SHIELDS, TYNE AND WEAR (N), originally included police offices, museum, bank and Mechanics' Institution (enclosing J. and B. Green's 1837 former Poor Law Guardians' Hall), Tudor, 1844-45; building is now Council Offices and Magistrates' Court [*NC*, 28 Mar 1845; Pevsner 1992, p.527]

1845-49
BANK HOUSE, NEWBIGGIN, MIDDLETON-IN-TEESDALE, COUNTY DURHAM, for John Hodgson Hinde, 1845 [Dobson, p.92]

CHATTON VICARAGE (NOW 'LONGSTONE HOUSE'), NORTHUMBERLAND, incorporating a 'pele tower', for Rev. Matthew Burrell, 1845 [*NC*, 10 Jan 1845; drawings in NCRO (1875/C); NCRO (ZAN/Bell/B1/61/1)]

CLEADON COTTAGE, NR. SOUTH SHIELDS, TYNE AND WEAR (D), classical house for Robert Swinburne, 1845, used as a hospital 1921-78, dem. c.1981 [Dobson, p.91; illustrated in Meadows and Waterson, p.37]

THE KNELLS, HOUGHTON, NR. CARLISLE, CUMBRIA, alterations (?) to classical house, for John Dixon, 1845 [*NDJ*, 16 Jan 1865]

ST. PAUL'S, WARWICK BRIDGE, CUMBRIA, neo-Norman, for Peter Dixon jnr., 1845 [*NDJ*, 16 Jan 1865]

ST. PAUL'S VICARAGE, WARWICK BRIDGE, CUMBRIA, Tudor, c.1845 [attributed on grounds of style, and proximity to building in previous entry]

ST. CUTHBERT'S, BENSHAM, TYNE AND WEAR (D), neo-Norman, 1845-48, north aisle added 1875 [*NC*, 28 Mar 1845; ICBS (No. 3581); plans and specifications in Society of Antiquaries, London]

BAPTIST CHAPEL, HOWARD STREET, NORTH SHIELDS, TYNE AND WEAR (N), neo-Norman, 1846 [*NDJ*, 16 Jan 1865]

CULLERCOATS, TYNE AND WEAR (N), rebuilding of breakwater, 1846 [*NC*, 27 Nov 1846]

REFORMATORY, NETHERTON, NORTHUMBERLAND, possibly identifiable with School, 1846 (?) [Dobson, p.130; Pevsner, 1992, p.402]

SETTRINGTON VICARAGE, NORTH YORKSHIRE, for Rev. C.M. Long, 1846 [*NDJ*, 16 Jan 1865]

TRINITY PRESBYTERIAN CHURCH, NEW BRIDGE STREET, NEWCASTLE UPON TYNE, Gothic, 1846-47, dem. [*NC*, 21 Aug 1846]

ALL SAINTS', FULWELL ROAD, MONKWEARMOUTH, TYNE AND WEAR (D), Gothic, 1846-49 [*NC*, 3 Jul 1846]

CENTRAL RAILWAY STATION, NEWCASTLE UPON TYNE, classical, for York, Newcastle and Berwick Railway Co., and Newcastle and Carlisle Railway Co., 1846-50, portico added 1862-63, station extended 1892-94 (see also entry for 1862) [*NC*, 15 Jan 1847; T.L. Donaldson, *Handbook of Specifications*, 1860, Part II, pp.842-66; drawings in Laing Art Gallery, Newcastle upon Tyne, and with Railtrack (Eastern)]

STATION, HALF MOON LANE, GATESHEAD, TYNE AND WEAR (D), railway station for York, Newcastle and Berwick Railway Co., 1846; construction delayed, building not completed until 1851, dem. [*NC*, 27 Apr 1849, 30 Aug 1850]

CHOLLERTON OLD VICARAGE, NORTHUMBERLAND, additions to house of c.1830 also by Dobson (?), 1847, for Christopher Bird jnr. [Pevsner 1992, p.233; drawings NCRO (1875/C)]

RIDING SCHOOL, NEWCASTLE UPON TYNE, classical, 1847, now converted into teaching accommodation for the University of Northumbria [*NDJ*, 16 Jan 1865]

ST. AUGUSTINE'S, ALSTON, CUMBRIA, restoration, 1847, rebuilt 1869-70 [Dobson, p.109]

ST. MARY AND ST. THOMAS AQUINAS (RC), STELLA, TYNE AND WEAR (D), additions, Gothic, 1847 [*NDJ*, 16 Jan 1865]

SCAR HOUSE, ARKENGARTHDALE, NORTH YORKSHIRE, Tudor-style house for Rev. John Gilpin, 1847 [*NDJ*, 16 Jan 1865; J. Hatcher, *Richmondshire Architecture*, 2nd edn., 1999, p.6]

CASTLETOWN HOUSE, ROCKCLIFFE, CUMBRIA, alterations, for George Gill Mounsey, 1847 (?) (see also entry for 1831) [*NDJ*, 16 Jan 1865; *CL*, 7 Sep 1989, pp.134-39]

CASTLE KEEP, NEWCASTLE, restoration, for Society of Antiquaries of Newcastle upon Tyne, 1847-48 [*NDJ*, 16 Jan 1865; *The Builder*, vol. xvii, 1859, p.583; *AA*, new series, vol. xi, 1886, p.177]

FLAX MILL, NEWCASTLE UPON TYNE, for R. Plummer, 1847-48, now converted to institutional use [*NC*, 6 Jan 1849]

NORTH SHIELDS, TYNE AND WEAR (N), warehouse for North Shields and Tynemouth Railway, 1848 [*NCh*, 16 May 1848]

QUAYSIDE, NEWCASTLE UPON TYNE, proposed new quay, Customs House, warehouses, etc., in collaboration with J. and B. Green and Mr. Brook (engineer to the Corporation), 1848 [*NC*, 28 Jul 1848]

ST. ANDREW'S, WINSTON, COUNTY DURHAM, restoration, 1848 [*NDJ*, 16 Jan 1865]

ST. JOHN'S, NEWCASTLE UPON TYNE, restoration, 1848 (see also entries for 1829, 1830, 1855, 1859) [*NC*, 2 Jul 1847]

ST. MARY'S, STAMFORDHAM, NORTHUMBERLAND, restoration and additions, probably in conjunction with B. Ferrey, 1848 (see also entry for 1830) [*NC*, 21 Apr 1848; ICBS (No. 3971)]

WELTON, NORTHUMBERLAND, Tudor-style Keeper's Cottage and Directors' Rooms for Whittle Dene Water Company, 1848 [*NDJ*, 16 Jan 1865]

NORMAL SCHOOLS, SOUTH SHIELDS, TYNE AND WEAR (D), Tudor, for J. Stevenson, c.1848, dem. [*NDJ*, 16 Jan 1865]

PRESBYTERIAN CHURCH, FREDERICK STREET, SOUTH SHIELDS, TYNE AND WEAR (D), Gothic, for J. Stevenson, 1848-49, dem. 1977 [*NJ*, 2 Sep 1848]

ST. CUTHBERT'S, SHOTLEY BRIDGE, COUNTY DURHAM, Gothic, 1848-50, north aisle added 1881-86 by J.W. Walton [*NC*, 1 Sep 1848; Fordyce, II, p.699; ground plan in ICBS (No. 3384); contract plans in church]

COLLINGWOOD MONUMENT, TYNEMOUTH, TYNE AND WEAR (N), addition of pedestals for guns, 1849 (see also entry for 1842) [*NCh*, 9 Feb 1849]

GATESHEAD, TYNE AND WEAR (D), main sewer, 1849 [Manders, p.180; *AA*, 4th series, vol. xlix, 1971, p.153]

MANORS STATION AND GOODS WAREHOUSE, NEWCASTLE UPON TYNE, railway station, warehouse, and associated buildings, for York, Newcastle and Berwick Railway Co., 1849, station enlarged 1886-87, all dem. [*NC*, 27 Apr 1849; T.L. Donaldson, *Handbook of Specifications*, 1860, Part II, pp.831-41.]

ST. JOHN THE BAPTIST'S, MELDON, NORTHUMBERLAND, restoration, 1849 [*NDJ*, 16 Jan 1865]

ST. MICHAEL'S, BISHOPWEARMOUTH, TYNE AND WEAR (D), addition of transepts, Gothic, 1849-50, church further reconstructed by A. Caroe, 1933-35 [*NCh*, 6 Jul 1849; plans in ICBS (No. 4148) and DCRO (EP/Biw866)]

1850-54

HOLY TRINITY, EMBLETON, NORTHUMBERLAND, restoration 1850, chancel added 1866-67 by F.R. Wilson [*NDJ*, 16 Jan 1865; *NJ*, 27 Sep 1887; ICBS (No. 3921)]

ST. ANDREW'S, BYWELL, NORTHUMBERLAND, alterations, 1850 (see also entry for 1830) [Pevsner 1992, p.204]

SCHOOLS, LYMM, CHESHIRE, 1850 [Dobson, p.116]

STOCKTON-ON-TEES, VICARAGE, CLEVELAND (D), 1850 [*NDJ*, 16 Jan 1865; DCRO (Queen Anne's Bounty Mortgage Papers, 39)]

BYWELL, NORTHUMBERLAND, cottages and schools for W.R. Beaumont, c.1850 [*NDJ*, 16 Jan 1865]

ELLISON MONUMENT, DONCASTER PARISH CHURCH, SOUTH YORKSHIRE, for R. Ellison, c.1850, evidently destroyed with church in fire of 1853; church later rebuilt by G.G. Scott, 1854-58 [*NDJ*, 16 Jan 1865]

GRESHAM PLACE, NEWCASTLE UPON TYNE, classical villa for James Morrison, c.1850, dem. [*NC*, 29 May 1857]

TYNEMOUTH, TYNE AND WEAR (N), Prior's Terrace, including house for Mr. Lawton, c.1850 [*NDJ*, 16 Jan 1865]

NEWCASTLE UPON TYNE, ST. PETER'S SHIPYARD, graving-dock for Messrs. T. & W. Smith, c.1850 or before [*The Builder*, vol. xxiii, 1865, p.28]

BARBER-SURGEONS' HALL, VICTORIA STREET, NEWCASTLE UPON TYNE, Italianate, 1850-51 [*NC*, 4 Oct 1850]

LYMM PARISH CHURCH, CHESHIRE, rebuilding, 1850-51; church subsequently rebuilt 1887-90 [*The Builder*, vol. ix, 1851, p.631; ICBS (No. 4315)]

BENFIELDSIDE VICARAGE, COUNTY DURHAM, Tudor, 1851 [*NJ*, 11 Jan 1851; DCRO (Queen Anne's Bounty Mortgage Papers, 38)]

BRICKLAYERS' HALL, CASTLE GARTH, NEWCASTLE UPON TYNE, Gothic, 1851, dem. [*NJ*, 22 Nov 1851]

CHURCH HOUSE, WINDSOR, BERKSHIRE, for Rev. Dr. Stephen Hawtrey, 1851 [*NDJ*, 16 Jan 1865]

DENE HOUSE, JESMOND, NEWCASTLE UPON TYNE, Dobson's house of 1818 rebuilt for Thomas (?) Cruddas, 1851, again rebuilt, in stages, by R. Norman Shaw, 1870-85, additions by F.W. Rich, 1896-97 (see also entry for 'Black Dene House', 1818) [Dobson, p.94]

MANBY HOUSE, WARRINGTON, CHESHIRE, additions, 1851 [Dobson, p.92]

NEWTON HALL (NOW MOWDEN HALL SCHOOL), BYWELL, NORTHUMBERLAND, alterations to 18th-century house, for W.H. Blackett, 1851, subsequently altered [Dobson, p.93]

OATLANDS HOUSE, WEYBRIDGE, SURREY, Tudor-style house for William Chapman Hewitson, 1851, dem. 1972 [*NDJ*, 16 Jan 1865]

PENNYTHORNE HOUSE, MIDDLESBROUGH, CLEVELAND, house for A. Topham, 1851 [*NDJ*, 16 Jan 1865]

RYTON, TYNE AND WEAR (D), additions to house for Robert Leadbitter, 1851 [*NDJ*, 16 Jan 1865]

ST. MARY MAGDALENE'S, GILSLAND, CUMBRIA, Gothic, 1851; the site architect was Stewart of Carlisle [*NDJ*, 16 Jan 1865]

ST. MARY'S ALMSHOUSES, SCHOOL AND CHAPEL, RYE HILL, NEWCASTLE UPON TYNE, Gothic, 1851, unexecuted design; buildings as executed were by B. Green, completed by J. Green jnr., 1856-59, some dem. [*NCh*, 22 Aug 1851]

STATION HOTEL, NEVILLE STREET, NEWCASTLE UPON TYNE, classical, 1851, later extended by Thomas Prosser, 1861-63, and by William Bell, 1892-94 [*NC*, 11 Jul 1851]

SUDBROOKE HOLME, LINCOLNSHIRE, large Tudor-style additions for Col. Richard Ellison, 1851, dem. [*NDJ*, 16 Jan 1865]

CHRIST CHURCH, COWPEN, NR. BLYTH, NORTHUMBERLAND, Gothic, 1851-52 [ICBS (No. 4401)]

ST. PAUL'S, HENDON, SUNDERLAND, TYNE AND WEAR (D), Gothic, 1851-52, dem. c.1970 (see also entry for 1860) [*NC*, 20 Jun 1851; ground plan in ICBS (No. 4342)]

THE LEAZES, HEXHAM, NORTHUMBERLAND, Tudor-style additions, etc., to house for William Kirsopp, 1851-53 [Dobson, p.95]

MONKWEARMOUTH, TYNE AND WEAR (D), planning and design of 400 houses in Ann Street, Barrington Street, Bloomfield Street, Dame Dorothy Street, Dock Street, Hardwicke Street, Milburn Place, Millum Terrace, Mulgrave Street and Normanby Street for Sir Hedworth Williamson, Bt., 1851-57, dem. [Fordyce, II, p.480]

COLLEGE OF MEDICINE, ORCHARD STREET, NEWCASTLE UPON TYNE, Tudor, 1852, dem. c.1889 [*NC*, 14 May 1852]

DILDAWN HOUSE, DUMFRIES AND GALLOWAY, house for Rev. Dr. Cowan, 1852 [*NDJ*, 16 Jan 1865]

FRIEDELHAUSEN, HESSEN, GERMANY, designs for Gothic castle for Adalbeit, Baron von Nordeck zur Rabenau, and his English wife, Clara Phillips, 1852, erected in altered form by the German architect Martin Unger, 1852-54 [drawings and correspondence in Hessisches Staatsarchiv, Marburg, Acc 1972/38, V,9, *ex inf.* A. Fowler]

PERCY CHAPEL, TYNEMOUTH PRIORY, TYNE AND WEAR (N), restoration, 1852 (see also entries for 1813, 1817) [*NCh*, 27 Aug 1852; *The Builder*, vol. xvi, 1858, p.194]

ST. PAUL'S RECTORY, HENDON, SUNDERLAND, TYNE AND WEAR (D), 1852, dem. [*NDJ*, 16 Jan 1865]

WESTMORELAND HOUSE, NEVILLE STREET, NEWCASTLE UPON TYNE, restoration in conjunction with building of Medical College, 1852, dem. c.1889 [*NDJ*, 16 Jan 1865]

SEATON BURN, NORTHUMBERLAND, Tudor cottages, c.1852 [drawing in Private Collection]

ST. MICHAEL'S, FORD, NORTHUMBERLAND, restoration, 1852-53 [*NDJ*, 16 Jan 1865; ICBS (No. 4455)]

ST. STEPHEN'S NATIONAL SCHOOL, MILE END ROAD, SOUTH SHIELDS, TYNE AND WEAR (D), for Rev. S. Brasher, 1852-53, dem. [*NC*, 27 Aug 1852; *The Builder*, vol. xi, 1853, p.167; plan in DCRO (E/SBP99)]

JOHN KNOX PRESBYTERIAN CHURCH, CLAYTON STREET WEST, NEWCASTLE UPON TYNE, Gothic, 1852-54, dem. c.1896 (see also entry for 1860) [*NC*, 24 Sep 1852; *The Builder*, vol. xii, 1854, p.425]

THE INFIRMARY, THE FORTH, NEWCASTLE UPON TYNE, alterations and new wing, 1852-55; dem. 1954 [G.H. Hume, *History of the Newcastle Infirmary*, 1906, pp.51-60; lithographed plan in NCRO (309/N2/25/7)]

BYKER LANE, NEWCASTLE UPON TYNE, planned new street nr. Byker Lane for manufactories and dwelling-houses in the area of St. Lawrence and St. Peter's Quay, 1853 [*NCh*, 4 Nov 1853]

CLEADON MEADOWS, NR. SOUTH SHIELDS, TYNE AND WEAR (D), house for Robert (or Richard) Shortridge, 1853, dem. [*NDJ*, 16 Jan 1865]

DIVINE UNITY CHURCH, NEW BRIDGE STREET, NEWCASTLE UPON TYNE, Gothic, 1853, dem. c.1936 [*NC*, 22 Apr 1853]

DOCKS, NEWCASTLE UPON TYNE, proposals made by Dobson and W. Brooks, C.E., 1853 [*NCh*, 2 Dec 1853]

HOLY CROSS CHURCH, CHATTON, NORTHUMBERLAND, restoration, 1853 [*NDJ*, 16 Jan 1865; illustration in NCRO (ZAN/Bell/B1/61/1)]

ST. MICHAEL'S RECTORY, BISHOPWEARMOUTH, TYNE AND WEAR (D), alterations to 18th-century house, 1853 [*NDJ*, 16 Jan 1865]

SCHOOL, WHIXLEY, NORTH YORKSHIRE, 1853 [Dobson, p.116]

THE CLOSE, NEWCASTLE UPON TYNE, rebuilding of warehouse destroyed by fire, 1853 [*NJ*, 16 Jul 1853]

WALLINGTON HALL, NORTHUMBERLAND, central hall, in courtyard of 17th- and 18th-century house, for Sir Walter Trevelyan, 1853-54 (see also entry for 1818) [*NDJ*, 16 Jan 1865; correspondence in Trevelyan Papers, University of Newcastle upon Tyne]

MUSEUM AND LIBRARY, WARRINGTON, CHESHIRE, classical, 1853; simplified version built, 1855-56 [Minutes of Warrington Council, 1853-54; drawings in Museum and Library, Warrington]

ARCHBOLD MONUMENT, ST. NICHOLAS'S, NEWCASTLE UPON TYNE, classical monument to James Archbold, 1854 [*NCh*, 21 Jul 1854]

RAGGED AND INDUSTRIAL SCHOOL, NEW ROAD, NEWCASTLE UPON TYNE, 1854, dem. (see also entry for 1858) [*NC*, 10 Mar 1854]

RECTORY PARK SCHOOLS, BISHOPWEARMOUTH, TYNE AND WEAR (D), Tudor, 1854, rebuilt by G.A. Middlemiss, dem. 1960s [*NC*, 14 Jul 1854]

ROYAL JUBILEE SCHOOL, CITY ROAD, NEWCASTLE UPON TYNE, "considerable alterations" to Dobson's 1810 building, 1854, dem. (see also entry for 1810) [*NCh*, 29 Dec 1854]

ST. MARY'S, GATESHEAD, TYNE AND WEAR (D), restoration after Quayside Fire, 1854-55, reconstructed 1980s [*NC*, 27 Oct 1854; *NCh*, 28 Sep 1855; *The Builder*, vol. xiii, 1855, p.477; Fordyce, II, p.760]

WEST VIEW CEMETERY, HARTLEPOOL, CLEVELAND (D), chapels and entrance, 1854-55, dem. [*NC*, 30 Jun 1854]

QUAYSIDE, NEWCASTLE UPON TYNE, plans for rebuilding after Quayside Fire, 1854-56 [*NC*, 27 Oct 1854, 4 Jul 1856; perspective in Laing Art Gallery, Newcastle upon Tyne]

1855-59

CASTLE KEEP, NEWCASTLE UPON TYNE, proposed conversion of Great Hall for museum, for Society of Antiquaries of Newcastle upon Tyne, 1855, not carried out [*Proc. Soc. Ant.*, vol. i, 1856, p.81]

ST. CUTHBERT'S SCHOOL, BENSHAM, TYNE AND WEAR (D), 1855 [*NC*, 5 Jan 1855]

ST. JOHN'S, NEWCASTLE UPON TYNE, refitting of chancel, involving oak panelling and railings designed by Dobson, 1855 (see also entries for 1829, 1830, 1848, 1859) [*NJ*, 27 Oct 1855]

SEGHILL VICARAGE, TYNE AND WEAR (N), Tudor, 1855 [*NC*, 20 Jul 1855]

WILLINGTON, COUNTY DURHAM, proposed new town, including streets, railway station, coal railway, market garden and parkland, for Viscount Boyne, 1855 [DCRO (D/Br/P117,118)]

ST. JOHN'S, OTTERBURN, NORTHUMBERLAND, Gothic, for Mrs. Askew and the Misses Davison, 1855-57 [*NCh*, 12 Oct 1855]

BLACK GATE AREA, NEWCASTLE UPON TYNE, proposed conversion of railway arches for museum use, with covered approach, for Society of Antiquaries of Newcastle upon Tyne, 1856, not carried out [*Proc. Soc. Ant.*, vol. i, 1856, p.85]

BLACK GATE, NEWCASTLE UPON TYNE, proposed conversion to museum, with new street frontage, Gothic, 1856, not carried out [*AA*, new series, vol. i, 1857, p.iii; *Proceedings of the Newcastle Council*, 12 Dec 1855 and 7 May 1856; watercolour in Private Collection]

GIBSIDE, TYNE AND WEAR (D), alterations to 17th-century house, for W. Hutt, M.P., 1856, house now ruinous (see also entries for 1814, c.1818) [*NDJ*, 16 Jan 1865]

LIVERPOOL, warehouses, 1856 [Dobson, p.126]

NATURAL HISTORY SOCIETY OF NORTHUMBERLAND, DURHAM AND NEWCASTLE UPON TYNE (Westgate Road, Newcastle upon Tyne), internal alterations, designed 1856, carried out by Thomas Austin, 1860 [T.R. Goddard, *History of the Natural History Society*, 1929, pp.65-67]

ST. COLUMBA'S PRESBYTERIAN CHURCH (NOW UNITED REFORMED), NORTHUMBERLAND SQUARE, NORTH SHIELDS, TYNE AND WEAR (N), Italianate, 1856-57 [*NC*, 22 Aug 1856; *The Builder*, vol. xiv, 1856, p.596]

WESLEYAN CHAPEL (UNITED FREE METHODIST CHURCH), HOWARD STREET, NORTH SHIELDS, TYNE AND WEAR (N), Italianate, 1856-57, now Council offices [Latimer, p.381; but also credited to B. Green in Pevsner 1992, p.527]

SUNDERLAND, TYNE AND WEAR (D), South Dock grain warehouse for George Hudson, 1856-58, dem. c.1989 [*NC*, 13 Jun 1856]

ST. NICHOLAS'S, CRAMLINGTON, NORTHUMBERLAND, proposed Gothic design, 1856, built in altered and enlarged form by Austin & Johnson, 1865-68 [*NDJ*, 16 Jan 1865; ICBS (No. 5137)]

CHATTON, NORTHUMBERLAND, alterations to 18th-century bridge, possibly involving the construction of "two [temporary?] wooden bridges over the Till", 1857 [*NC*, 23 Jan 1857; Pevsner 1992, p.217]

INGLETHORPE HALL, EMNETH, NORFOLK, Tudor-Gothic house for Charles Metcalfe, 1857 [*The Builder*, vol. xviii, 1860, p.12]

STATION HOTEL, LEEDS, WEST YORKSHIRE, 1857 [Dobson, p.118]

WHITBY, NORTH YORKSHIRE (WEST CLIFF), hotel, terrace and crescent, including East Terrace, and Royal Crescent, for George Hudson, 1857 [*NC*, 31 Jul 1857; site plan in Whitby Literary and Philosophical Society; drawing for elevation of Royal Crescent in North Yorkshire County Record Office, Northallerton (ZW (M) 8/20)]

ST. PAUL'S, ELSWICK, NEWCASTLE UPON TYNE, Gothic, 1857-59 [*NC*, 27 Nov 1857; *The Builder*, vol. xvii, 1859, p.796; ground plans in ICBS (No. 5050) and TWA (No. 530)]

LAMBTON CASTLE, COUNTY DURHAM, major structural repairs and rebuilding of I. Bonomi's early 19th-century house, for the 2nd Earl of Durham, 1857-62, completed by Sydney Smirke, 1862-66, partly dem. 1930 [*NC*, 9 Oct 1857; drawing in Laing Art Gallery, Newcastle upon Tyne]

HOLEYN HALL, WYLAM, NORTHUMBERLAND, large additions to slightly earlier 19th-century house, for Edward James, 1858 [*NDJ*, 16 Jan 1865]

HYLTON CASTLE, TYNE AND WEAR (D), survey for repairs, etc., for John Bowes, 1858 [DCRO (Gibside Estate Memo Book)]

NEWCASTLE COURANT OFFICE, GEORGE YARD, NEWCASTLE UPON TYNE, 1858, dem. [*NC*, 12 Feb 1858]

RAGGED AND INDUSTRIAL SCHOOL, NEW ROAD, NEWCASTLE UPON TYNE, additions to Dobson's 1854 building, 1858, dem. (see also entry for 1854) [*NC*, 10 Sep 1858; plans in TWA (719)]

ST. MICHAEL'S RECTORY, BISHOPWEARMOUTH, TYNE AND WEAR (D), installation of antique staircase,

1858 [*The Builder*, vol. xvi, 1858, p.319]

SHAWDON HALL, NORTHUMBERLAND, lodges and alterations for John Pawson, 1858 (see also entry for 1825) [*NDJ*, 16 Jan 1865; NCRO (530/20/478)]

ST. MICHAEL'S, HOUGHTON-LE-SPRING, COUNTY DURHAM, restoration, 1858-59 [*NC*, 12 Feb 1858; ICBS (No. 5071); plans in DCRO (EP/Ho694,695)]

PRIORY CHURCH OF ST. ANDREW, HEXHAM, NORTHUMBERLAND, restoration of choir and east end, partly in conjunction with A. Salvin, 1858-60 (see also entries for 1817, 1828) [Dobson, p.100; ground plan in ICBS (No. 5266)]

FREEMASONS' LODGE, MIDDLESBROUGH, CLEVELAND, classical, 1858-61, dem. [*The Builder*, vol. xix, 1861, p.84]

JESMOND PARISH CHURCH, NEWCASTLE UPON TYNE, Gothic, 1858-61, vestry added by R.J. Johnson, 1874 [*NJ*, 9 Apr 1859; *The Builder*, vol. xvii, 1859, p.796]

BLACK GATE, NEWCASTLE UPON TYNE, proposed conversion to museum, with new street frontage, Gothic, 1859, not carried out [*AA*, new series, vol. iv, 1860, p.153]

LITERARY AND PHILOSOPHICAL SOCIETY, NEWCASTLE UPON TYNE, addition of lecture theatre, 1859, reconstructed 1966 [*The Builder*, vol. xvii, 1859, p.275; illustrated in C. Parish, *The History of the Literary and Philosophical Society of Newcastle upon Tyne*, II, 1990, facing p.72]

ST. JOHN'S, NEWCASTLE UPON TYNE, restoration, 1859 (see also entries for 1829, 1830, 1848, 1855) [Dobson, p.104]

ST. NICHOLAS'S, NEWCASTLE UPON TYNE, rebuilding of east end, 1859 (see also entries for 1817, 1823-24, 1827, 1832-34, 1862) [*AA*, new series, vol. iv, 1860, pp.152-53]

SCHOOL AND MASTER'S HOUSE, BRANDON, COUNTY DURHAM, 1859 [*NC*, 12 Aug 1859]

GAOL, CARLIOL SQUARE, NEWCASTLE UPON TYNE, major additions, 1859-61, dem. c.1929 (see also entries for 1822-28, 1839) [*The Builder*, vol. xvii, 1859, p.460; *NC*, 8 Feb 1861; drawings in TWA (782)]

OFFICE AND WORKERS' COTTAGES, NORTHUMBERLAND DOCK, NORTH SHIELDS, TYNE AND WEAR (N), classical, for Tyne Improvement Commissioners, 1859-61, dem. [*NC*, 27 May 1859]

1860-62

JOHN KNOX PRESBYTERIAN CHURCH, CLAYTON STREET WEST, NEWCASTLE UPON TYNE, addition of galleries, 1860, dem. c.1896 (see also entry for 1852-54; *NC*, 18 May 1860]

'MAGDALENE GARDENS', proposed street to continue St. Mary's Place, Newcastle upon Tyne, 1860, not carried out [*NC*, 13 Jul 1860]

ST. GREGORY'S, KIRKNEWTON, NORTHUMBERLAND, restoration and rebuilding, 1860 [*NJ*, 22 Apr 1860; ground plan in ICBS (No. 5529)]

ST. LAURENCE'S, WARKWORTH, NORTHUMBERLAND, restoration of nave, 1860 [*NJ*, 20 Oct 1860]

ST. PAUL'S, HENDON, SUNDERLAND, TYNE AND WEAR (D), additions to Dobson's 1851-52 church, 1860, dem. c.1970 (see also entry for 1851-52) [ICBS (No. 5139)]

ST. PETER'S, OXFORD STREET, NEWCASTLE UPON TYNE, completion of tower and spire to Dobson's 1840-43 church, Gothic, 1860, dem. c.1936 (see also entry for 1840-43) [*NC*, 16 Mar 1860]

SEATON DELAVAL HALL, NORTHUMBERLAND, repairs after fire, for Lord Hastings, 1860 (see also entry for 1814-17) [Dobson, p.26]

TYNEMOUTH, TYNE AND WEAR (N), proposed crescents, etc., at Tynemouth Lodge for William Linskill, 1860 [prospectus in NCRO (ZMD 68/7)]

UNTHANK HALL, NORTHUMBERLAND, additions, for Dixon Dixon, 1860, rebuilt 1862, reduced 1965 (see also entry for 1815) [Dobson, p.75]

JESMOND DEAN [*sic*], NEWCASTLE UPON TYNE, additions, including separate Italianate Banqueting House, for Sir William Armstrong, 1860-62, dem. c.1930 except for Banqueting House (now ruinous) [Dobson, p.96]

ST. EDWARD'S, SUDBROOKE HOLME, LINCOLNSHIRE, neo-Norman, for R. Ellison, 1860-62 [*NDJ*, 16 Jan 1865]

ST. MARY'S, TYNE DOCK, SOUTH SHIELDS, TYNE AND WEAR (D), Gothic, 1860-62, completed under the superintendence of Thomas Austin, dem. 1982 [*NC*, 8 Feb 1861]

GREENWOOD, EASTLEIGH, HAMPSHIRE, house for George Palmer, 1861, dem. [*NDJ*, 16 Jan 1865]

ST. MARY'S, COWPEN, NR. BLYTH, NORTHUMBERLAND, Gothic, 1861, completed in modified form by Austin & Johnson, 1864 [*NC*, 20 Dec 1861]

GAS COMPANY OFFICE, NEVILLE STREET, NEWCASTLE UPON TYNE, Italianate, 1861-62, dem. c.1971 [*NDJ*, 16 Jan 1865; drawing in TWA (1193)]

MECHANICS' INSTITUTE, ELSWICK, NEWCASTLE UPON TYNE, for Sir William Armstrong, 1862 [*NC*, 2 Sep 1862]

ST. NICHOLAS'S, NEWCASTLE UPON TYNE, proposed restoration of steeple, 1862, not carried out (see also entries for 1817, 1823-24, 1827, 1832-34, 1859) [*AA*, 4th series, vol. ix, 1932, p.145]

CENTRAL STATION, NEWCASTLE UPON TYNE, addition of portico, from 1862, executant architect Thomas Prosser (see also entry for 1846-50) [drawings in Laing Art Gallery, Newcastle upon Tyne, and with Railtrack (Eastern)]

GROAT MARKET AREA, NEWCASTLE UPON TYNE, proposed remodelling of street frontages, Gothic, c.1862, not carried out [Dobson, p.71; watercolour in Private Collection]

Undated Works

CHESTER, CHESHIRE, house [*NDJ*, 16 Jan 1865]

EBCHESTER, COUNTY DURHAM, house for Matthew Robert Bigge, possibly identifiable with 'Prospect House', Station Bank [*NDJ*, 16 Jan 1865; N. Pevsner and E. Williamson, *The Buildings of England: County Durham*, 1983, p.260]

HYLTON LODGE, CHIRTON, TYNE AND WEAR (N), house for Thomas Hughes, dem. [*NDJ*, 16 Jan 1865]

MILBURN (MILBOURNE?) HALL, NORTHUMBERLAND, bridge [*NDJ*, 16 Jan 1865]

NETHERWITTON OLD VICARAGE, NORTHUMBERLAND (now known as 'Mill Race House'?), alterations to 18th-century house (?) [*NDJ*, 16 Jan 1865]

NORTH SHIELDS, TYNE AND WEAR (N), plans and sections, for North Shields and Tynemouth Railway [*NDJ*, 16 Jan 1865]

RECTORY (KINGSLEY HOUSE), MIDDLEHAM, NORTH YORKSHIRE, extensions (north range with canted bays), for Rev. M. Birch [*NDJ*, 16 Jan 1865; J. Hatcher, *Richmondshire Architecture*, 2nd edn., 1999, p.159]

RECTORY, WEST BOLDON, TYNE AND WEAR (D), extensive improvements, including "an elegant stone front, having two hexagonal projections", for Rev. N.J. Hollingsworth [Fordyce, II, p.738]

SOUTH SHIELDS, TYNE AND WEAR (D), new quay [Dobson, p.127]

TEMPERLEY GRANGE, NR. CORBRIDGE, NORTHUMBERLAND, alterations, for Mr. Hopper [*NDJ*, 16 Jan 1865]

WIDDRINGTON CASTLE, NORTHUMBERLAND, alterations (?); castle largely dem. by 1832 [*NDJ*, 16 Jan 1865]

KEY EVENTS IN THE LIFE OF JOHN DOBSON

1787: (9 December): Dobson born at Chirton, near North Shields

1797: (9 October) birth of Richard Grainger, in High Friar Lane, Newcastle

c.1804: Dobson enters into an apprenticeship with the Newcastle architect David Stephenson

1807: Belsay Hall, Northumberland, begun to the designs of its owner, Sir Charles Monck

1807: construction begins of Ravensworth Castle, near Gateshead – based on designs by John Nash

1809: Dobson travels to London after completing his time with Stephenson to further his architectural and artistic education

1810: Dobson returns to the North East and sets up practice on Tyneside, initially at Chirton

1810: he designs his first executed building, the Royal Jubilee School, Newcastle

1810-12: construction of John and William Stokoe's neoclassical Newcastle Moot Hall

1811: Dobson joins the Literary and Philosophical Society of Newcastle upon Tyne

1812: he moves to an office in Pilgrim Street, Newcastle

1812: construction of John Stokoe's new bridge across the Pandon Dene, Newcastle

1813: the architect Ignatius Bonomi comes north to take up the post of Durham County Bridge Surveyor

c.1813: Dobson makes measured drawings of the old Castle Keep, Newcastle; travels in England, Wales and France

1815: Dobson joins the recently founded Society of Antiquaries of Newcastle upon Tyne

1815: he designs Prestwick Lodge, Northumberland, one of his earliest neoclassical villas

1815: Thomas Oliver begins work as Dobson's first pupil and assistant

1816: Dobson marries Isabella Rutherford of Gateshead

1816: Richard Grainger sets up as a builder in Newcastle

1817: Thomas Rickman publishes *An Attempt to Discriminate the Styles of English Architecture*

1818: Dobson exhibits at the Royal Academy a watercolour of Seaton Delaval Hall, Northumberland, following the abandonment of his scheme to enlarge and remodel the Hall

1818 (December): he accompanies the Mayor of Newcastle, Archibald Reed, on a fact-finding visit to London prior to obtaining the commission to design the new Gaol in Newcastle (built 1822-28)

1819: Dobson's friend Sydney Smirke wins the Royal Academy Gold Medal for architecture

1819: death of David Stephenson

c.1819-20: Richard Grainger builds Higham Place, Newcastle

1820: Dobson's contemporary John Green sets up as an architect in Newcastle

1820-24: construction of Cresswell Hall, Northumberland (Green acting as clerk of works for its architect, John Shaw of London)

1821 (January): Thomas Oliver begins independent practice in Newcastle as a "Land Surveyor and Architect"

1821: Dobson wins a competition for the design of the Northumberland Gaol at Morpeth (built 1822-28)

1821-23: publication of Augustus Charles Pugin's *Specimens of Gothic Architecture*

1822 (March): Dobson wins a competition for the design of the Carlisle County Gaol, only for his plans to be rejected soon afterwards

1823: Dobson designs the neoclassical Mitford Hall, Northumberland, although it is not built until 1828-29

1823: Dobson designs his own house (from where he practised thereafter) in New Bridge Street, Newcastle, and other adjacent classical villas

1824: he designs Longhirst Hall, Northumberland

c.1824-25: Dobson evolves an ultimately unsuccessful proposal for the redevelopment of central Newcastle

1825: commencement of Eldon Square, Newcastle, Dobson's first major work for Richard Grainger

1827 (24 July): Dobson's design for St. Thomas's, Newcastle, is selected by the Newcastle Corporation (it is built 1827-30, his first major church)

1827: publication of Eneas Mackenzie's *Descriptive and Historical Account of Newcastle upon Tyne*; it has the benefit of Dobson's architectural advice

1828: Dobson designs Lilburn Tower, Northumberland, his first major Tudor-Gothic house

1828 (November): foundation stone is laid of the new town and harbour of Seaham, County Durham, planned largely by Dobson for the 3rd Marquess of Londonderry

1829: Leazes Terrace, Newcastle, is begun to the designs of Thomas Oliver, for Richard Grainger

1830: issue of Thomas Oliver's first engraved map of Newcastle

1831: Dobson helps set up the Northern Society of Painters in Watercolours

1831: commencement of St. James's, Benwell, Newcastle, Dobson's first church in the neo-Norman style; he becomes cited in the infamous "Benwell Intrigue"

1831 (June): work begins on Dobson's Newcastle Royal Arcade, for Richard Grainger

1833 (30 July): a public dinner is held in Newcastle in honour of Grainger

1834 (29 January): issue of Prospectus for a "Cemetery in Jesmond Fields" designed by Dobson (built in altered form as the Newcastle General Cemetery, 1834-36)

1834 (May): Richard Grainger presents his plan for the redevelopment of central Newcastle to the Common Council, while in negotiation for the purchase of Anderson Place

1835 (24 October) Dobson attends a grand dinner to commemorate the opening of Newcastle's new Market, designed by himself as part of Grainger's redevelopment

1834-37: construction of Grey Street, Newcastle, for Grainger (the lower east side between Shakespeare Street and Mosley Street is by Dobson)

1836: publication of A.W.N. Pugin's *Contrasts*

1838: Dobson exhibits in Newcastle a watercolour of Seaton Delaval Hall in its restored state

1840: his unbuilt proposal for a classical chapel at Elswick, Newcastle, is his last design for Richard Grainger

1840: the noted architect Sydney Smirke marries Dobson's eldest daughter Isabella

1841: publication of A.W.N. Pugin's *The True Principles of Pointed or Christian Architecture*

1841: founding of the magazine *The Ecclesiologist*

1841 (September): Richard Grainger leaves Newcastle to avoid arrest for bankruptcy; he survives the crisis but from now on his career goes into decline

1842: Dobson designs the Collingwood Monument at Tynemouth

1843: he submits an unexecuted proposal for a high level bridge over the Tyne at Newcastle

1844: he unsuccessfully campaigns for the restoration of the historic Hospital of St. Mary the Virgin (demolished for the widening of Neville Street, Newcastle)

1844: Dobson is involved as an arbitrator in the case of Lord Londonderry versus Ignatius Bonomi, following the latter's rebuilding of Wynyard Park

1845: Dobson becomes a Fellow of the Institute of British Architects

1846 (23 February): at a meeting of the Board of the Newcastle and Berwick Railway Company, Dobson is appointed architect for the Newcastle Central Station (built 1847-50, portico added 1862-63)

1846: death of Dobson's wife Isabella

1848 (3 August): Dobson attends a celebratory banquet in the Castle Keep, Newcastle, following his restoration of the building for the Society of Antiquaries

1849 (7 June): completion of the Newcastle High Level Bridge, designed by Robert Stephenson and Thomas Harrison

1849: construction of Dobson's Manors Goods Station, warehouse, etc., a major example of his 'engineering architecture'

1850 (30 July): Dobson attends an inaugural dinner at the Newcastle Central Station

1850 (29 August): official opening of the Central Station by Queen Victoria and Prince Albert; Dobson presents drawings to the Queen

1850: Dobson exhibits a view of the Central Station's proposed "arcades and portico" at the Royal Academy

1850: Dobson's son Alexander is elected ARIBA.

1851: Dobson wins an Honourable Mention at the Great Exhibition in London for exhibiting a model of the Newcastle Central Station roof

1851-52: Dobson inspects hospitals in Manchester, Liverpool, Birmingham, London and Brussels prior to obtaining the commission to add a new wing to the Newcastle Infirmary

1852: Dobson goes to Germany, accompanied by his daughter Margaret, to prepare designs for a Gothic castle (the Neues Schloss, Friedelhausen, built in altered form 1852-56)

1852 (August): Dobson takes members of the Archaeological Institute of Great Britain and Ireland on a tour of Newcastle's antiquities and gives a paper on his recent restoration of the Percy Chapel, Tynemouth

1853: John Johnstone and W.A. Knowles win a competition for the design of Newcastle's New Town Hall, a project strongly opposed by Dobson

1853: Dobson produces a largely abortive design for the Warrington Museum and Library, Cheshire (built in a simplified form 1855-56)

1854 (6 October): Alexander Dobson is killed in the disastrous Newcastle and Gateshead Quayside Fire

1854 (November): Dobson publishes plans for rebuilding the Newcastle Quayside

1855: Dobson exhibits various designs at the Newcastle Fine Art Exhibition

1856: he designs the South Dock grain warehouse at Sunderland for George Hudson

1856: Ignatius Bonomi retires from practice and leaves Durham

1857: Dobson exhibits drawings of his first, unbuilt design for the Newcastle Central Station at the Manchester Art Treasures Exhibition

1857: he is called in by the Earl of Durham to underpin Lambton Castle and design major new extensions

1858-60: Dobson undertakes a controversial reconstruction of the choir and east end of Hexham Abbey, Northumberland

1858: Dobson is elected the first President of the newly-founded Northern Architectural Association, based in Newcastle

1858-61: construction of Jesmond Parish Church, Newcastle, one of Dobson's most elaborate Gothic designs

1859 (April): Dobson delivers his inaugural Address to the Northern Architectural Association

1861 (25 April): the architect R.J. Johnson gives a paper to the Northern Architectural Association criticising contemporary restoration practice

1861: Sydney Smirke is appointed Professor of Architecture at the Royal Academy

1861 (4 July): death of Richard Grainger; a public funeral follows

1861 (September): Dobson is commissioned by the North Eastern Railway Company to design a reduced version of his original portico for the Newcastle Central Station (this final scheme is built in modified form 1862-63)

1862: Dobson is obliged to retire from practice following a stroke

1865 (8 January): death of Dobson; he is buried at the Newcastle General Cemetery (Jesmond Old Cemetery) following a private funeral

1865: Thomas Austin and R.J. Johnson purchase Dobson's practice

GLOSSARY OF TERMS

aisle A part of a church running parallel to the nave (on either or both sides) and usually separated from it by arches or columns.

antae (singular *anta*) Pilasters at the ends of a colonnade, portico or other feature; columns in between these pilasters are described as *in antis*, so a portico *in antis* typically has two columns flanked by pilasters.

apse A semicircular or polygonal projection in a building, often referring to the east end of a church.

arcade A row of arches supported on columns or piers.

ashlar Stonework laid in regular courses, with flat, even surfaces and right-angle joints, as opposed to rubble masonry of roughly cut stones of differing shapes and sizes.

attic In architectural terminology, a storey above the main entablature of a building; in everyday usage, the word refers to the space within the sloping roof of a house.

balustrade A low decorative railing supported on bulbous posts (balusters).

baroque An exuberant style of architecture characteristic of 17th-century Europe and sometimes revived in later times.

barrel vault. A vault with an uninterrupted semicircular section, like that of a tunnel (tunnel vault is an alternative name).

bay A vertical division or compartment of a building or part of a building, usually one marked by some regularly repeated constructional feature or unit of design such as a row of arches, columns or windows; thus a church nave with four arches along each side and corresponding windows above is described as having four bays. The term is not to be confused with a bay (projecting) window; a curved bay window is known as a bow window.

blind arch An arched shape applied to the surface of a wall as a decorative motif.

bow window See bay.

bracket A small projecting piece of stone or other material used as a support.

broach spire A spire that is square in plan at the base but becomes octagonal further up, the transition being effected by sloping triangular faces (broaches).

buttress A solid, upright mass of stone or brick built against a wall to strengthen and support it.

capital The topmost part of a column, pilaster or pier, often carved in various distinctive forms.

castellation The use of battlements to give a building a romantic, medieval look.

chancel The eastern part of a church containing the altar (or the main altar); in a cross-shaped church the term generally refers to the whole of the building east of the central crossing.

chantry A small chapel in or attached to a church in which Masses are said for the soul of the founder of the chapel or for the souls of other specified people.

classical A very broad term referring to ancient Greek and Roman architecture and all later architecture that is derived from it.

clerestory The upper part of the main longitudinal walls of a church, above the aisle roofs, pierced with a row of windows.

coffering A decorative treatment of ceilings or similar surfaces, consisting of recessed panels arranged in geometrical patterns.

column An upright, fairly slender supporting member, usually consisting of a base, a cylindrical shaft (often tapering slightly towards the top) and a crowning capital.

colonnade A row of regularly spaced columns supporting arches or an entablature.

Composite See Order.

corbel A bracket projecting from the face of a wall to support a parapet, beam or other horizontal member.

Corinthian See Order.

cornice A projecting band of ornament at the top of a wall or other feature; more specifically, in classical architecture the term refers to the topmost part of the entablature.

crow-steps Step-like profiles ornamenting the sloping sides of a gable.

Decorated See Gothic.

dentil A small projecting block used as a repeated, closely spaced decorative motif in classical cornices, producing an effect somewhat like a row of teeth.

Doric See Order.

drip moulding See hood moulding.

Early English See Gothic.

ecclesiology The study of churches, especially their architecture and decoration; in the context of 19th-century English art, the word often refers specifically to the Ecclesiological Society, which was influential in promoting the Gothic style.

elevation A facade or side of a building.

Elizabethan Architecture of the reign of Elizabeth I (1558-1603) or in a style imitating it.

entablature In classical architecture, the broad horizontal band of ornament that surmounts a row of columns; it consists of three parts: (from bottom to top) architrave, frieze and cornice.

facade The front face of a building, particularly when it is treated as a prominent architectural feature.

fenestration A collective term for the design and general arrangement of windows in a building.

fluting A series of shallow vertical grooves (flutes) decorating a column or pilaster.

frieze A horizontal band of ornament, more specifically the middle section of an entablature.

gable The triangular section of wall at the end of a pitched roof.

Gothic The style of architecture prevalent in Europe in the late Middle Ages, characterised most obviously by the use of pointed arches. English Gothic architecture is conventionally divided into three phases (all of which were imitated during the Gothic Revival): Early English (c. 1175-c. 1275), Decorated (c. 1250-c. 1350), and Perpendicular (c. 1330-c. 1530).

Gothic Revival A fashion for the imitation of the Gothic style of the Middle Ages; it began in the 18th century and became a major strand in 19th-century architecture.

Gothick A term sometimes used to describe the style of buildings erected in the early days of the Gothic Revival; these buildings tend to be rather playful in spirit, with medieval forms used superficially, whereas 19th-century Gothic Revival architects were generally much more serious in approach.

Greek Revival A fashion for the scholarly imitation of the style of ancient Greek buildings, at its peak in the 1820s and 1830s; it is an aspect of neoclassicism.

groin vault A square or approximately square vault formed when two barrel vaults intersect at right angles (the groins being the edges or ridges created at the points of intersection).

ha-ha A trench, sometimes lined with a wall, that forms a boundary to an estate or garden but because it is below ground level does not interrupt the view.

half-column A column integrated with a wall, so that only half of it projects.

hipped roof A roof in which the end faces, as well as the sides, slope inwards.

hood moulding A projecting moulding over a window, door or arch, serving to divert the flow of rainwater; it can also be called a drip moulding or dripstone.

in antis See antae.

Ionic See Order.

Jacobean Architecture of the reign of James I (1603-25) or in a style imitating it.

keystone The central wedge-shaped block at the top of a stone arch, often given prominence through decorative carving.

kneeler A projecting stone at the base of a gable to stop the stones on the slope above from slipping.

Lady Chapel A chapel dedicated to the Virgin Mary (Our Lady).

lancet A tall narrow window with a plain pointed head without any tracery, one of the most characteristic features of the Early English style.

machicolations In fortifications, a series of openings in a projecting parapet through which defenders could drop missiles onto attackers at the foot of the wall below; they were sometimes used decoratively in Gothic Revival buildings.

moulding A band of ornament used in various architectural contexts, for example to accentuate or enrich the outline of a door or window; there are many distinctive types of moulding characteristic of different styles and periods.

nave A term applied to the western limb (usually the largest section) of a cross-shaped church, as opposed to the eastern limb (the chancel), and more specifically to the central division of the western limb, as opposed to the aisles that generally flank it.

neoclassicism A broad movement in European art and architecture in the late 18th and early 19th centuries characterised by a revival of the forms and spirit of the art of ancient Greece and Rome.

neo-Gothic An alternative term for Gothic Revival.

neo-Norman A style imitating the rugged architecture of the Norman period in England (11th-12th centuries).

neo-Renaissance A style consciously evoking the style of the Italian Renaissance, specifically the opulence of Italian palaces of the 16th century; it was popular in England in the mid 19th century for certain types of buildings, including banks, country houses and gentlemen's clubs.

neo-Tudor A style imitating the architecture of the early Tudor period.

Norman See Romanesque.

Order In classical architecture, a unit of design described mainly in terms of the type of column used. The ancient Greeks used three types of column – Doric, Ionic and Corinthian – which are progressively slimmer and more ornate; and the Romans added two more –– Tuscan (a starker form of Doric) and Composite (the most elaborate of all, combining features of Ionic and Corinthian).

oriel window A bay window projecting from an upper storey and overhanging the wall below.

Palladian A term applied to architecture influenced by the style and ideas of the Italian architect Andrea Palladio (1508-80), whose dignified and graceful buildings were regarded by many admirers as setting unsurpassable models for civilised living; his influence was particularly strong in 18th-century England.

parapet A low protective wall or balustrade built where there is a sudden drop, for example along the edge of a roof.

pediment A triangular area over a portico or a similar feature above a window.

pendentives The curved triangular areas between the arches that support a dome and the rim of the dome.

Perpendicular See Gothic.

Picturesque A term used in the 18th and 19th centuries to describe buildings and landscapes that were considered attractive in a rough, irregular or quaint way.

pier A substantial vertical supporting member of stone or brick, thicker than a column.

pilaster In classical architecture, a kind of flattened column, attached to a wall and projecting slightly from it.

pinnacle A pointed decorative termination common in Gothic architecture, for example at the top of buttresses.

porte-cochère A portico that is big enough for a wheeled vehicle to be driven through it.

portico A large, formal entrance porch, usually with a roof supported by columns.

quoins The stones or bricks forming an external corner of a building, particularly when they are emphasised in some way (for example by using stone quoins on a brick building).

Renaissance See neo-Renaissance.

Romanesque The style of architecture prevalent in Europe in the 11th and 12th centuries, characterised most obviously by massiveness of construction and the use of round-headed arches; Romanesque architecture in Britain is often described as Norman, as it was intro-

duced largely as a consequence of the Norman conquest of England in 1066.

rustication Stonework that is given a rough-textured effect or cut with deep grooves between the blocks to produce a feeling of rugged strength.

segmental arch An arch with a fairly shallow curve – one that is part of a segment of a circle.

spandrel A triangular area with one or more curved sides, such as the surface between two adjacent arches.

spirelet A slender spire rising from the roof of a church rather than from a tower.

string-course A moulding or band of masonry running horizontally along a wall.

stucco A type of light plaster used for sculpture and architectural decoration.

swag An ornamental carving in the shape of a graceful sweep of drapery suspended between two points.

tracery An openwork pattern of stone embellishing the upper part of a window, one of the most distinctive features of Gothic architecture.

Tudor Architecture of the Tudor period or in a style imitating it; in this context the word usually refers to the early Tudor period (1485-1558), when the final phase of the Gothic style (Perpendicular) was still prevalent in England (hence the term Tudor-Gothic), as later Tudor architecture, which was more classical in style, is generally distinguished as Elizabethan.

Tuscan See Order.

Wyatt window A distinctive type of window named after the English architect James Wyatt (1746-1813), who invented it in about 1780; it consists of three sections (the middle one wider than the other two) beneath a segmental arch.

INDEX

(Note: page numbers in bold refer to illustrations.)

Newcastle upon Tyne, churches and chapels in